Order and Disorder - International Conference Proceedings -

Edited by
Sihem Arfaoui, Noureddine Fekir and J.S. Mackley

New Edition 2025 Published by Isengrin Publishing

ISBN-13: 978-1-917130-11-0

To the memory of our late colleague ***Najib Fadhlaoui*** *to whom we bid farewell in 2015 and with whom we sowed the seeds of the first ideas for the Order Disorder events from 2014.*

To the blessed soul of ***Professor Lynn Hannachi*** *who left us in 2017, after inspiring a tradition of conferences in the Department of English since her participation in the first one on Indigenous Languages in 2011.*

To both, our love and gratitude

Contents

Acknowledgements

Sihem Arfaoui
Conference Organizer

A few words need to be said to acknowledge the dedication and perseverance of a dynamic team who has done an excellent job and worked hard through several challenges – spatial, temporal as well as virtual – in order to allow this collection to take shape. We owe a debt of thanks to all the contributors for their incessant patience and cooperative spirit, starting with ISSHJ Director Ridha Ben Rejeb for almost imposing the challenging tradition of organizing a research gathering on an annual basis in each department of ISSHJ; hence, the Study Day (April 21st 2015) followed by the International Colloquium (November 6-7th 2015) on Order and Disorder, as well as his engagement in allowing the selected reviewed papers to see the light of publication. In addition, we would like to thank several people who generously critiqued this volume and provided invaluable help. Among the reviewers, Narjess Saidi Doutreligne, Dorra Bassi and Faress Talbi kindly commented on the French parts of the manuscript. We are also grateful to the advice and recommendations of Abderrazak Dourari and Sondess Hamdi on the articles in English. Among our editors, Noureddine Fekir carefully read the articles and offered many thoughtful suggestions. We are most grateful to Jon Mackley for his problem-solving skills, enthusiastic engagement, and diligence in formatting and editing this compilation.

Introduction: "The well-deserved reward of an ordered mind"? (Márquez)[1]

Sihem Arfaoui, Noureddine Fekir, and J.S. Mackley

The Proceedings on Order and Disorder are the fruit of two consecutive scientific encounters in April and November 2015. These encounters were organized by the Department of English in the Higher Institute of Humanities of Jendouba (Jendouba University, Tunisia). On April 21st 2015, the HIHJ hosted 14 presenters and presentations in the context of a Study Day on Order and Disorder. The study day was the outcome of the idea that the Arab uprisings have shifted not just the socio-political paradigm, but also the academic scene and have opened a space for yet provocative debates. The heavy involvement of youth in the uprising calls for the necessity to ponder a number of issues previously unasked: the way the use of technology is dramatically transforming perspectives towards learning; the shifting perspectives toward traditional teaching methods and, therefore, the (dis)satisfaction with these methods, the relationship between generations which affects teacher/learner interaction, and the university as a democratic space.

During the study day, we explored many questions, including: How do we understand signs of order and disorder on campus? Does order always imply peace and harmony? In what sense has disorder on campus become the de-facto legitimate order? Can we conceive of disorder as a necessary step that precedes the harmony which characterizes order? How can we find the balance between order and disorder? How to balance the teachers' self-interest with the interests of the learners and that of the community? How do political changes transform disorder on campus into a different kind of order? Where do order, freedom and responsibility intersect? Can we continue to teach the way we did before, while ignoring what the digital revolution offers,

---

[1] Gabriel García Márquez, *Memories of My Melancholy Whores* (London: Jonathan Cape, 2005), p. 65.

for instance? How often should curricula be updated? Under the threat of the present ideological conflicts, can and should we still incorporate banned and controversial books such as *Moll Flanders, The Scarlet Letter, Lolita, and The Satanic Verses* among others, into the literary corpus? Or should we cater for the students' ideological stumbling block? Due to ideological blockage, what role do censorship and auto-censorship play in keeping or threatening order?

Other questions considered the teaching-learning process: where should teaching and learning be placed in the order of priorities? Where is the teaching-learning value in the LMD system which is rather focused on continuous testing? Does the teacher have to be in control of everything in class or just track off the learners? Questioning teaching orders, is the teaching order more a question of networking the students through a bottom-up approach than controlling one's own knowledge?[2]

Several participants were enthusiastic about the theme and presented an important selection of papers which covered such panels as reflections on order and disorder in the literary imagination, innovation and education, formation and information, social and political order in the contemporary world.

During the debriefing session at the end of the order-disorder study day, we observed that we needed to pursue the investigation into these fields but also to extend it to other spheres such as art and linguistics. Thus, the Department of English called for an extended investigation of the theme of "Order and Disorder" in different fields through its third colloquium scheduled for November 6-7, 2015. The call for papers observes: Painting, music, dance and more generally the live performing arts are less often present in our conferences than our traditional disciplines of literature, cultural studies or civilization and linguistics. After the so-called "Arab spring", in particular in Tunisia, the focus (especially in the media) has been political and economic more than cultural. As Khaled Tebourbi highlighted in his article in

[2] Study Day on Order and Disorder in April 21st, 2015 In the memory of the late Najib Fathlaoui CFP. 15-1-2015. http://call-for-papers.sas.upenn.edu/cfp/2015/01/15/update-study-day-on-order-and-disorder-in-april-21st-2015-in-the-memory-of-the-late

La Presse Magazine, April 26th 2015: “The political shows have thrived and multiplied since the revolution (…) but how can we explain that at the same time the cultural matter in all its forms has regressed everywhere and has dramatically shrunk to virtually nothing?”[3] Yet the arts in general have always been the locus of struggle between the conventional order of established conventions and the disorder or innovation. By challenging the accepted rules new trends have moved from figurative to abstract, tonal to atonal, bourgeois to urban and street art, and they are, in their turn, establishing the new rules of an alternative order. As articulated by the Columbian novelist Gabriel García Marquez, order can mirror disorder, and vice versa: “I discovered that my obsession for having each thing in the right place, each subject at the right time, each word in the right style, was not the well-deserved reward of an ordered mind, but just the opposite: a complete system of pretense invented by me to hide the disorder of my nature.”[4]

Culminating in 33 papers, the two–day symposium furthered the debate on order and disorder through international and interdisciplinary contributions, which bridged the domains of socio-psychoanalysis, linguistics, arts, literature, cultural studies, and gender. It brought together a group of scholars from the first International Conference on **Indigenous Languages** (2012) and the second one on **Myth and Power** (2014).

This compilation is a selection of 15 contributions out of the 47 original papers being presented. It is the result of an intensive intercultural cooperation between the editors and a selection of contributors. The present volume covers a wide range of order and disorder dialectics across language, world politics, metaphysics, philosophy, media, poetry, drama and a wide range of fiction from classical to contemporary. The enclosed articles pose questions about the philosophical dimensions of order and disorder but, also explore

---

[3] Khaled Tebourbi, *La Presse de Tunisie*, 26th April 2015.

[4] Order and Disorder Symposium, 6-7 Nov 2015, ISSH of Jendouba, Université de Jendouba, Jendouba CFP. 11-5-2015. URL: http://call-for-papers.sas.upenn.edu/cfp/2015/05/11/full-title-order-and-disorder-symposium-date-6-nov-7-nov-2015-location-issh-of

their intricate common terrains, particularly, when in dialogue with the contemporary world orders. The key-note address by Dr Nouraddine Fekir, "Criticism or the Mythological Creation of Dis/order in the Literary Text: the Humanist Project under Erasure", shows that the order and disorder duality "is a conspiratorial construct," often used as a marginalizing mechanism. It "unveils the fallacy of the Order/Disorder dichotomy and relates the rise of humanism, as the logical outcome of modernity, to the political situation of the modern world."

The first cluster of articles is a discussion of **Dis/orders Between Metaphysics and Classicism**. J.S. Mackley explores the order of two hells hell presented in the Judas episode of the Anglo-Norman reworking of the *Voyage of St Brendan*, while Farah Stiti considers Bonaventure Des Périers' *Les Nouvelles Récréations and Joyeux Devis* as a representation of the conflicts between the individual and society. The second cluster, entitled **Contemporary Imaginings and Performances of Clashing Dis/orders**, includes an article by Bachar Aloui which re-examines "linguistic detours" and "the chaos of diction" in an elegy posing "as an orderly form of lamenting expression" from the perspective of a significant glitch on psychic conflicts *a la Freudienne*. The second piece by Sihem Arfaoui, "Shahriar Mandanipour's *Censoring an Iranian Love Story*", offers a scrutiny of the pains and pleasures of literature once "usurped by or, in some cases, anticipates and perpetuates censorship as a religiously and politically-encompassed order of things." In the last piece in this group, "The Apollonian and the Dionysian in *The Great God Brown*" Welid Hmeissia accounts for the mythological and philosophical origins of order and disorder, demonstrating that they remain "antagonistic and yet complementary."

The next group, entitled **Aesthetic Readings of Order and Disorder**, begins with a close reading entitled "'Now they shake hands without hearts": Order and Disorder in Gabriel Okara's 'Once Upon a Time'" in which Asma Dhouioui provides a close reading of Okara's poem through from postcolonial and modernist lenses, exploring the overlapping issues of the past, alienation and an authentic Nigerian identity. Similarly, Farhat Benamor's examination "Between the

Ethics of Order and the Aesthetics of Disorder" sets out to unravel, among other things, "the despicable dissonance built between the ethical dimension of the story envisaged in redressing the orderly nature of the chain of being."

In our fourth group we move onto **Problematics of Order and Disorder in Language**, firstly through Ons Abdi's investigation "Tunisian Students' Conception of Structural Order in the English Argumentative Essay", in which she explores third-year Tunisian students' beliefs about structural order in English argumentative essays through the analysis of a questionnaire presented to 48 respondents. Mounir Jouini's "Constraints on the Order of Final Consonants in Tunisian Arabic" examines these constraints within the framework of Optimality Theory, focusing on the order of the consonant sequence as governed by the Sonority Sequencing Principle, which requires that final consonants exhibit a falling sonority. In "Speaking Anxiety, Order or Disorder?" Zeineb Ayachi considers the fear of negative evaluation and self-perception as sources of skill-specific anxiety for a group of ESP Tunisian learners in relation to the new Tunisian order yielded by the disorder that took place during the Jasmine revolution of 2011. Finally, in "La polysémie du verbe *porter*", following Victorri and Fuchs' observation that more than 40% of words in the *Petit Robert* dictionary are polysems, Hajer Ochi explores the multiple and contrasting uses of the verb "porter".

Our final cluster brings the collection to its full circle with **Dialectics of Order and Disorder from World Politics and Media to Philosophy**. This group begins with Mohamed Anouar Barouni's article "A New Order of Zionist Lobbying: A Statistical Approach for the Jewish Pressure Groups during Ronald Regan's Presidency" which considers the implications of the shift of Jewish lobbies from the Democratic Party to the Republican Party during the Reagan administration. In the second paper, Majdi Chaoiachi considers the media aspect of an incessant disorder wherein it is difficult to keep clear boundaries between information and opinion in "Chevauchement des genres rédactionnels journalistiques", and finally Aya Somrani asks the question: "Why are Order and Chaos Part of Man's Inescapable Doom?" suggesting that our existence relies on them in equal measure, considering this paradox through the lens of the New World Order and Hegel's Management Theory.

We feel very lucky to have worked as a team on compiling and editing such a collection of articles on Order and Disorder which we hope you will enjoy exploring through the variety of languages and disciplines this volume offers.

Works cited

Márquez, Gabriel García. *Memories of My Melancholy Whores*. London: Jonathan Cape, 2005.

Order and Disorder Symposium, 6-7 Nov 2015, ISSH of Jendouba, Université de Jendouba, Jendouba CFP. 11-5-2015. URL: http://call-for-papers.sas.upenn.edu/ cfp/2015/05/11/full-title-order-and-disorder-symposium-date-6-nov-7-nov-2015-location-issh-of

Tebourbi, Khaled. *La Presse de Tunisie*. 26th April 2015.

Study Day on Order and Disorder in April 21st, 2015 In the memory of the late Najib Fathlaoui CFP. 15-1-2015. http://call-for-papers.sas.upenn.edu/cfp/ 2015/01/15/update-study-day-on-order-and-disorder-in-april-21st-2015-in-the-memory-of-the-late

Introduction

Narjess Saidi d'Outreligne

Le Centre National des Ressources Textuelles et Lexicales définit l'ordre par «Rapport intelligible, satisfaisant aux exigences de l'esprit, pouvant être saisi ou institué entre différents éléments». Et son contraire le désordre est un «Manque d'ordre; défaut de rangement, de disposition fonctionnelle ou esthétique». Ne peut-on pas envisager le désordre non comme un antonyme d'ordre mais plutôt la possibilité de faire, d'accomplir des «prouesses» dans un monde où, celui qui sort des normes est considéré comme un paria dans le sens où il ne se plie pas à l'ordre / aux ordres? Le désordre ne doit en aucun cas être considéré comme annulant l'ordre. A travers l'histoire, les courants littéraires et artistiques qui se sont succédé nous montrent qu'un ordre n'est jamais immuable et que le désordre est aussi une forme d'esthétique:

> L'espace comme le temps ne peuvent être toujours alignés sur des droites et des cercles, des surfaces et des angles; ils s'ouvrent parfois aussi sur d'autres parcours et se laissent pénétrer par des points de condensation, des stries, des feuilletages, tout aussi indispensables pour comprendre l'ordre et le désordre du monde.[1]

Le présent colloque montre l'évolution de ces deux concepts, les différents domaines dans lesquels les contributeurs qui ont analysé, répertorié, organisé des textes, des articles et des discours ont apporté leurs pierres à l'édifice. Du «Chevauchement des genres rédactionnels journalistiques» qui aborde l'amalgame entre la presse d'information et celle d'opinion en passant par le «Désordre dans *Les Nouvelles Récréations et Joyeux Devis* de Bonaventure Des Périers» qui présente De Périers «derrière une façade légère qui refuse la pesanteur d'un quelconque enseignement, les nouvelles de Des Périers s'avèrent, «paradoxalement» (au sens étymologique du terme), riches de significations». «La polysémie du verbe porter: de l'ordre vers le désordre et vice versa», quant à elle analyse la richesse du verbe

[1] Jean-Jacques Wunenburger, *La Raison contradictoire, sciences et philosophie modernes, la pensée du complexe* (Paris: Albin Michel, 1990), p. 258.

«parler» selon des «données aussi bien linguistiques qu'extralinguistiques». L'ordre implique donc l'autorité, les mesures coercitives; le désordre, au contraire, est une forme de liberté, au sens large du terme que les auteurs ont essayé mettre au grand jour.

Ces contributions nous apprennent que la pensée est remodelée selon les époques, les écrivains, les artistes et que l'*épistémè*, selon Michel Foucault, est de «saisir les transformations d'un savoir à l'intérieur à la fois du domaine général des sciences et, également, à l'intérieur du domaine en quelque sorte vertical que constitue une société, une culture, une civilisation à un moment donné».[2]

---

[2] Michel Foucault, *Les mots et les choses* (Paris: Gallimard, 1966).

Bibliographie

- Foucault, Michel (1966). *Les mots et les choses*. Paris: Gallimard.
- Wunenburger, Jean-Jacques (1990). *La Raison contradictoire, sciences et philosophie modernes, la pensée du complexe*. Paris: Albin Michel.

Narjess Saidi d'Outreligne

The Humanist Project Under Erasure

Criticism or the Mythological Creation of Dis/order in the Literary Text: The Humanist Project under Erasure

Noureddine Fekir, University of Carthage, Tunisia

Abstract

Towards the second half of the twentieth century, essentialist theories of criticism, such as New Criticism, Archetypal criticism and Structuralism, were haunted by the desire to systematize the text and impose a mythological order on it, one which existed only in the minds of those who were influenced by the project of modernity. The vision of an order became possible once the political grasp of Christianity had been displaced. The above-mentioned schools sought to establish order upon the disjunctive texts created by writers who gradually loosened themselves from the controlling power of the "Inquisition" which operated even as late as the end of the 18th century. This article considers the order of literature and the way modern theory has tried to impose its own order on literature, as if literature could be ordered, systematized and objectified. The article shows that this duality between order and disorder is a conspiratorial construct. It has always been used to marginalize certain aspects of life, to discredit others only to revitalize them at times when the adepts of the mythological or occult order thought that they should be celebrated. The article unveils the fallacy of the Order/Disorder dichotomy and relates the rise of humanism, as the logical outcome of modernity, to the political situation of the modern world.

Keywords: rationality, system, order, disorder, humanism, conspiracy, literature.

Many attempts have been made since the 1940s to find a frame that encompasses and accounts for the nature and understanding of literary works. The Formalist project, which highlighted the aesthetic side of literature as formulated by the Moscow Linguistic Circle and the New Criticism as well as by Northrop Frye and the French Structuralists, failed to provide a sustainable system that accounted for the idea of literature as a discourse that had an origin and a rationale of its own. This desire to categorize the essentials of literary creation or production was informed by a rationalistic drive to conceive of literature as an order of words that necessarily abided by a certain number of restrictions and prohibitions. Such a drive was inherited from Neoclassical thought and was coincident with the start of the Enlightenment era. Alexander Pope, in his "Essay on Man", spoke of criticism as that which casts method on literature in just the same way that nature was analyzed systematically by the emerging scientists:

> First follow nature and your judgment frame
> By her just standard, which is still the same.
> Unerring nature still divinely bright,
> One clear, unchanged and universal light, (68–72)
> ....
> Those rules, of old discovered, not devised,
> Are Nature still, but nature methodized;
> Nature, like liberty, is but restrained
> By the same laws which first herself ordained. (88–91)

Criticism became haunted by the scientific credo that it should emanate from the imitation of the order of nature. Just as literature imitates human nature, so too critical judgment must be based on whatever methods are abstracted from the observation of the laws that govern human nature. A successful critic, according to neoclassical standards, must then follow nature and its rules and see whether the artist has followed the order that binds human nature. Hence, to proclaim an artist as great or mediocre, the critic must ensure that the artist has followed the extent to which his work holds the mirror to nature. The order of nature reflects itself in the order of literature which in turn is reflected in the judgment of the critics who follow the same rules which, by the same token, they had never devised but they had merely inherited from the Classicists.[1]

What is striking here is the way Pope resorts to a series of words: "judgment, frame, just, standard, unerring, still, rules, methodized, restrained, laws, ordained". These words denote the existence of an intrinsic system that literature and criticism have to abide by. In not more than eight lines, eleven words related to the importance of order are used, which sheds light on the necessity to make literature fit into the ideological framework of the Augustan age, an age that firmly believed that Europe could never recover the glory of its Roman past without subjecting all the aspects of its life and culture to a strict regimentation governed by reason and order.

The Enlightenment period led to the splintering of scientific research into several areas of specialization, and although the Romantic movement strove hard in the early nineteenth century to undermine all orders imposed by the mind, there arose in the twentieth century a belief that spread among the men of letters. This belief stipulated that literature could itself be subsumed and made to fit under some specific molds that were not governed by nature. Such forms in the Neoclassical period, which strictly required that literary works should be faithful to human nature, but by the very descriptive categories of linguistics, since literature itself came to be seen as an order of words.[2] In this way literature could become a separate discipline that would be studied on its own, one that would develop its own tools of criticism and analysis. Gone was the time when literature had to be subservient to history or ethics; for now the concern was with the literariness of the discipline and not with literature as an entertaining or didactic message to be vehicled to the masses.

Whilst the New Critics invented a series of characteristics that served to distinguish the ideal literary text from other discourses, the Canadian critic Northrop Frye argued in his *Anatomy of Criticism* that literature is an 'order of words' and that criticism must no longer be seen as a parasitic or supplementary form of knowledge, since true

---

[1] The reference here to Aristotle's "Poetics", Horace's "Ars Poetica' and Longinus' "On the Sublime".

[2] One can refer here to the works of Roman Jakobson and the French structuralists such as Roland Barthes and Gerard Genette.

criticism can only emanate from the institution of literature. In no way should a critic project criticism onto a text from outside the enterprise of literature. Rather he should look back into the origins of literary production and relate the text to the mythoi from which it originates. Frye thus developed a form of generic criticism which could have shed light on the true nature of literary discourse had he delved deeper into analyzing the origins of the order of literature.

Frye undertakes an approach that conceives of criticism as a science derived from literature: "If criticism exists, it must be an examination of literature in terms of a conceptual framework derivable from an inductive survey of the literary field. The word 'inductive' suggests some sort of scientific procedure. What if criticism is a science as well as an art?" (*Anatomy* 7) Nothing could be more ideal than this wish, for it betrays Frye's desire to devise a scientific anatomy for the analysis of literature while not relinquishing his belief in the uniqueness of the experience generated by art.

Frye, who was influenced by William Blake's symmetrical vision of life, tried to reproduce this in literary criticism. He devised a system of broad mythoi that purportedly accounts for all literary works. Thus, tragedy is represented by the mythos of autumn, and comedy by spring. Between these two mythoi satire and irony are set in the season of winter whilst romance is associated with summer, the season of ripeness and completeness. It is easy for any reader of Classical mythology to discern here a myth derived from the Eleusinian rituals which also tend to associate comedy and romance with the seasons of rebirth and light, the six months which Persephone spends with her mother Demeter while autumn and winter are the seasons she spends with Pluto, the god of the underworld.[3] Frye, it is true adopts a Christian reading of this myth, but like T.S. Eliot in his poem, *The Waste Land*, he sees an affinity between pagan and Greek mythology and Christian eschatology.[4] In fact, Eliot, before his conversion to Catholicism, used to think that all the myths of the past shared a

[3] See Manly P. Hall, *The Secret Teachings of All Ages* which historicizes Greek mythology by referring to all the politics underlying its ramifications.

[4] See Frye's *The Great Code* which betrays a sense of the author's inability to systematize criticism and literature without falling into what I would call the metaphysics of the occult.

common trait with Christianity which is that the death of the god (such as Dionysus, Osiris or Christ) is necessary for the process of the rebirth of nature and the continuity of mankind.

Frye argues that literature, unlike nature, is informed by a design which criticism must uncover and lay bare: "It is clear that criticism cannot be a systematic study unless there is a quality in literature which enables it to be so. We have to adopt the hypothesis, then, that just as there is an order of nature behind the natural sciences, so literature is not a piled aggregate of "works," but "an order of words" (*Anatomy* 17). This means that literature is informed by a structure of recurrent motifs and reveals a pattern of recognizable archetypes that can easily be detected by the critic. Frye never reflects on the underlying design behind what he calls the order of words. He remains silent on the issue in *The Anatomy* and even later in *The Educated Imagination*, he does not develop the issue convincingly. He merely states therein that literature springs from the human desire to survive and that literature is based on the imitation of rituals. He does not say that these rituals could be the Eleusinian rituals or the Dionysian rites that led to the emergence of tragedy.

Frye does not go deep in the analysis of the origin of ritual, because as a Christian humanist he is divided between showing his loyalty to the secular academy that employs him and the Christian religion he believes in. He probes into the origin of literature but dares not investigate the matter thoroughly and say that the origin of literature is pagan and that storytelling, from its inception, has always been associated with the human attempt to rival the monotheistic version of the creation. While he makes a step forward in reconstituting the origin of literature as fiction, as a discourse that was primarily meant to create an alternative discourse to the version provided in the Hebrew Bible, Frye finds no fault with attributing the origin of literature to rituals and fails to point to the pagan nature of such rites as well as to the hidden secrets embedded in the practice of such rituals. As Robert Alter states in his review of Blake's *The Great Code*:

> *The Great Code* makes one wonder whether Christian typology may not have been the ultimate model on which *Anatomy of Criticism* was based. To be sure, Frye's frame of reference for typology is more modern anthropology

> than medieval theology. Writing with a sense of historical perspective, he does not seriously imagine that the authors of the tale of the binding of Isaac in Genesis and of the dead and resuscitated son of the Shunamite woman in Kings were explicitly adumbrating the story of the crucifixion and resurrection. (Alter 20)

Frye sharply condemns the New Critics who seek to find a hidden meaning in the literary text. He is against considering the text as a mysterious, hermetic and ambiguous structure of words that conceal some esoteric meaning which only erudite critics can unveil. "The assertion that the critic should confine himself to 'getting out' of a poem exactly what the poet may vaguely be assumed to have been aware of 'putting in,' is one of the many slovenly illiteracies that the absence of systematic criticism has allowed to grow up." Frye does not believe that meaning lies in the text but that it is projected by the critic onto the text (17) If Frye insists on highlighting the status of literature as the basic imitation of rituals, it is because as an erudite scholar, he cannot remain mute on the true origin of literature, but as an academician he cannot say more, for that would threaten his reputation as a scholar who is bound by what has been commonly agreed upon in the West as forming the basis of the dominant discourse that issues forth truth statements. As a critic, Frye is one of the first to have drawn attention to the mythical origin of literature; but myth itself is nothing but a disguised manifest version of the latent secret knowledge that was at the root of all literary production. Having read Blake, Yeats and most literature starting from the Greek period, one can only wonder why he has been seduced by Madame Blavatsky, the writer of *Isis Unveiled* and one of the most articulate matrons of occult knowledge.[5]

If there were to be a second volume of additional figures whom Frye admired for one reason or another but about whom he wrote nothing sustained, it might well include another dozen or so: Jacob Boehme, François Rabelais, Madame Blavatsky, Martin Buber, Jane Ellen Harrison, Mircea Eliade, John Stuart Mill, Thomas Carlyle,

---

[5] See Leon Surette. *The Birth of Modernism: Ezra Pound, T.S. Eliot, W.B. Yeats, and the Occult.* Montreal: McGill-Queen's University Press, 1994.

Oscar Wilde, Alfred North Whitehead, G. F. W. Hegel, Nicolò Machiavelli, and the Mahayana Sutras (Avatamsaka, Lankavatara) (Denham 2).

Why did Frye never write explicitly about Jacob Boehme, the mystic thinker and theosophist? What is his relationship with the Jewish Lurianic Kabbalist Martin Buber? Why was he interested in Giordano Bruno who was excommunicated by the Lutherans and executed by the Inquisition for his heretic views? In short, why was Frye who knew Richard Burton and Carl Jung unable to proclaim that literature is fraught with Kabbalistic lore through and through? The aim here is not to assert a judgment upon Frye on the basis of those whom he read or those he was concerned with, but to show that his work is deeply fraught with a scheme that was thoroughly inspired by paganistic lore and not by a scientific and an objective tool of representation.

After Frye, it was the French structuralists who provided another vain attempt to systematize literature and impose order on it. A. J. Greimas, Roland Barthes, and Tzvetan Todorov firmly believed that literature had an underlying structure very similar to the structure of language which scholars such as Ferdinand de Saussure had laboriously worked to find in language. The structuralists believed that the task of the critic is to uncover the constants of all literary texts and that models derived from linguistics could help in finding the common denominator between all narratives or poems. Even after the publication of Jacques Derrida's three books on the demise of the structuralist agenda, structuralism continued to be in vogue for more than two decades throughout the academic world.[6]

What is ironic is that one of the founders of the structuralist methodology for the analysis of literature, namely Todorov, poses today as one of the most fervent critics who resist the existence of ordered analysis in literature. In an article published less than a decade ago and entitled "What is Literature for?" in which he questions the

---

[6] Poststructuralist critics under the influence of Derrida advocated that literature is a discursive field that resists being subjected to any system or form of closure. There ensued an epistemic shift which insisted that no order can be imposed on literature, a discourse that is marked by indeterminacy, unsystematicity and the lack of uniformity.

structuralist beliefs and methodology to which he subscribed in 1960s and methodology and after having spent more than two decades with Gerard Genette and Roland Barthes trying to build what Barthes called "une science de la literature". Todorov, who gradually receded from the structuralist project sharply refuted this methodology that had long tried to dissect the text and reduce it to its minimal constituents and criticized the way students, whether at high school or at university studied the formal properties of the literary text, 'a closed object made of language, self-sufficient and absolute) (21). Todorov ironically asks, "[why] study literature when literature is only an illustration of the tools to study literature?" (21). Todorov is now amazed at how the structuralists neglected the message conveyed by literary texts and cared only about the structural codes that deliver meaning. He considers: if literature has any value, it lies in the meaning that the reader must find, for that "will permit him to better understand human beings and the world, to discover in them a beauty that enriches his existence" (23). The structuralist activity had simply killed the humanist dimension of literature. The efforts which Todorov and his fellow structuralists had so elaborately deployed have now turned into ashes, as the critic ultimately declares that literature must replenish our soul, our vision of life and the world.

All this proves that the order and systems these critics have tried to establish were mere taxonomic and formal gestures cast by the rationalistic drive in its urge to control every single bit of knowledge or linguistic praxis. Perhaps it is the postmodern drive that prompted Todorov to swerve from the path he had battled for during more than two decades with a view to disseminating it in literary studies. The New Historicism, Deleuzian theory, Derrida's later thought, feminism, and the return of ethical criticism have perhaps all served to bring Todorov back to consider literature as a field for acquiring human experience. While in the 1960s critics sought to impose order on the literary text, the 1970s saw a surge in the critics' attempt to view the text as an emblem of ambivalence, of inter-warring forces, a site for ideological views in conflict with essentialist doctrines and hegemonizing views. The order that was imposed by Frye and the Structuralists was meant to shed light on literature which seemed to be an ambiguous, fragmented, unclear discourse. The postmodernists viewed this ambivalence as a viable quality in the text, more to be celebrated than a site that would cause anxiety to the critic who seeks to decode its meanings. This shift from the dream to find the ideal order that could account for all literary texts to a celebration of the chaotic nature of literature occurred at a moment not distant from the moment when politicians would launch the call for a new world order. In fact, the call was launched by William Butler Yeats in his poem "The Second Coming," in which he announced the start of a new era some eight decades before G.W. Bush proclaimed it in 1991 with the outbreak of the Gulf War when he declared that a new world order has now entered center stage.

The reference to Yeats is significant in as much as it points to the way this poet has ever endlessly drawn attention to the haunting influence of occult knowledge upon the vast body of literary texts. Yeats even contributed to spreading and disseminating this knowledge through the use of symbols that date back to the ancient Greek and Egyptian times. In the above-mentioned poem, he states:

> Turning and turning in the widening gyre
> The falcon cannot hear the falconer;
> Things fall apart; the centre cannot hold;
> Mere anarchy is loosed upon the world,
> ……………………………………
> Surely some revelation is at hand;
> Surely the Second Coming is at hand.
> The Second Coming! Hardly are those words out
> When a vast image out of Spiritus Mundi
> Troubles my sight: a waste of desert sand;
> A shape with lion body and the head of a man,
> A gaze blank and pitiless as the sun,
> Is moving its slow thighs, while all about it
> Wind shadows of the indignant desert birds.

Various scholars have recently referred to the way several symbols such as the beast, and 'spiritus mundi' both point to the way Yeats was providing an interpretation that was derived from paganism and not from Christianity. The 'gyre' which Yeats has always promoted is not to be simply seen as a symbol for the alternation between an age of subjectivity (disorder) followed by an age of objectivity (order), but must be interpreted as the site where the interpenetrating cones denote a sexual image very much similar to the way the Kabbalists describe the act of 'giving' required of anyone who wishes to repeat the eternal act of creation as embodied in sexuality.[7] In this context, one needs only to mention the works of Leo Surette, Marsha Schuchard and Manly P. Hall who have all studied the huge influence many writers such as Yeats, William Blake, Ezra Pound, and an infinite number of modernist writers have had in promoting the rituals of secret societies in literature.

Such a realization is perhaps what stands behind Todorov's sharp critique of the structuralist project. Todorov changed his aesthetic affiliations not under the duress of postmodern shifts but because he realized, during his life – more specifically after the emergence of what is now called the ethical turn that was itself consolidated by Jacques Derrida himself – that three were hidden orders behind the institution of literature and that criticism has greatly contributed to mystifying such a concern. Criticism tried to develop frameworks for the analysis of literature, but these frames remained unscientific and subjective because the critics did not analyze all the backgrounds associated with literary production and refused to delve into the institution of literature, its origins and modern affiliations. Objectivity in the analysis of literature cannot be achieved if the historical, religious and political contexts are discarded from the analysis of texts.

This notion of order and disorder is not reliable. Those who accuse postmodernists of being rejecters of all commonsensical notions of order are victims of a fallacy, since even those who tried to find order in the humanities merely contributed to the development of the plot or conspiracy which Todorov spoke of in his introduction to his study, *Imperfect Garden: The Legacy of Humanism*. Todorov sees humanism as a development of the human desire to replace God with man. He declares:

> It was revolutionary to claim that the best justification of an act, one that makes it most legitimate, issues from man himself: from his will, from his reason, from his feelings. The center of gravity shifts, here, from

---

[7] Michael Laitman, *A Guide to the Hidden Wisdom of the Kabbalah* (Toronto: Kabbalah Publishers, 2009).

> cosmos to anthropos, from the objective world to the subjective will; the human being no longer bows to an order that is external to him but wishes to establish this order himself. The movement is therefore double: a disenchantment of the world and a sacralization of man; values, removed from one, will be entrusted to the other. (9–10)

Before proceeding to support this argument about how the shift occurred from the centrality of God to that of Man, it is necessary to relate the way humanism as a philosophy worked in conjunction with this desire to impose order in order to undermine the dominant version offered by Christianity. Humanism as a term first appeared to refer to that tendency in the Renaissance period which sought to encourage certain disciplines related to man and his achievements. Peter Burke defines it in the following terms: "[h]umanism is the movement to recover, interpret and assimilate the language, literature, learning and values of ancient Greece and Rome. Correspondingly, [...] a humanist is someone who was actively involved in the movement regardless of his professional position in the society" (Burke 2). This implies that the humanist focuses on developing knowledge about man in order to displace the centrality of the divine.

Todorov in turn explains:

> The term humanist has several meanings; ... it refers to the doctrines according to which man is the point of departure and the point of reference for human actions. These are "anthropocentric" doctrines, just as others are theocentric, and still others put nature or tradition in this central place. The term humanist figures, perhaps for the first time in French, in a passage by Montaigne in which he uses it to characterize his own practice, in contrast to that of the theologians. Though he grants the theologians their right to respect, and certainly to existence, he prefers to separate the two domains and reserve a new field for the 'humanists,' which consists of strictly human activities or 'fantasies,' of 'purely human' writings, those concerning subjects that are 'matters of opinion, not matters of faith,' treated in 'a lay not clerical manner'. (*Legacy of humanism* 6)

He further adds that "Humanism is the ideology underpinning modern democratic states; but this very omnipresence makes it invisible or insipid. Because of this, although everyone today is more or less a "humanist," the doctrine in its original form can still surprise and enlighten us" (6–7).

The extent to which Todorov seems disillusioned by this

philosophy which he apparently describes in objective terms is clear in his setting off the humanists from the theologians. The introduction to his *Legacy of Humanism* contains a parable about how humanism first appeared as the work of conspirators to counteract the rise of Christianity is surprising but daring, issued as it is from one of the earliest proponents of structuralist analysis. One can only wonder at the reasons behind such a radical revisionist stance on the part of Todorov and one may well speculate as to whether behind this is his discovery of the occult and how it is deeply rooted in the scholarship of those who declare they are the objective analysts of modern culture.

Writers of diverse persuasions have established a link between humanism and the Renaissance. Marx himself acknowledged in 1844 that "he was formulating a radical humanism ('to be radical is to grasp things by the root. But for man the root is man himself') (qtd. in Davis 11–12). In his turn J. A. Symonds advocated the necessity to dissociate the rational from the theological in order to understand the essence of humanism. He saw that "classic literature alone displayed human nature in the plenitude of intellectual and moral freedom" (52) and attributed its rise to the intellectual desire to fight "ecclesiastical despotism" (52). The dissociation of humanism from Christianity went smoothly because the proponents of this trend were very careful not to arouse the animosity of the Church.

It is in the modern period that the rift between these two conceptions of life became apparent to all eyes. With the decline of the Church and the proliferation of published materials, it was very easy to associate the radical ideas of the humanists with the secular projects of establishing democratic states that were no longer curbed by the authority of the Church. Some even went so far as to foster the link between paganism and humanism. In his *Occultism and the New Age humanism* Gary North argues:

> C. S. Lewis makes the observation in *The Abolition of Man* (1947) that occultism and humanism appeared in Western history at about the same time, during the Renaissance. Humanist philosophy and occultism were two sides of the same revival of paganism. Thus, he argued, occultism and humanistic rationalism are not enemies in principle but rather cooperating philosophies that are united against Christianity and Christian civilization. This is the theme of his great masterpiece, the novel *That Hideous Strength.*

(4)

Humanism is an issue that is raised each time the religious question comes to the fore. Postmodern thinkers and Marxists alike view it as just another essentialist philosophy that conceives of man as the center. Yet when theo-centrism is at stake, humanism is the first thing that is resorted by philosophers and thinkers alike to refute the theistic thesis.

What is at stake here is that literature has been promoted to highlight the following values: reason, anthropocentrism, and order. Even though literature celebrated disorder, criticism came to impose order upon human thought which swerves between the longing for the divine and the desire to affirm its centrality. Literature and criticism are not just expressions of the personal or objectives drives of reason. They have often been used to serve either the anthropocentric drive in man, or the agendas of occultism, pantheism and satanic worship.

My argument in this article has been that even criticism is at times manipulated by secret societies as is the case with a major critic such as Frye who is a Biblical scholar and a preacher. The order which he sought to find in literature and which he proclaimed to be based on a scientific urge, is a reflection of the secret agenda he believed in or partly shared and which cannot be refuted seeing his extreme thrust in the study of Blake whom he saw as his guru. To substantiate this claim, one may only need to refer to Harold Bloom who openly and fervently bases most of his recent interpretations of literature on the Jewish Kabbalah.

Whilst Edward Said has sought to produce some form of contrapuntal criticism, one that reads the text against its grain in an attempt to unmask the ideology of the Western Gaze and the imperial project, the present work seeks to consolidate some efforts undertaken by such writers as Leon Surette, Hugh McDiarmid, and Marsha Schuchard who confronted the academy with evidence that the greatest writers and producers of literature were disseminators of occult beliefs or at best were complicitous with secret societies through and through.

The task of literary criticism is not to categorize literature, find some sense of order or disorder in it or merely find meaning in it. The task of the critic is to find the truth in the writing and behind the writing, to excavate and recover the hidden agendas that have monitored people's beliefs for centuries in the many stories recounted to people along the ages. Theories may be useful in this undertaking only insofar as they shed light on the way language ideologically manipulates readers (especially when it is aesthetically constructed through rhythmic variations, plot complexity and rhetoric). The critic is to take advantage of such theories that circulate in the academic world, but in no way should he conceive of them as the very end of research. Not until criticism has delved into the symbology vehicled by all artists and men of letters (from *Gilgamesh* to the *Twilight* Saga) can the reader aspire to have come close to the reasons behind the production of so many literary texts that have haunted the minds of people throughout the ages.

It is not objective on the part of critics to remain silent on the occult beliefs and symbols in their writings under the pretext that these are unverifiable. The Age of the New Criticism, which was the age when critics had to isolate the writer from his beliefs and era and focus on the 'words on the page' in a textualist fashion that is based on close reading is now a bygone age. The critic must not dispense with any detail, whether autobiographical or historical, so long as it is authentic. The argument that such details add nothing to the nature of understanding the achievement of the text is obsolete in the age of the New Historicism, Post-Marxism and Derrida when everything is proclaimed to be nothing more than a text. Everything is a text and therefore even the idealization of literature is a Platonic dream that has nothing to do with scientific research and material evidencing.

Nobody can deny today that many founders of Western thought and literature were indebted in the development of their works to the teachings of secret societies, to the occult lore of the Indians, the Egyptians and the Greeks. Plato and Pythagoras before him were both initiates of Egypt's Gizah temple from which they derived their wisdom. Nobody can deny that tragedy, the supreme genre in literature was a mere imitation of the ritual in honor of the god Dionysus, and that literature as it first appeared among the Greeks and as clarified by Frye himself, is an imitation of a pagan ritual and not just any ritual.

This article has shown that it is not only literature that is contaminated by traces of the occult, but that criticism is equally deeply marked by the tendency to mask its course with ambivalent moves that paradoxically subscribe to both mythological-cultic thinking and rationalistic discourse. To do this, criticism constantly shifted its strategies masquerading at times as the proponent of mimesis and at others as the custodian of humanist values. What is noteworthy is that very few critics dared broach the pagan roots of literature and by doing that they fell into the same trap, that of ever-endlessly acknowledging their debt to Greek Sophia from which they all derive their precepts. The result is the production of a body of knowledge that is schizophrenic in that it proclaims its allegiance to enlightened philosophy even as that philosophy has always remained caught in the tangles of the occult, the Kabbalistic and the mythical.

Works cited

Burke, Peter. 'The Spread of Italian Humanism' in *The Impact of Humanism on Western Europe.* Eds. A. Goodman and A. MacKay. London and New York: Routledge, 2013. 1–22.

Denham, Robert D. *Northrop Frye and Others: Twelve Writers Who Helped Shape his Thinking*. Toronto: Toronto UP, 2015.

Davies, Tony. *Humanism*. London: Routledge, 1997.

Frye, Northrop. *The Anatomy of Criticism*. Princeton: Princeton UP, 1957.

----- The *Educated Imagination*. Bloomington: Indiana UP, 1964.

----- *The Great Code.* Toronto: Toronto UP, 2006.

Laitman, Michael. *A Guide to the Hidden Wisdom of the Kabbalah.* Toronto: Kabbalah Publishers, 2009.

Hall, Manly P. *The Secret Teachings of All Ages*. San Francisco: H.S. Crocker, 1928.

Pope, Alexander. "An Essay on Man" in *Selected Poetry and Prose.* Ed. Robin Sowerby. New York: Routledge, 1988. 68–99.

North, Gary. *Unholy Spirits. Occultism and New Age Humanism*. Fort Worth, Texas, Dominion Press, 1986.

Schuchard, Marsha Keith Manatt. *Freemasonry, Secret Societies and the Continuity of the Occult Traditions in English Literature*. The University of Texas at Austin. Unpublished Ph. D., 1975.

Surette, Leon. *The Birth of Modernism: Ezra Pound, T.S. Eliot, W.B. Yeats, and the Occult.* Montreal: McGill-Queen's U. Press, 1994.

Symonds, J.A. *The Renaissance in Italy.* 2 vols. London: Smith Elder and Co, 1898.

Todorov, Tzvetan. *Imperfect Garden: The Legacy of Humanism.* Trans. Carol Cosman. Princeton: Princeton UP, 2002.

------"What is literature for?" *New Literary History*, Vol. 38, No. 1, (Winter, 2007): 13–32.

Yeats, W.B. *The Collected Poems*. London: Wordsworth Library, 2000.

Disorders Between Metaphysics and Classicism

The Order of Hell in the Judas Episode of the Anglo-Norman *Voyage of St Brendan*

J.S. Mackley, University of Northampton, England

Abstract

The twelfth-century Anglo-Norman version of the *Voyage of St Brendan* presented a discussion of the nature of salvation and damnation by offering an exciting narrative showing St Brendan's voyages to the Otherworld. One of the most memorable encounters is when St Brendan discovers Judas Iscariot on a rock in the middle of a tempestuous ocean. This scene is unique to the *Voyage* and provides vivid descriptions of a volcanic hell as witnessed by Brendan himself. However, when Brendan discovers that Judas Iscariot is given a "day of respite" on a rock in the middle of a tempestuous ocean, he learns of the geography of the Otherworld. Judas describes that there are two hells in which he suffers.

This article examines Judas's descriptions of the order of his weekly routine where his torture is alternated each day between the fiery and freezing hells, along with the non-canonical "day of respite" that Judas receives on account of the good deeds he performed in his lifetime. It considers some of the Biblical and classical sources which may have influenced this scene, including the Classical Otherworld and the different depictions of Hell in the Bible and the apocryphal *Apocalypse of Paul*.

This rhetorical means of discussion – which were reproduced in medieval texts – provided a forum to discuss the natures of salvation and in the vernacular when discussion of ecclesiastical matters was almost always in Latin.

Keywords: St Brendan, Judas Iscariot, Hell, otherworld

Introduction

This article considers the representation of Hell with specific reference to the Judas episode in the Anglo-Norman version of the *Voyage of St Brendan.*[1] Originally written at the end of the tenth century and often known by its Latin name, the *Nauigatio Sancti Brendan*, the *Voyage of St Brendan* tells the story of Brendan, a sixth century Irish abbot, who wishes to see the wonders of Paradise and the torments of Hell before he dies. The queen of Henry I of England requested this story to be translated in the first quarter of the twelfth century (Wooding 9–26). At a time when all educational and ecclesiastical matters were conducted in Latin, the translation of a text into the vernacular was a significant event in making stories accessible to the aristocratic court. Despite being a story containing many marvels, three of the surviving six manuscripts begin with a Christian hagiographic title: *Incipit vita Sancti Brendani* – "Here begins the Life of Saint Brendan". There are other Latin and Irish hagiographic texts that describe the pious deeds that Brendan performs: the Irish texts are known as the *Vita Brendani*, and the *Betha Brénnain.* The Anglo-Norman *Voyage* is not merely a translation of the Latin *Nauigatio*: the monk named at the beginning as 'Dom Benedeit' (l. 8), rewrote the story in octo-syllabic rhyming couplets. He excised materials from his Latin source text, either because they were lengthy liturgical lists, or because Benedeit himself was unfamiliar with the symbolism of the text he was reworking. He also added Christian maxims throughout, so that the cautionary message was as clear to the twelfth-century audience as it was to the monks who traveled with Brendan. Significantly, Benedeit greatly expands Brendan's encounter with Judas Iscariot. The focus of this article considers St Brendan's experiences of Hell as a physical location and his subsequent meeting with Judas Iscariot who has been granted a short respite from the tortures he experiences in *two* Hells because of the good deeds he has performed in his lifetime.

According to the legends of St Brendan, Judas is released from the

[1] All translations of the Anglo-Norman *Voyage* are taken from J.S. Mackley, *The Anglo-Norman Voyage of Brendan: Bilingual Edition* (Createspace: Isengrin Press, 2013); all references to the *Nauigatio* are from John J. O'Meara (ed. and trans.). "The Latin Version" in *The Voyage of St Brendan: Representative Versions of the Legend in English Translation.* Ed. W.R.J. Barron and Glyn S. Burgess. (Exeter: University of Exeter Press, 2005): 26–64, hereinafter referred to as the *Nauigatio.*

punishments of Hell for one day each week; on one of these respite days Brendan finds him and learns about the *two* Hells from one who has experienced them first hand. Judas's description of Hell in the Anglo-Norman *Voyage of St Brendan*, along with relevant comparisons with the earlier Latin *Nauigatio* and other antecedents describing a vision of the Otherworld, is the focus of this article.

The Anglo-Norman version of the *Voyage*, for the most part, follows the plot of the *Nauigatio*. Brendan is inspired to understand the mysteries of Heaven and Hell before he dies. He chooses fourteen companions to travel with him. In addition, three late-coming (or supernumerary) monks demand to join the crew, even though Brendan warns that they will not complete the quest. Together, they travel for seven years encountering many marvels at principal points of the liturgical calendar. These encounters include an island of giant sheep and a Paradise of Birds who are angels that sided neither with God nor Lucifer in the War in Heaven. The brethren also see a fish so large that it is mistaken for an island; and a perfect monastic community by which Brendan is almost tempted away from his quest. The brethren return to these locations at the same time on major liturgical feast days each year. Once they have travelled for seven years, the brethren cross into the Otherworld where they see a towering crystal pillar and a terrifying, demonic smith on the shores beside a flaming mountain. Brendan's final encounters are with the traitorous Judas Iscariot and then a holy hermit named Paul. Having understood the Christian maxims as demonstrated to him during his oceanic encounters, Brendan follows a Divine guide through a mist-barrier that conceals Paradise and sees *some* of the Divine mysteries; however, the human mind is unable to comprehend *all* the mysteries, and Brendan returns to Ireland with the promise that he will see the final mysteries after his death (Mackley 2013 64–201).

The Descriptions of Hell

After circling the ocean for seven years, the monks see a towering crystal pillar, which marks Brendan's crossing into the Otherworld (Mackley 2008 183). This tranquil encounter, a location where the monks say Mass in what seems to be a gigantic crystalline cathedral, acts as a juxtaposition to the violence of the Smitth of Hell; it is only in the Latin version that Brendan describes this as the "confines of Hell" (*Naugiatio* 55). Conversely, the Anglo-Norman version gives a more detailed, sensory description, of "putrid fumes, stinking more than rotting flesh" (ll. 1109–10) which leads to a hellish illustration of:

> The island alight
> And covered in smoke
> They see several thousand demons
> They hear the cries of the damned and weeping
> The stench comes to them, exceedingly great,
> From the smoke which spreads through the air. (ll. 1169–74)

The demon smith who inhabits this location disgorges fire from his throat (l. 1145) then hurls a metal blade at the monks' vessel – in fact, it lands far *beyond* the monks, highlighting the danger that the monks face (l. 1152). If the physical danger facing the monks was not sufficient, in the following scene, one of the late-coming, supernumerary monks is dragged away by a hundred demons "on account of [my] sins" (l. 1204) and shortly afterwards the surviving brethren see

> Hell quite open,
> Hell discharges fire and flames
> Burning poles and blades of metal
> Pitch and sulphur right up to the clouds
> And sucks them back in again, because they belong there. (ll. 1210–14)

Escaping the Smithy of Hell, the monks see a figure, a naked man, "plucked bare and battered" (l. 1227) clinging to a rock in a tempestuous sea, where even the elements appear to be attacking him:

> He clung to the stone,
> So that the waves would not drag him under;
> The waves of the sea struck him strongly
> So that his death knew no end.
> One struck him to the point that he nearly perished;
> The other, behind him, threw him upwards;
> Danger in front; danger above,
> Danger behind, danger below; (ll. 1231–38).

In addition to pain delivered by the waves, the man's face is whipped by a cloth. The man pleads to Jesus to intercede on his behalf. Brendan calms the waves, then asks what crime he has committed to warrant such a punishment. The man replies that he is Judas Iscariot, betrayer of Christ. There is a degree of irony in Judas's invocation of Jesus; but this is an act of desperation on his part. He says

> I do not know whether I ought to cry for mercy,
> I cannot, or dare not, for I did so much wrong
> That judgment has already been passed on me. (ll. 1252–54)

He continues by explaining his transgressions, and this follows the descriptions from the Bible: "the man who sold my saviour" (l. 1273), who was "pretending love by giving a kiss" (l. 1276); "I am he who kept his money" (l. 1277); then he describes himself as a "traitor who hated God" (l. 1287). He tried to return the pieces of silver as detailed in Matthew's Gospel (Matthew 26:15). Matthew is the source of the events which lead towards Judas's demise. In the Gospel narrative, Judas sees that Jesus has been handed over to Pilate, and although he attempts to reverse the situation by returning the coins to the priests, they refuse to accept them, and, in his despair, Judas hangs himself (Matthew 27:5). In the Anglo-Norman *Voyage*, Judas describes Jesus's trial, where He is "worshipped with derision, and [they] crowned him with thorns" (l. 1293–94); Judas also sees Jesus "suspended on the cross" and the "blood flow from his tender side" (ll. 1298–99). It is at this point, according to the *Voyage*, that Judas goes to the priests to return the thirty pieces of silver, but, as with Matthew's Gospel, they are "unwilling to accept repayment" (l. 1302). Admittedly, the act of returning money when Jesus is already dead seems like a futile gesture, unless this is part of the "madness" of which Judas speaks, which takes him over and leads him to kill himself (l. 1304). It is this suicide without confession that leads Judas to be "damned for all eternity" (l. 1306).

While Judas's betrayal of Jesus is well-known, in his account of the betrayal and Crucifixion in the *Voyage*, he repeats the phrase 'when I saw' (ll. 1289–1300). This is mirrored by the six days of torture that Judas suffers in Hell. However, Judas tells Brendan that the situation that he experiences – being lashed by the tempestuous seas, and whipped around the face and eyes – is nothing compared to the torments of Hell (l. 1308), and reveals: "I am given a respite from my danger that I receive on Saturday evening. [And] on Sunday, all day" (ll. 1309–11). He also lists other occasions – dates in the Monastic Calendar – when he is released from Hell, which include the fifteen days of Christmas, the Assumption of Mary, Easter, and Pentecost. Thus, Judas is released from his torture for 100 days each year.

The episode describing the meeting between Brendan and Judas is included in the earlier Latin *Nauigatio*, but here, Judas's suffering is discussed in a single sentence: "I burn, like a lump of molten lead in a pot, day and night, in the centre of the mountain you have just seen" (*Naugatio* 57). In the Anglo-Norman *Voyage*, the scene is greatly expanded – it occupies 282 of the 1840 lines of the full text, just over a sixth of the narrative – to reveal the structure and the punishments of Hell.

While the traditional image of Hell is one of fire and brimstone, the Anglo-Norman *Voyage* draws on an older tradition. Judas explains that there are two Hells: the first is situated on a mountain top, the other is in a valley; the two are separated by the sea. He says that he is the only one who suffers in both (ll. 1341–42). These descriptions evoke a sensory response, for example, the first Hell is described as hot and sweaty and is the more painful; the second Hell is cold and stinking, which is the more horrible of the two. These types of contrast echo a binary opposition that is reflected throughout the *Voyage*, for as we have seen above, the tranquility of the ice pillar is juxtaposed with the violence of the fiery mountain.

Judas relates how his tortures vary on a daily basis: on Monday in the mountain-hell, he is "turned on the wheel", at the speed of the wind.[2] His second punishment, having been hurled into the valley-hell, is to be chained to a bed of spits. He is then crushed with rocks and lead and his body is "all pierced through by being spitted there" (ll. 1359–68). His punishment on Wednesday in the mountain-hell is to be boiled in pitch then burned in a fire so intense that it would melt marble, and presumably Judas would have been blinded and suffocated by the pitch as it formed a mask around his face, but Judas's body cannot perish in the flames; by contrast on Thursday, when he is hurled again

[2] For a more detailed discussion of how the tortures inflicted on Judas resemble those contemporary with the writing of the Anglo-Norman *Voyage*, see J.S. Mackley, 'The Torturer's "Art" in the Judas Episode of Benedeit's *Voyage of St Brendan*', *Notes and Queries*, March 2007: 24–27.

into the valley, he is frozen so intensely that, ironically, he longs for the fires of the previous day.

Judas's fifth torture is an amalgamation of suffering: he is flayed until nothing remains of his skin, then pushed into a compound of salt and soot with a burning stake. However, the flesh grows back after each bout of torture so the torment can be repeated. He is then forced to drink molten lead and copper (l. 1415). This is in anticipation of Saturday's punishment, when he is hurled into the valley-hell and imprisoned in a dark, filthy dungeon; however, he swells with nausea and is unable to vomit because of the molten metal he has ingested. Instead, he says "my skin stretches ... I almost split" (ll. 1429–30). Although his Sunday is spent away from the two Hells, he still receives a comparative physical torture through being lashed by the waves and the cloth. His tortures also take on a further dimension: once Brendan has calmed the seas and the winds in a manner equating to Jesus calming the storms, Judas's punishment ceases to be physical (cf. Matthew 8:23–27; Mark 4:37–41; Luke 8:22–25). He knows what tortures will be inflicted upon him on a day-to-day basis and so part of the torture is the anticipation of knowing what comes next. His respite gives him time to reflect on past transgressions and his future suffering. Thus, the torture becomes a psychological anguish. However, Judas has the additional relief that his rock in the ocean is sufficiently far away from the two Hells that he is unable to hear the hellish torments from there (l. 1332).

The Respite

When Brendan asks about the items that Judas has with him, he discovers how this encounter with Judas is possible. While Brendan had first thought that Judas was suffering some infernal torment on the rock, Judas's descriptions of the two Hells in which he normally suffers reveals that this day of excruciating agony is a comparative relief compared to his daily measure of punishments. It is echoed later by Mephistopheles in Marlowe's *Doctor Faustus*, who, when questioned about how he is out of Hell, the demon replies "Why this is Hell, nor am I out of it!" (Scene III, l. 74). Judas has the anticipation of returning to his punishment: "Damned for all eternity" (l. 1306).

After Judas's descriptions of his daily tortures, Brendan asks Judas about the things he has with him. Judas explains that these represent the good deeds that he performed in his lifetime. He says that the alms he received (presumably from stealing from the other disciples' purse, as decribed in John 12:6) were used to buy "a cloth for a naked wretch" (l. 1456); however, because it was bought with stolen money, it was not his to give away. Consequently, the cloth causes physical pain and whips him across the eyes and face; on the other hand, Judas used it for a kind gesture, so it prevents Judas from drowning and eases his pain when he is hit by the waves. Furthermore, it is of no use to him in Hell (l. 1461). Conversely, the rock that Judas clings to represents a "hillock" which he placed in a watercourse, after which he built a "strong little bridge over it" (l. 1464) and thus helped travelers avoid a significant detour on their travels. This sounds a little elaborate for one of Judas's good deeds. In the Latin version, Judas explains "with the rock on which I sit I filled a trench in the public road to support the feet of those passing by, before I was a disciple of the Lord" (*Nauigatio* 58). It is these good deeds that secure Judas a weekly respite from Hell; but, however much the objects help him in this liminal space between Heaven and Hell, where Judas is not *in* Hell, but neither is he *out* of it, their significance is governed by how they were obtained and used in Judas's lifetime.

Such good deeds performed by Judas are found neither in the Bible nor in the Apocrypha. Indeed, in the Bible, when Judas appears, there is normally a foreshadowing of the future events. Judas is cast as Christ's betrayer. He is also called a thief because he stole from the disciples' money bag. Consequently, when considering other medieval stances towards the punishment of their archetypal betrayer, it is unusual to hear an account of him given in positive terms, rather than to focus on his damnation (although the Anglo-Norman *Voyage* does spend considerable time describing his punishment). Instead it is a means of demonstrating Christ's mercy by showing that even Judas, most grievous of sinners, receives a comparative relief from the tortures of Hell because of the good deeds that he performed in his lifetime. The Latin *Nauigatio* includes additional detail of Judas's good deeds. Judas says that he had given the cloth to a leper, but observes that it was not his to give, so it gives him no relief. As observed above, he "filled a trench in the public road" (*Nauigatio* 58). The *Nauigatio* has Judas perform an additional good deed: he gave the priests of the temple two iron forks to hold up cooking pots, and these are also on Judas's rock, with the cloth fixed to it to save him from drowning. It is easy to see why Benedeit omitted this additional material as it does not add anything to the scene, and it is confusing. Why would Judas give the forks to the temple priests? (*Nauigatio* 58) However, these "good deeds" that Judas performed provide additional characterization, generating empathy for Judas who is always last in line when the disciples are listed.

Nightfall soon approaches after Judas has described his tortures and his good deeds, and the demons return to take him back to Hell. Brendan, who has been moved to tears throughout this encounter, intercedes on Judas's behalf and secures an additional day of relief for him. Even so, one of the devils attempts to catch Judas with a crook (perhaps an inversion of the imagery of Jesus as Good Shepherd) but is prevented when Brendan invokes Christ as his protector. The following morning, the devils come forward again and threaten to inflict twice the normal amount on Judas, but again, Brendan forbids it and the devils depart with Judas (l. 1492).[3]

In the scene which follows Brendan's encounter with Judas, the brethren discover that one of the late-coming, supernumerary, monks has mysteriously disappeared. This is one of the monks whe Brendan predicted would not complete the voyage. Although there is no explanation as to what has happened, it is implicit that the devils took him away with Judas. That said, Brendan repeats the words that Judas uses earlier when doubting whether he dares to beg Christ for mercy. As noted above, Judas says "judgment has already been passed on me" (l. 1254), and Brendan observes of the third supernumerary monk:

> Judgment has been passed on him,
> Either for rest or for torment. (ll. 1509–10)

Thus, the Judas scene in the Anglo-Norman *Voyage* is bookended by the departure, and apparent damnation, of one of the supernumeraries.

[3] The *Nauigatio* also mentions that the devils are punished in Judas's place (58).

However, this is where the violence in the narrative ends. Just as the tranquil scene at the crystal pillar preceded the violence of the smoke-capped mountain, so the horrific dascription of Judas's torment is followed by a peaceful account of the encounter with extreme monastic aestheticism through the life of abstinence, as described by the pious hermit called Paul. Having heard of the horrors of damnation from Judas, the subsequent narrative from Paul the Hermit leads Brendan to truly understand the mysteries of Hell and Heaven.

Sources

Brendan's meeting with Judas and the latter's discussions of his torments in Hell are arguably the most popular and memorable of Brendan's encounters and appears in most vernacular translations of the *Voyage of Brendan*, as well as being incorporated into some of the *Vitae* describing Brendan's Holy deeds. This is remarkable as these devotional works are expected to focus on the holy deeds that Brendan performed, rather than the exciting tales of Brendan's life. Indeed, one scribe laments that he is unable to include all the marvelous details of Brendan's voyage, but must instead focus only on the hagiographic details of Brendan's life (Heist 329).

The Judas episode appears in a different form in the earliest texts of the *Vita Brendani*: while traveling through inclement weather, one of the brethren asks Brendan if the weather in Hell could be so awful (Moran 22). Brendan describes how he once saw Judas on a rock, beaten by both fiery and icy waves, but once he realized that this was a comparative release from Hell, he concluded that the weather in Hell was indeed worse than that in which the monks were travelling Plummer I 147). Here, then, Brendan only alludes to his meeting with Judas and the nature of Hell itself, and the audiences of the *Vita* could identify with the kinds of punishment Brendan describes. At this stage, the story is insufficiently developed to include Judas's good deeds or Brendan's intercession on Judas's behalf.

When considering the torments of Hell, it is worth giving s brief consideration to the later Dutch version of *The Voyage of Brendan*.[4]

[4] *De Reis van sint Brandaan*: The story has a different emphasis: Brendan is so incredulous when he reads a Book of Wonders, that he hurls it into the fire. Brendan

Only a handful of the encounters that appear in the Anglo-Norman *Voyage* are repeated in the Dutch *Reis,* but one of these is the meeting with Judas. As with the Latin and Anglo-Norman versions, Judas is found on a rock in the ocean with the cloth whipping his eyes and face. What is notable here is the description of Judas's body: "one of his sides was frozen to the bone, the other one was scorched by the rock" (Gerritsen and King 120). Clearly the motif of heat and cold associated with the torments of Hell was a well-rehearsed trope as it was transmitted to later reworkings of the legend.

The description of Brendan travelling to the Otherworld draws on many antecedents. We might consider Classical descriptions of the Otherworld, including the Greek and Roman depictions of Hades, and those heroes who traveled to – and returned from – that realm such as Odysseus or Aeneas. Here, the heroes must cross the river Styx to reach the Otherworld. In addition to the oceans and the mist barrier that appear in Brendan, there is a further water barrier – a river – in the *Nauigatio*: at this point Brendan and his monks realize that they cannot continue, but a Youth tells them "before you lies the land which you have sought for a long time" (*Nauigatio* 63). Having *seen* the land is enough for Brendan and he returns to Ireland to share what he has learned with his other monks, certain in the knowledge that he will soon reach that paradise.

One of the major influences on the Brendan narratives, which, as D.D.R. Owen argues, was "responsible more than any other single work for fixing the terrific detail of Hell in the Medieval eye", (Owen 3; cf. Patch 91–93) comes from the third century apocryphal text called the *Apocalypse of Paul*. This text was influenced by the Apostle Paul's Second letter to the Corinthians: Paul explains that he knew "a man" (most likely Paul himself) "such as one caught up to the third Heaven" (1 Corinthians 12: 1–5). Paul admits that he is uncertain whether he experienced this vision as a physical form, or as one whose

is then punished for his disbelief and charged to sail the ocean until he has replaced the book, cf. Willem P. Gerritsen and Peter K. King (ed. and trans.). "The Dutch Version" in *The Voyage of St Brendan: Representative Versions of the Legend in English Translation.* Ed. W.R.J Barron and Glyn S. Burgess. (Exeter: University of Exeter Press, 2005): 107–130.

soul had separated from the body (see below with reference to Dante). Even though Paul had reached this Paradise, he also suffered a thorn in his flesh, described as a torment from "a messenger of Satan", and even though Paul pleaded three times to be free of this thorn, Christ did not oblige, replying "My power is made perfect in your weakness" (2 Corinthians 12:7–9). These themes of a vision of the Otherworld, torment and an appeal to Christ for some clemency from the tortures all appear in the *Apocalypse of Paul* and the Latin and Anglo-Norman versions of the Brendan legend. The early part of this biblical passage is also positioned at the start of the *Apocalypse* to contextualize it. As with the canonical *Book of Revelation* (or *Apocalypse*) of St John the Divine, Paul is led through his vision by an angel. In the *Apocalypse*, Paul says to his guiding angel "I would see the souls of the righteous and the sinners as they depart" (James 530). Paul soon sees "a great cloud of fire spread over the whole world", representing unrighteousness. This quickly moves Paul to tears, just as Brendan laments on hearing Judas's punishment.

Paul is taken down into the various circles of Hell: "I saw there a river of fire burning with heat, and in it was a multitude of men and women sunk up to the knees, and other men up to the navel; others also up to the lips and others up to the hair" (James 542). Each figure is immersed according to the heinousness of their sin. There is also "a place of ice and snow" where the men and women stand naked with their hands and feet cut off (James 544). Although this is only one of several examples of Hell in the Apocalypse, here we see an example of the two opposing Hells, one of fire, the other of ice, which may have been the source of inspiration for the depiction of the two Hells that Judas visits (Owen 3). Of course, in these examples the sinners stay in their own Hell allocated in accordance with the type of sin they have committed, unlike Judas who suffers in both Hells in the Anglo-Norman *Voyage*. One of Judas's torments on the rock in the *Voyage* – being whipped by the blanket – might have been inspired by the description of a bishop in Hell: "four evil angels" smote him with stones and wounded his face like a tempest. In the previous passage in the *Apocalypse* the angel Aftemeloukos "came with a great fork of fire" and "pierced the entrails of the old man" James 542). Thus the characters in the Apocalypse are punished according to their immoral acts during their lifetime, whereas, in the Anglo-Norman *Voyage*, Judas is rewarded because of the good deeds he performed. Given that Judas had three items associated with his good deeds in the earlier *Nauigatio*, it is reasonable to assume that the author of the *Nauigatio* had the images in the *Apocalypse* in mind, although in the *Nauigatio*, the forks benefit Judas, rather than harm him.

Likewise, Judas's Wednesday and Thursday tortures in the Anglo-Norman *Voyage* seem to be a reversal of the scene of torture in the *Apocalypse of Paul* where the sinners are plunged into a river of fire. In the vision of Hell, Paul begs Christ to intercede on behalf of the souls; however, Christ rebukes Paul, asking "Art thou more merciful than the Lord God?" (James 546). The souls of the dead then call upon Christ: "he that hast granted refreshment unto all that are in Heaven and earth; have mercy on us likewise" (James 548). When Paul asks Christ to intercede and offer the damned some respite, Christ asks of the sinners "[w]hat *good* works have ye done that ye should ask me for refreshment?" But because of prayers and oblations, as well as Christ's own goodness, he grants a day of respite on Easter Monday: "on that day whereon I rose from the dead I grant unto all of you that art in torment refreshment for a day and a night forever" (James 548).

Although the *Apocalypse of Paul* is seen to be a principal influence on the *Nauigatio* and the Anglo-Norman *Voyage*, there are many other later examples of the Otherworld in literature. Often, the characters' visions are a result of serious illness for example the "angelic vision" of St Furseus (Gardiner 51–55). On some occasions the person who experiences the vision has already died, but who, after experiencing a vision of the Otherworld is then restored to life so that they can amend their own ways, or pass on the knowledge, as in the example of St Drythelm (who also witnessed Heaven and Hell, but who was refused access to Paradise) – and Tundale, who is restored to life so that he can confess his sins and live a pious life (Gardiner 57–63; 149–95). The *Vision of Tundale*, like the Anglo-Norman *Voyage* and the *Apocalypse of Paul*, describes two Hells of fire and ice. Another way of accessing the Otherworld is through a dream rather than vision, as seen in later texts, such as *The Vision of Piers Plowman* and a devotional text called *Pearl*. Written in the fourteenth century, *Pearl* describes how the "Jeweller" loses his "pearl" in a garden: this could be an allegory for the narrator lamenting the death of his infant daughter, as she "left" before she was three years old (Andrew and Waldron l. 483). The Jeweller has a dream in which he sees the pearl-maiden – his daughter – in Heaven and although they are separated by a stream, they discuss theology and the redemption of the Jeweller. Again, we see the stream as a barrier which prevents the traveller from going any further, so that he only sees and hears things that the human mind can process. When he tries to cross, he falls into the water and wakes up. As with the *Voyage of Brendan*, *Pearl* deals in the vernacular with some challenging ecclesiastical issues, such as the nature of salvation at a time when it was considered heretical to do so. The dream vision was a form that was accessible to anyone. In the *Purgatorio*, Dante describes how dreams may be prophetic at a time just before waking when our souls become liberated from our bodies, and, unhindered by our physical forms, our minds are open to influences and "visions that are almost divine" (Dante, *Purgatorio*, Canto IX, II.16–18; cf. Seroni 50–59). Even this is derived from classical writers such as Virgil and Homer who believed that the dreamer and the ghost were both disembodied souls.

Biblical Hells

The concepts of *two* Hells is not found in the Bible although Owen notes that references are made in Pope Gregory the Great's *Dialogues* (VI, 42) and Honorius Augustodunensis's *Elucidarium* (3, 13 §447) (Owen 60). However, while these may be interpretations of Psalm 86 which refers to a "lower hell" (*inferno inferiori*), there are, in fact, three different words that are translated as "Hell" in the King James Bible. These are *Hades* (*Sheol* in Hebrew); *Tartarus* and *Gehenna*.

Hades corresponds to the modern word 'grave'. In this condition there is no awareness of the state of death (Ecclesiastes 9:5, 10. Cf. Psalm 16:10; Ezekiel 32 27–29; Matthew 11:23; 16:18; Acts 2:31). This is where the dead will sleep until Resurrection. *Tartarus* in Greek mythology is the name of a prison where the wicked are punished: it is the place where Sisyphus pushes his boulder up the hill. The Bible uses the verb *tartaroo* – to imprison. Peter the Apostle explains that fallen angels were cast into 'gloomy dungeons' to await judgement

(2 Peter 2:4; cf. Jude 6, 7). James notes the word *Tartar-uchi* is used in the description of the Hell inflicted on a priest who had not fulfilled his ministry (James 543). Paul says that the priest is stood in a river of fire where he is caught by the throat by angels, keepers of Hell who "pierced the [priest's] entrails" (James 543).

Gehenna refers to a real place south west of Jerusalem, the Valley of Hinnom, where in the Old Testament the Israelites sacrificed their children (Jeremiah 32:35 Matthew 5:29, 30; James 3:6). Later it was a place where Jerusalem's rubbish was destroyed in constantly burning fires. It was also the place where city inhabitants would dispose of anything unclean, including the bodies of executed criminals; thus, it is a term that links the image of the burning fires in Hell with the total annihilation of the soul. Therefore, the Anglo-Norman *Voyage*'s description of Hell in a valley is not canonical. In Revelation, this distinction of different Hells is made most clear where John describes how 'death and Hades were thrown into the lake of fire. The lake of fire is the second death' (Revelation 20:14). The 'second death' is total annihilation: those who do not suffer the second death live with Christ in eternal life.

Of these three concepts of Hell, then, only two suggest torture: in Hades, the soul is oblivious until the Day of Judgement: this is not Judas's fate. It is the other two Hells that he suffers in the Anglo-Norman *Voyage*. Judas is denied the oblivion of Hades. Instead, his description of how in one Hell he is 'removed and roasted, bound to a post between two fires', is likely to have been influenced by the understanding of Gehenna. He then describes how he is put in a dungeon where he endures the tortures ascribed to that day: this description is probably based on Tartarus (l. 1419).

In other descriptions of Hell, Judas arrives only moments after all the other residents of Hell are released, that is, at the time of Christ's Harrowing of Hell. Or Judas is found in the very heart of Hell, suffering the worst of punishments. The message from the Biblical and Anglo-Norman representations of Judas is that his principal crime was to despair of Christ's mercy. His punishments in the Otherworld are measured (or indeed, *without* measure) because of the sinful deeds Judas committed in his lifetime; however, Judas's good deeds are considered and it is these that the Anglo-Norman *Voyage* explore to present Judas as an example of God's mercy.

Conclusion

Brendan's encounter with Judas is one of the most memorable scenes in the different versions of the *Voyage of Brendan*. The Anglo-Norman reworking of the original Latin text provides a discursive space in which to explore the nature of salvation and damnation in a safe, and importantly *vernacular* environment. Judas is in a space where he is neither in Hell, nor out of it. The day of respite provides an opportunity for him to describe his experience of the two Hells as a didactic caution to those still alive. In addition, the accounts of Hell describe a routine approach to Judas's daily tortures. There is a structure to Hell and punishment therein, which, in turn, brings order to the chaos of damnation. Hell becomes structured.

As we have seen, the Judas episode demonstrates indebtedness to the themes witnessed in the apocryphal *Apocalypse of Paul.* The idea of any kind of release from Hell was *anathema* to the Church Fathers and the Apocalypse was condemned in the *Gelasian* Decree, written in the sixth century, while the encyclopedist, Vincent of Beauvais (writing around a century after the *Voyage* was circulated) described the Apocalypse as 'full of fables' (James 525). On the other hand, later critics such as D.D.R. Owen and Jacques Le Goff, note its importance in creating the imagery of Hell and Purgatory (Owen 3; Le Goff 35).

Likewise, the story of Judas's respite from Hell is not canonical, and was censured by the Church. In the deposition of Bernard Raymond Barahon in 1274, Barahon explained to his inquisitors that he believed Paradise was a place of rest because he had read of it in the *Life of Brendan.* Following the Inquisition, Barahon handed his two books over to the inquisitors: a copy of the Brendan legend (perhaps the Occitan version), and an Occitan poem called *La Bible* (Biller et al. 583–589).

The idea of Hell being organized in terms of punishment, rather than chaos, was used by Dante in his *Inferno*, where punishment is meted out according to the sins of the damned. Virgil tells Dante: "Hope not ever to see Heaven. I have come to lead you to the other shore; into eternal darkness; into fire and into ice" (Dante, *Inferno*, Canto III, II. 85–87) with the ice being in the lowest circle, freezing Lucifer up to his chest (Dante, *Inferno*, Canto XXXIV, II.29, 90). Dante uses sources that have also influenced the encounters in the Brendan narrative; Dante observes that "the chosen vessel went there" – meaning Hell – and Dante compares himself with other travelers to the Underworld, explaining "I am not Aeneas, neither am I Paul" (Dante, *Inferno*, Canto XXXIV, I.32.).

The legend of Brendan in its various forms, shows a rather liberal approach to theology, much to the chagrin of commentators such as Vincent, and, more particularly, the Inquisition. Neither version is condemnatory of the transgressor of the Bible, but instead, both generate sympathy by adding depth to their characters. Ultimately, however, the message to those transgressors against God – even through apathy – is that they face Limbo; waiting instead for possible respite or even salvation. Rather than restricting itself to punishment for the sins one commits in life – and even Brendan berates himself for failing to achieve perfection – the Judas episode also speaks of rewarding the good deeds that one does. Even so, Judas is punished for his sins, and the respite gives only comparative relief.

Judas's respite echoes Brendan's journey. When Judas is released from Hell at Easter, Brendan travels from an island of giant sheep to the back of an enormous fish that the monks initially mistake for an island. By Pentecost, he has reached the Paradise of Birds which is the abode of angels that sided neither with God nor Lucifer, and were cast out of Heaven for their apathy. The parallel is clear: the angels have been removed from Heaven, and Judas has been granted a release from Hell. The characters are in motion, but they are uncertain about their fate.

Works cited

Alighieri, Dante. *La Divina Commedia.* Ed. by Umberto Bosco and Giovanni Reggio. 3 vols. Florence: Le Monnier, 1979. Print.

Andrew, Malcolm and Ronald Waldron. Ed. and trans. *The Poems of the Pearl Manuscript: Pearl, Cleanness, Patience, Sir Gawain and the Green Knight*. Exeter: University of Exeter Press, rev. 5th ed. 2007. Print.

Biller, Peter, Caterina Bruschi and Shelagh Sneddon eds. *Inquisitors and Heretics in Thirteenth-Century Languedoc: Edition and Translation of Toulouse Inquisition Depositions, 1273–1282.* Leiden: Brill, 2011. Print.

Eileen. Gardiner. *Visions of Heaven and Hell before Dante.* New York: Italica Press, 1989. Print.

Gerritsen, Willem P. and Peter K. King. ed. and trans. "The Dutch Version" in *The Voyage of St Brendan: Representative Versions of the Legend in English Translation.* Ed. W.R.J Barron and Glyn S. Burgess. Exeter: University of Exeter Press, 2005: 107–30. Print.

Heist, W.W. ed. *Vitae sanctorum Hiberniae*. Brussels: Société des Bollandistes, 1965. Print.

James, Montague Rhodes. ed. and trans. "The Apocalypse of Paul". *The Apocryphal New Testament*. Oxford: Clarendon Press, 1924. 525–55. Print.

Le Goff, Jacques. *The Birth of Purgatory*. Trans. Arthur Goldhammer. Chicago: University of Chicago Press, 1984. Print.

Mackley, J.S. 'The Torturer's "Art" in the Judas Episode of Benedeit's *Voyage of St Brendan*". *Notes & Queries*, (March 2007): 24–7. Print.

Mackley, J.S. *The Anglo-Norman Voyage of Brendan: Bilingual Edition.* Createspace: Isengrin Press, 2013. Print.

Mackley, J.S. *The Legend of St Brendan: A Comparative Study of the Latin and Anglo-Norman Versions*. Leiden: Brill, 2008. Print.

Marlowe, Christopher. *Doctor Faustus: The A Text*. Ed. John O'Connor. 2nd Ed. Harlow: Pearson/Longman, 2003. Print.

Moran, Patrick F. *Acti sancti Brendani: Original Latin Documents connected with the Life of Saint Brendan, Patron of Kerry and Clonfert.* Dublin: William Kelly, 1872. Print.

O'Meara, John J. "The Latin Version". *The Voyage of St Brendan:*

Representative Versions of the Legend in English Translation. Ed. W.R.J Barron and Glyn S. Burgess. Exeter: University of Exeter Press, 2005. 26–64. Print.

Owen, D.R.R. *The Vision of Hell: Infernal Journeys in Medieval French Literature.* Edinburgh and London: Scottish Academic Press, 1970. Print.

Patch, Howard Rollin. *The Other World According to Descriptions in Medieval Literature*. Cambridge, Mass. Harvard University Press, 1950. Print.

Plummer, Charles. ed. *Vitae Sanctorum Hiberniae*. 2 vols. Oxford: Clarendon Press, 1910. Print.

Seroni, Charles 'Dante's Prophetic Morning-Dreams.' *Studies in Philology* 45 (1948): 50–9. Print.

Wooding, Jonathan M. "The Date of Nauigatio S. Brendani Abbatis". *Studia Hibernica*, 37 (2011): 9–26. Print.

Du «Désordre» dans Les Nouvelles Récréations et Joyeux Devis de Bonaventure Des Périers

Farah Stiti Haddad

Résumé

Chez Des Périers, la notion de « désordre » est intéressante, non seulement par la fréquence de ses manifestations, mais aussi parce qu'elle est chargée d'intention. En effet, sous couvert de compositions légères dépourvues d'enseignement, les *Nouvelles Récréations et Joyeux Devis* de Des Périers s'avèrent, «paradoxalement» (au sens étymologique du terme), riches de significations.

Le premier volet de notre communication, que nous avons pris le parti d'intituler «Une esthétiuqe du «désordre» », traitera des différentes manifestations du désordre qui rythment les *Joyeux Devis.*

Le deuxième volet de notre étude, intitulé «Des interlocutions faussement joyeuses», tentera de lever le voile sur la dimension subversive qui sous-tend l'œuvre de bout en bout. Pour ce faire, nous nous appuierons sur les outils qu'offre la discipline de l'analyse du discours et essentiellement sur les travaux de Dominique Maingueneau.

L'originalité foncière de l'œuvre de Des Périers réside dans la fonction assignée au désordre. Loin de renvoyer à une «faiblesse esthétique» – conception communément admise – le désordre renvoie, chez Des Périers, à l'acte d'écriture. En réalité, tout se passe comme si les personnages (mais également le narrateur-conteur lui-même), ne pouvaient s'exprimer que par le biais de détours et de distorsions. Ainsi, le désordre n'est pas envisagé comme un écart par rapport à une norme, il est inhérent à toute création littéraire.

En ce sens, le désordre intronise, dans l'écriture de Des Périers, un nouveau rapport au langage. Loin de constituer un frein à l'intelligibilité d'un énoncé, il permet –paradoxalement- de traduire au plus près la relation conflictuelle que l'auteur entretient avec la société dans laquelle il évolue.

Mots-clés: Désordre, Genres, Rire, Carnavalisation, Subversion

«Ouvrez le livre: si un compte ne vous plaist, hay à l'autre. Il y en ha de

> tous bois (…) Et ne me venez point demander quelle ordonnance j'ay tenue. **Car quel ordre fault il garder quand il est question de rire**? Qu'on ne me vienne pas non plus faire des difficultez: Oh ce ne fut pas cestuy cy qui fit cela: Oh cecy ne fut pas faict en ce cartier la: je l'avoys desja ouy compter: celafut faict en nostre pays: Riez seulement, et ne vous chaille si ce fut Gaultier ou si ce fut Gargouille. Ne vous souciez point si ce fut à Tours en Berry, ou à Bourges en Touraine. Vous vous tourmenteriez pour neant.»[1]

Dans son adresse au lecteur, Des Périers annonce d'emblée la couleur: ses nouvelles ne suivront aucun ordre préétabli. Loin de guider le lecteur, cette «autonomie» des nouvelles le déroute car il ne peut s'appuyer sur aucun type d'ancrage.[2]

En effet, dans les *Nouvelles Récréations et Joyeux Devis*,[3] le souci de la vraisemblance est constamment concurrencé voire détrôné par ce que les critiques s'accordent à appeler «le plaisir de la conversation». C'est d'ailleurs dans ce sens que Jean-Claude Arnoud avance dans son article intitulé «Le joyeux devis des nouvelles récréations» les propos suivants:

> La plasticité du recueil, la versatilité du rapport à la vérité sont certes des traits du genre facétieux, en pleine harmonie avec la mobilité des acteurs et la volubilité du narrateur. Elles reçoivent cependant ici une signification plus profonde: l'indifférence du réel par rapport au narré, déjà proclamée par le prologue. Au fond, il est égal que les choses n'aient pas été telles qu'elles sont contées, «c'est tout un.» Car l'enjeu véritable de la performance n'est pas le réel mais la narration elle-même; il n'est pas la véracité de cette narration mais la «bonne grâce» avec laquelle elle s'accomplit et produit des effets sur l'auditoire, le centre de gravité se déportant ainsi franchement de son contenu vers l'échange qu'il permet entre auteur et lecteur (…).[4]

En outre, par le biais de l'interrogation rhétorique qui clôt l'affirmation de Des Périers, «*Car quel ordre fault il garder quand il est question de rire?*», l'auteur explique que le ton humoristique de son recueil exclut toute forme de rigueur formelle.

---

[1] Bonaventure Des Périers, *Les Nouvelles Récréations et Joyeux Devis*, p. 11.

[2] Ni temporel, ni spatial, ni même thématique.

[3] NRJD: Abréviation pour *Les Nouvelles Récréations et Joyeux Devis.*

[4] Article de Jean-Claude Arnoud intitulé «Le joyeux devis des nouvelles récréations», in Boudou Bénédicte (dir.) et Dominique Bertrand, *Lire les Nouvelles Recréations et Joyeux devis de feu Bonavanture Des Périers*, Presses de L'Université Blaise Pascal de Clermont Ferrand, 2009, p. 32.

De quelle manière l'expression du «désordre» se manifeste-t-elle dans les NRJD? Ya-t-il des enjeux sous-jacents au projet de Des Périers? Ou bien s'agit-il d'une entreprise ludique qui n'aspire qu'à dérider le lecteur? Telles seront les principales questions auxquelles nous tenterons de répondre au cours de notre communication.

Chez Des Périers, la notion de «désordre» est intéressante, non seulement par la fréquence de ses manifestations, mais aussi parce qu'elle est chargée d'intention. En effet, derrière une façade légère qui refuse la pesanteur d'un quelconque enseignement, les nouvelles de Des Périers s'avèrent – paradoxalement – riches de significations.

C'est d'ailleurs dans cette perspective que nous avons choisi d'articuler notre travail autour de deux axes.

I. Une esthétique du désordre:

Le premier volet de notre communication, que nous avons pris le parti d'intituler «Une esthétique du désordre», traitera des différentes manifestations du désordre, qu'elles soient d'ordre microstructural (de manière ponctuelle, c'est-à-dire des phénomènes à petite échelle, à l'intérieur de l'œuvre) ou macrostructural (donc dans une perspective plus large, à l'échelle de l'œuvre entière).

En ce qui concerne l'architecture globale du recueil, nous nous attarderons sur certaines pratiques qui confèrent au recueil son aspect «chaotique».

Pour ce faire, nous nous sommes intéressée au problème du/des genre(s) au(x)quel(s) l'œuvre appartiendrait.[5]

Réfractaire à toute tentative de classification, les NRJD constituent une œuvre atypique tant le métissage générique y est prononcé et tant l'héritage dans lequel elle puise y est composite.

Non sans flottement, Des Périers hésite à qualifier ses anecdotes de «*Comptes*»,[6] «*Propos*»,[7] ou encore «Nouvelles».[8] Autant de substantifs, qui ne peuvent nous laisser indifférents face à ce que

---

[5] L'emploi du conditionnel est ici délibéré.

[6] «*Pour venir à nostre **compte***» p. 38; «*Et s'il gaigna ou perdit* (…) *le **compte** n'en dit rien.*» p. 91; «(…) *le **compte** dit qu'il* (…)» p. 69; «*On dit de luy, tout plain de bons **comptes**,* (...)» p. 192; «*On dit du mesmes Pontalais un **compte**,* (…)» p. 143.

[7] «Je vous gardoys ces joyeux **propos** à quand la paix seroit faicte (…)» p. 13.

[8] Ce terme figure dans le titre de la première nouvelle: «*Premiere **Nouvelle** en forme de preambule*».

semble vouloir nous présenter l'auteur-narrateur comme une véritable «palette synonymique» du processus narratif. Cette tendance[9] qui consiste à déployer tout un attirail de synonymes était d'ailleurs monnaie courante chez les auteurs de la Renaissance.

Les critiques peinent également à s'entendre sur une même qualification pour désigner cette œuvre haute en couleur. Si Furretière parle de «facéties», Lionel Sozzi préfère le mot «contes», et Bénédicte Boudou celui de «nouvelles».[10] Bref, autant d'appellations qui ne cessent de donner du fil à retordre aussi bien aux théoriciens qu'aux lecteurs les plus avertis.

Parallèlement à ce problème de taxinomie qui crée déjà assez de confusion dans l'esprit du lecteur, nous avons relevé un autre phénomène – assez récurrent dans l'économie du recueil- à savoir, la non-correspondance entre le nombre de nouvelles (qui est de 90) et celui des anecdotes qui les composent (qui s'élève à plus de 150). En effet, dans une seule et même nouvelles peuvent se succéder ou s'enchâsser deux, trois anecdotes voire plus. Et le titre, lacunaire, ne fait souvent allusion qu'à une seule d'entre elles, laissant au lecteur le soin de les découvrir au fur et à mesure. Est-ce par négligence? Est-ce un oubli? Ou bien est-ce une manière de créer une certaine hiérarchie entre les anecdotes (autrement dit, de mettre en exergue les plus importantes)? Une chose est sûre, cela participe de cette esthétique du désordre si chère à Des Périers.

De surcroît, le passage d'une anecdote à une autre (et à une échelle plus grande: d'une nouvelle à une autre, à part quelques cycles tels que le cycle des coupeurs de bourses et le cycle des Poitevins) se fait le plus souvent de manière brutale et sans transitions, semant davantage le doute dans l'esprit du lecteur.

Toujours dans cette perspective, l'impression de désordre naît des différents commentaires métalinguistiques qui balisent l'œuvre. En effet, à plusieurs reprises, Des Périers se contredit, rectifie certaines

---

[9] A ce sujet, Mireille Huchon affirme d'ailleurs dans son œuvre intitulée «*Histoire de la langue française*» qu' «Au XVIème siècle, la perfection d'une langue se mesure à l'étendue de son vocabulaire, au nombre de ses synonymes.»

[10] Pour ne citer que ceux-là des critiques qui se sont penchés sur le cas des NRJD de Des Périers.

«maladresses», et réajuste ses commentaires: il dit une chose puis son contraire, ouvre des parenthèses, et va même jusqu'à récuser âprement ce qu'il affirmait quelques lignes plus haut. En effet, Des Périers affirme une chose pour aussitôt la réfuter et à y voir de plus près, c'est souvent ce qu'il récuse violemment qui constitue le fond de sa pensée.

En retouchant systématiquement ses propos, ce dernier nous met sur la piste d'une écriture qui se cherche et qui commente et pointe constamment ses propres défaillances.

A ce stade du travail, certaines questions s'imposent: Est-ce les traces d'une œuvre qui voit le jour sous les yeux du lecteur? Ou est-ce justement un artifice qui veut nous faire croire à l'«imperfection» inhérente à toute œuvre littéraire? Là encore, une chose est sûre: l'entreprise de Des Périers semble n'avoir qu'un seul mot d'ordre: faire de l'oralité et du badinage, les *stylèmes*[11] de ces devis.

C'est d'ailleurs en ce sens qu'il feint souvent dans ses «haltes commentatives»[12] de comprendre certaines attitudes de ses personnages et va même jusqu'à tenter de les justifier. En réalité, nous avons fréquemment affaire, dans les *Joyeux Devis*, à un fonctionnement antiphrastique des commentaires qui crée une confusion dans l'esprit du lecteur. Ainsi, au lieu d'éclairer, ces derniers ne font bien souvent que brouiller davantage les pistes et déjouer *l'Horizon d'attente* [13] du lecteur.

Par ailleurs, si l'œuvre de Des Périers accuse un aspect «décousu», c'est très souvent à cause du nombre vertigineux de proverbes qui ponctuent les nouvelles. Les articles de J. W. Hassell Jr.[14] et d'Alina

---

[11] Stylème: «Comment qualifier le genre de faits que l'on trouve, que l'on détecte, que l'on cherche en tout cas à isoler, dans ce domaine du stylistique? Puisqu'il ne suffit pas de dire qu'on trouve un mot, une distribution, un système narratif … toutes choses qui sont des réalités ou précisément linguistiques ou généralement langagières, mais en aucune façon spécifiquement stylistiques. On répond: on cherche des «caractérisèmes de littérarité»; acceptons de donner le nom de «*stylème*» à un tel caractérisème.» in G. Molinié, (1997), p. 203.

[12] C'est ainsi que qualifie Lionelle Sozzi les nombreux commentaires qui ponctuent l'œuvre de Des périers, l'apparentant le plus souvent à une conversation à bâtons rompus dans son œuvre intitulée « Les contes de Bonaventure Des Périers».

[13] Terminologie de Jauss dans son ouvrage: *Pour une esthétique de la récéption*, (Gallimard, 1978).

[14] J. W. Hassell Jr, «The Proverb in Bonaventure des Périers' short stories», *The Journal of American Folklore*, vol. 75, n° 295 (1962), pp. 33–47.

Lewicka[15] offrent d'ailleurs un éclairage intéressant sur ces tournures proverbiales qui parasitent les devis et leur confèrent cet aspect décousu. Il n'est d'ailleurs que de citer la nouvelle 5 pour s'en convincre.[16]

Il en est de même pour les nombreuses digressions qui scandent le recueil de bout en bout. En effet, par le truchement de ces structures parenthétiques, le narrateur intronise un nouveau rapport aux propos qu'il tient: il bifurque, s'écarte de son dessein initial et prend des libertés quant à son thème principal. Cette démarche est d'ailleurs souvent assimilée à une activité involontaire, accidentelle que le conteur tente tant bien que mal de maîtriser.

Dans la mesure où elle émerge à l'insu du conteur de façon presque inconsciente, la digression constitue un espace privilégié de la subjectivité où s'esquissent les pensées, les positions et les partis-pris de ce dernier. En témoigne la nouvelle 82 dans laquelle l'intervention finale du conteur en dit long sur sa position quant aux hommes de loi: «(…) *Surquoy le Prevost (car telles personnes ne sont pas voulentiers renvoyees devant l'Evesque) luy dit en riant* (…)».[17] Il en est de même pour la nouvelle 74 dans laquelle le narrateur-conteur tourne cette fois en dérision les érudits et tous les pédants qui prétendent détenir un savoir en ces termes:

> (…) mais comme il advient que les hommes sçavans ne font pas voulontiers des enfans des plus spirituelz du monde, (je croy que c'est parce qu'ilz laissent leur esprit en leur estude, quand ilz vont coucher avec leurs femmes) celuy dont nous parlons (…)[18]

Dans une œuvre qui relève de l'esthétique de la «brièveté»[19] et du

---

[15] Alina Lewicka, «Un exemple de comique subversif: l'emploi du proverbe dans les Nouvelles récréations de Bonaventure des Périers», *Le comique verbal en France au XVIème siècle*, éd. de l'Université de Varsovie, 1981, pp. 219–32.

[16] Dans la nouvelle 5 intitulée «*Des trois Seurs nouvelles espouses qui respondirent chascune un bon mot à leur mary la premiere nuict de leurs nopces»,* les répliques à caractère proverbial des trois épouses constituent le «point culminant» de l'anecdote, autrement dit le moment où la tension est à son comble.

[17] NRJD, p. 289.

[18] NRJD, p. 265.

[19] Le «Principe de Brièveté»: «De ses origines, la nouvelle garde un caractère oral, ce qui suppose une autre caractéristique: la brièveté: «C'est le seul trait que retiendra dans son évolution le genre de la nouvelle aux dépens de la notion étymologique de nouveauté» (in Thomine M-C., L'Heptaméron, Neuilly, Atlande, 2005.) Dubuis le rappelle in Sozzi, 1981, 24): la brièveté est une nécessité sociologique, une manière

fragment, il convient de s'interroger sur la légitimité et la place de ces entités digressives qui, en tant que développements, engendrent des effets de ralentissements et perturbent par là même la construction régulière et accélérée des contes.

Tout cela sans oublier le recours systématique aux latinismes ainsi qu'aux «*langages individualisés*»[20] qui rendent souvent la tâche du lecteur plus difficile. Il s'agit là d'autant d'éléments qui font des NRJD une œuvre éminemment «polyphonique».

II. Des interlocutions faussement joyeuses:

Dans le deuxième volet de notre travail intitulé «Des interlocutions faussement joyeuses» nous tâcherons de dégager la dimension ludique des *Devis* qui n'est, en réalité, qu'apparente.

Pour ce faire, nous nous appuierons sur les outils qu'offre la discipline de l'analyse du discours et essentiellement sur les travaux de Dominique Maingueneau qui affirme que l'acte de création «poétique» [21] implique fatalement une dimension polémique.[22]

Toutefois, le substantif «Récréations» présent dans le titre du recueil met d'emblée l'accent sur la finalité récréative et ludique de l'œuvre aux dépens du genre, du sujet, d'une dimension didactique ou encore moins polémique.

Nous nous sommes, par conséquent retrouvée, confrontée à un paradoxe: cette œuvre, placée sous le sceau du comique s'achève sur une nouvelle tragique où un mari jaloux tue sa femme infidèle. C'est cette place de choix accordée à la seule et unique nouvelle tragique du recueil qui nous a mise sur la piste d'une entreprise faussement joyeuse. En effet, tout se passe comme si le narrateur invitait son lecteur, dans la dernière nouvelle, à relire l'œuvre sous un nouveau jour.

---

de soutenir l'attention du public, d'éveiller son intérêt, de ne pas lui déplaire. Associée au plaisir narratif, la brièveté se rattache à une esthétique de la *varietas.* Cette brièveté nous conduit aussi au public auquel s'adresse la nouvelle, à cette « société conteuse» in Boudou B. et Halévy O., *Bonaventure Des Périers, Nouvelles Récréations et Joyeux Devis,* Atlande, 2008, p. 60.

[20] C'est en ces termes que Lionnel Sozzi qualifie le langage de la vieille «vieillois», du chien «cagnesque» de Caillette «le cailletois» qui balisent de bout en bout le recueil.

[21] A prendre au sens étymologique du terme, autrement dit de «création littéraire».

[22] Au sens de «controversé».

Nous allons donc tenter, à ce stade du travail, de démontrer que, malgré la frivolité apparente des *Devis*, on décèle rapidement les caractéristiques d'un discours qui s'érige «*contre*».

Puis, nous tenterons de démontrer, à la lumière de la théorie Bakhtinienne de carnavalisation, que toutes les interlocutions qui jalonnent le recueil, participent d'une volonté plus large de guérir le lecteur grâce aux vertus thérapeutiques du rire.

Nous nous intéresserons d'abord au traitement que fait la discipline de l'analyse du discours de la notion d'*Ethos*.[23] L'Ethos est la manière avec laquelle l'orateur construit son discours et la façon dont il se montre dans le texte. Autrement dit, il s'agit du «rôle» ou encore du «masque» que porte l'énonciateur.

C'est d'ailleurs en ce sens que le narrateur des NRJD feint souvent de comprendre certaines attitudes et va même jusqu'à tenter de les justifier. En effet, le narrateur affirme souvent tolérer l'attitude des femmes mariées qui se laissent séduire alors qu'une analyse stylistique rigoureuse de ses propos révèle qu'il est loin de la cautionner.

Cela nous amène à la dimension ludique de l'œuvre. En effet, à l'instar de ses personnages qui se jouent les uns des autres, le narrateur s'amuse souvent à induire son lecteur en erreur, et fait, là encore, du désordre une caractéristique inhérente à son esthétique.

«L'unité d'analyse pertinente n'est pas le discours mais un espace d'échanges entre plusieurs discours»:[24] en avançant ces propos, Dominique Maingueneau reconstruit la notion d'«interdiscours». Selon lui, l'acte de création «poétique» implique fatalement une dimension polémique. Autrement dit, loin de créer une situation d'entente, le discours littéraire ne peut qu'engendrer une activité agonistique. D. Maingeneau pose donc le postulat suivant: à partir du moment où un auteur écrit, il écrit *contre*. Tout l'intérêt de l'analyse du discours réside dans ce versant social.

Or, dans notre cas, Des Périers affirme dès «*La premiere nouvelle en forme de preambule*» qu'«*il n'y ha point de sens allégoricque, mistique, fantastique*» et invite par là son lecteur à s'en tenir au sens

---

[23] Dominique Maingueneau, *Le discours littéraire. Paratopie et scène d'énonciation* (Paris: Armand Colin, 2004).
[24] Maingueneau, *Le discours littéraire*, p. 38.

littéral que véhicule son recueil. De même, ce dernier met l'accent quelques lignes plus loin sur la gratuité de son entreprise qui n'a d'autre préoccupation que de faire rire son lecteur «*Riez seulement, et ne vous chaille si ce fut Gaultier ou si ce fut Gargouille. Ne vous souciez point si ce fut à Tours en Berry ou à Bourges en Touraine*». Nous sommes donc, *a priori,* bien loin de l'univers de la querelle suggérée précédemment et de l'idée selon laquelle tout énonciateur, quel qu'il soit, doit avoir une «vocation énonciative».[25]

Dans ce contexte, la notion de «Paratopie»[26] prend tout son sens puisqu'elle constitue une marque d'identité importante du positionnement de l'énonciateur et qu'elle caractérise souvent sa démarche littéraire, philosophique ou encore artistique. A ce sujet D. Maingueneau affirme que chaque énonciateur «(…) nourrit son œuvre du caractère radicalement problématique de sa propre appartenance à la société».[27]

C'est d'ailleurs cette idée de malaise, de mal-être et de rapport conflictuel avec la société à laquelle le discours vient porter secours que l'on retrouve dès les premières lignes des NRJD:

> Je vous gardoys ces joyeux propos à quand la paix seroitfaicte, affin que vous eussiez dequoy vous jouir (…). Mais quand j'ay veu qu'il s'en falloit le manche, et qu'on ne sçavoit par ou le prendre: j'ay mieux aymé m'avancer, pour vous donner moyen de tromper le temps, meslant des resjouissancesparmy vos fasheries, en attendant qu'elle se face de par Dieu: Et puys je me suys avisé (j'ai réalisé) que cestoiticy le vray temps de les vous donner: car c'est aux **malades** qu'il fauta **medecine.**[28]

Cette affirmation met l'accent sur l'idée de « moment opportun ». Des Périers insiste dans ce passage sur le contexte qui nécessite des attentes de la part du public. Ses «*joyeux propos*», tel qu'il les qualifie lui-même, émergent donc dans un cadre critique qui est celui de la guerre. L'insistance sur la finalité récréative du projet prend ainsi tout

---

[25] Autrement dit, il tente d'entrer dans un débat social avec son lecteur.

[26] Paratopie: Dans son Glossaire, Dominique Maingueneau définit la Paratopie en ces termes: «La paratopie caractérise à la fois la «condition» d'un discours constituant (religieux, esthétique, philosophique…) et celle de tout créateur qui construit son identité à travers lui: il ne devient tel qu'en assumant de manière singulière la paratopie du discours constituant dont il tire cette identité créatrice».

[27] Maingueneau, *Le discours littéraire*, p. 38.

[28] NRJD, p. 13.

son sens: les «*comptes*»[29] font office de «remède» pour panser des lecteurs moralement atteints par les atrocités de la guerre.
La métaphore de la maladie qui clôt la citation ci-dessus et que le narrateur file tout au long de l'œuvre, va d'ailleurs de pair avec cette idée. Les termes de «*maladie*», «*malade*», «*remede*» (et son dérivé «*irremediable*») hantent les nouvelles et y reviennent comme de véritables leitmotive.

Cette métaphore de la maladie devrait, à notre sens, être rapprochée de l'exclusivité réservée au rire. Profitant d'une place de choix dans l'économie du recueil, le rire se voit assigner dans les NRJD une fonction cathartique. La nouvelle 89 en constitue d'ailleurs un exemple probant. En effet, guéri non pas grâce au remède préparé par ses médecins, mais par le rire engendré par les gambades folâtres de son singe (qui a bu le remède à sa place), le malade de cette avant-dernière nouvelle célèbre les bienfaits du rire et ses pouvoirs curatifs et salvateurs.

Ainsi, par-delà l'apparente gratuité que semble prôner Des Périers, les NRJD offrent une certaine cohérence interne qui confère à l'ensemble son unité. Ce fil d'Ariane est la dimension subversive. En véritable principe fondateur du texte, le mouvement subversif d'inversion constitue l'un des traits de caractérisation fondamental de l'esthétique de Des Périers et s'offre à lire comme le seul moyen à même de conférer, paradoxalement, un certain «ordre carnavalesque» dans le «désordre scriptural».

[29] Terminologie employée par Des Périers pour désigner ses nouvelles.

Bibliographie

- L'édition de référence est celle de Krystyna Kasprzyk: *Nouvelles récréations et joyeux devis: I-XC.*, Paris, STFM, 1980.

-Boudou Bénédicte et Olivier Halévy, *Bonaventure Des Périers, Nouvelles Récréations et Joyeux Devis,* Atlande, 2008.

-Boudou Bénédicte (dir.) et Dominique Bertrand, *Lire les Nouvelles Recréations et Joyeux devis de feu Bonavanture Des Périers*, Presses de L'Université Blaise Pascal de Clermont Ferrand, 2009.

-Montagne Véronique et Marie-Claire Thomine-Bichard, *Bonaventure Des Périers, conteur facétieux,* Paris, PUF, 2008.

-Mikhaïl Bakhtine, *L'Œuvre de François Rabelais et la culture populaire au moyen âge et sous la Renaissance*, Gallimard, 1970.

-Dominique Maingueneau, *Le discours littéraire. Paratopie et scène d'énonciation*, Paris, Armand Colin, 2004.

Contemporary Imaginings and Performances of Clashing Dis/orders

Cryptic Poetics and Significant Glitches: The Elegiac in Dis/Order

Bachar Aloui, University of Jendouba, Tunisia

Abstract

This article examines the fissures generated within the grieving expression of traumatic loss by reading an elegy. Operating within a metapsychological framework informed by the linguistic rooting of secrets, it seeks to open the cryptic verbiage to scrutiny. The analysis focuses on the ambivalent resistances that this obscure and obscuring intrapsychic mechanism generates within what otherwise poses as an orderly form of lamenting expression. While, according to Freud, mourning is the preferred outcome of traumatic loss, it is argued that linguistic regressions create ebbs and flows towards melancholia, the less desired and virtually muted psychic affliction. Otherwise put, the elegy's unsuspected flight to tropical reversals – as in the literalization of the figural, for instance – marks a precocious, muddled entombment. It is a vivisepulture of the love object signifying, via linguistic detours, hinting at an "origin," which is the dead-as-cipher. Thus, a superficially harmonious text encodes the inability to progress beyond the love object's disappearance. The ensuing verbal reintegration is a hybrid state of attachment, transpiring in the chaos of diction. Nonetheless, this maneuver does not suppress the psychic conflict, thus engendering significant glitches. Moreover, this readjustment lends credence to the Derridean view that the (indefinitely confronted) impossibility of mourning corresponds to its success. This psychoanalysis attempts to reveal how the absurdity of the poetic vehicles the vicissitudes of the shattered elegiac idiom. Born out of identification paradoxes and linguistic debris, the psychic entanglements (between self and other) shape the salutary form of lyrical anamnesis: total fidelity must be untoward.

Keywords: metapsychology; crypt; mourning; incorporation

"No absurdity is impossible for psychoanalysis" – Freud (qtd. in Abraham and Torok 108)

This exegetical commentary begins by the allusion to an intriguing absurdity; namely, the question of death.[1] Indeed, death is an enfolded conundrum. It is an articulate *address* that interpellates one in a fashion reminiscent of Freudian (*ergo*, Caruthian) conceptions of trauma as a transfiguring call. Death generates limitless philosophical reactions. In the *Phaedo*, Plato considers it a welcome respite from a life in which the soul is weighed down by corporal whims: a "true votary of philosophy … is always pursuing death and dying" (958). Death would be a misidentified blessing, and the wise should "be of good cheer" before it, for it is a harbinger of "the greatest good" (958). Death is discussed in Shakespeare as well: dying "is common," reflects Hamlet, pondering the spectacle of mourning and its ritualized, sanctioned practices: "customary suits of solemn black"; "windy suspiration of forced breath"; and "the fruitful river in the eye" (*Hamlet* 1.2. 72–83).

In Freudian psychoanalysis, the psychic reactions revolving around death offer valuable insight into the ego's links to traumatic repetition and cathectic investment. Death is not simply an anticipated byproduct of being; it is reconceptualized as the ultimate aim of life in Freud's seminal *Beyond the Pleasure Principle.*[2] Death epitomizes disagreeable experiences and episodes of "unpleasure," revealing their constitutive role in mental life. The Freudian "death drive" itself is a primordially instinctual momentum, exposing "an urge inherent in organic life to restore an earlier state of things which the living entity has been obliged to abandon" (30). It is a matter of resetting, of recuperating a previous condition. The vigorous yearning for inertness, Freud asserts, means that the "aim of all life is death" (32). Consequently, he places the "repetition compulsion" at the core of the psychic function – driven by a potent imperative to recapture past, preorganic plenitude.

---

[1] I am grateful to Bessem Cherni, the elegist, and to Anouar Barouni, for the Arabic-to-English translation. At times, I use my own translation to highlight the Arabic nuance of meaning. This article is dedicated to the memory of Nejib Fadhlaoui.

[2] Hereafter referred to as *BTPP*.

The fact that an elegy, as defined by *The Oxford Dictionary*, is a "poem of serious reflection, typically a lament for the dead" already signals its entanglement with several representational pressures. While loss can be met with the stoic perseverance of rhymes, one might wonder about the kind of poetics befitting the abysmal reset. This article claims that the elegy under scrutiny lyrically deflects attention away from its thematic kernel to mask a failed psychogenic separation.[3] It acts as a verbal effacement attending to its own devices, since it is unable to pronounce the departed dead. Thus, it presents itself as aposiopesis, as a sudden invasion of speech by muteness. It invites an abruptly suspended order – both as arrangement and command – to permit anamnesis (a loyal perpetuation of memory). In other words, the poem must decimate signification to succeed in its "encounter" with death. This is what the examined elegy erratically does: it succeeds lamentably to lure the reader via its detours. At other times, it fails gloriously to misdirect the reader and reveals its true content, the deceased – in line with the Derridean conception of proper mourning. Hence, the reading must refrain from fetishizing the address *per se*, as it threatens to be fatal to the (death) letter(s).

"Each death," according to Derrida, "is unique … and therefore unusual" ("Work" 193). Hence, the question of an always already unknown death becomes the very sign of disorder. Death is disturbance, a linguistic strain upon commemorative poetic diction. This analysis attempts to highlight the to-and-fro motion that contemplates death, and its traumatic *après-coup*, in the elegiac. It aspires to assert disordered enunciation as the required tribute to the dead. The chaotic intrusion of grief, it contends, is more suitable than a normalized situation of resignation and closure: an affective settling down obstructs memorialization efforts by facilitating the transition from the (re)called to the call itself.

Dispersed amidst its letters, the elegy cannot but become a cryptic memorial – hidden in plain sight. Oscillating between excess and impotence, it unfathomably aspires to entertain the (possibility of the) survival of the name. The text becomes an "expression of the inertia"

[3] As shown in the appendix below, the elegy has no title.

that designates possession by the figure of death (*BTPP* 30). The focus will hereafter be on death as a trauma inviting, but also challenging, representation. Then, a textual explication will fore-ground the interplay of mnemonic and cryptic elements – *à la* Nicolas Abraham and Maria Torok. It highlights the ways in which the elegiac acts as a retreating and misleading linguistic labyrinth. The last section will briefly comment on the mourning process – as conceived by Freud, and rethought by Derrida.

Trauma in Death

Death is a remarkably encumbered concept. It is an intensely fraught fact of existence, whose reverberations cannot easily be subsumed in textuality. This aspect derives from its numerous incapacitations and traumatic aftereffects. Death is multiple enigma, disappearance, cessation, loss, extinction, passing, destruction, and demise. One does not comprehend it. It is puzzling, a horizon that does not lend itself to straightforward contemplation. Death invokes the idea of belonging elsewhere, otherwise – which acts as a barrier to our curious wonder. It is a termination impacting ontology and episteme-ology, an abrupt stoppage. Indeed, Zygmunt Bauman asserts that it is "impossible to define death, as death stands for the final void, for that non-existence which, absurdly, gives existence to all being" One could rehash the dense network of effects around dying: a moment of loss and absence diminishing the world of those who remain behind. "Death is the absolute other of being, an unimaginable other, hovering beyond the reach of communication," Bauman comments. Death is a hybrid, an unfathomable transition, spatially and temporally. Death ruins the very metaphors employed to illustrate its ripples: "death is *not* like other 'others' – those others which the ego is free to fill with meaning" (3). It is a black hole of signification.

Because it is fraught with elements that resist unproblematic classification, death remains a quintessential trauma: recurrent, (scantily) normalized, at odds with the very possibility of total control. It challenges our senses, our orders, and our sense of order. Indeed, death intensifies the impossibility of cognition, which is specifically the psyche's plague in trauma: the mental apparatus's incapacity to grasp its encounter with destruction, at the onset of the traumatic episode, is also endless in death. Death equals subjective passivization, rejection of control, and profound altering of referential terms. In the shattering of one's temporality and otherwise rooted situatedness, death is trauma *par excellence*.

Trauma in Freud is conceived and couched in narrative terms as irretraceable violation that is assigned a deadly finality. The traumatic assault, emphasizing the traumatic unknown as the core element of the experience as such, liberates a voice from the wound that alerts one to tormented alterity. In his treatment of trauma, Freud retells Tasso's *Gersalemme Liberata* as a prime example of the repetitive encounter with injurious episodes, an embodiment of those moments of a "passive experience, over which [one] has no influence" (*BTPP* 16). These cases seemed to reveal "some 'daemonic' force at work," by which Freud introduced an indomitable drive, seemingly bypassing the ego's incessant quest for gratification (29). Alluding to the fictional, Freud exposes a puzzling feature of trauma: it fractures subjective temporality. Its damaging force is not registered as it happens but rather is re-lived belatedly. It is misrecognized, experienced paradoxically for the *first* time as it *returns*: only when Tancred unwittingly reiterates the aggression against his beloved, does he hear her voice "complaining" (16). Bearing in mind the Greek etymology of "trauma" as the term for "wound," the Freudian interpretation of the repeated infliction of the wound as the effect of unsuspected cathexis – or libidinal energy – becomes unmistakable.

The repetition compulsion and the attendant cry from the wound are key precepts in the temporal unfolding of traumatic experiences. While delving into what he labels the "dark and dismal" issue of traumatic neuroses, Freud notes how inescapable the intrusive reiteration of literal, pristine experience is. He further likens it to some "malignant fate" (16). This cycle reflects the attempt to grasp the event itself, to tardily integrate it within one's life story. Similarly, narratives of trauma are obsessively preoccupied by a craving for hindsight – to retrieve a tense past, unavailable for psychic assimilation. Attempting to regain control, *post factum*, over the violent scene of trauma, and to supplement the psychical reaction belatedly, *nachträglichkeit*, is as central to the Freudian model of psychic function as it is to trauma writing, for they are both projects of (re)staging.

In her commentary on trauma's intrinsic paradox, Cathy Caruth highlights the initial misidentification of the experience (perceived as non-event) as the sign of dissociation. The manifold traumatic occurrence intriguingly shatters the psyche's chronology. Caruth attempts to transcend the Freudian reference to traumatic neurosis, via a retracing of traumatic gaps and toward a temporally-displaced narrative address. She defines trauma as "much more than a pathology, or the simple illness of a wounded psyche". Indeed, she reconfigures the import of the traumatic experience as the crisis of missing knowledge and recurring address. Thus, trauma is "always the story of a wound that cries out, that addresses us in the attempt to tell us of a reality or truth that is not otherwise available … [of] what remains unknown in our very actions and our language" (4).

Freud conceptualizes trauma as the result of the initial unpreparedness of the mental apparatus's "protective barrier" in the face of excessively violent stimuli (*BTPP* 29). This "breach" explains not only the incessant re-emergence of the event, but also its psychogenic fixation. Its unbidden nature places it outside the control of the psyche, upon which it "is constantly forcing itself" (7). This is an invasive iteration of the event as a surplus of gap-engendering energy. Trauma is trespass, without "any possibility of preventing the mental apparatus from being flooded with large amounts of stimulus" (23–24). As far as mental control is implied, trauma is a structurally-doubled conundrum, pushing the psyche toward compensatory after-the-fact re-enactments of devastating wounds. Accordingly, Caruth queries about the extent to which this time gap makes the events (un)available for knowing, barely accessible in their (re)occurrence. Trauma's indirectness is magnified by delayed literality, which produces undeniable concerns about textualizing it. How can an event's unmediated rawness be submitted to the structural, referential requirements of the narrative? Or, to transpose it onto the interest of this very analysis, how can the order of the elegy meet the chaos of death?

Exegesis: (De)Stabilizing the Idiom

Death is (chronological) excess: it hovers as a supplement, without life. It is therefore only open to monologues, unidirectional verbiage. By burdening the linguistic, it negates the very likelihood of a conversation. The delicate task of casting into language its resisting antagonism – the plethora of traumatic details disabling their own registration – is a challenge. It amounts to a re/construal. It is a re/composition that confronts death as de/composition. For Dori Laub, the process of unearthing the traumatic experience from under the layers of muteness demands attention to the unstated and to an idiom that is stretched powerless: there "are never enough words or the right words … to articulate the story that cannot be fully be captured in thought, memory, and speech" (78).

Ever-fleeting, the traumatic moment strenuously hollows language – not only does it resist verbal depictions, it also creates antithetical currents of expression. The medium implodes due to what Judith Herman refers to as an inner "conflict between the will to deny horrible events and the will to proclaim them aloud" (1). These competing tendencies, of denial and obsession with articulation, are central to any exegetical reading. They offer the potential to reveal secret implications of what, on the surface, would like to solemnly present itself as a masterly text that is utterly in charge. In the face of such resistances, textuality variously attempts to formulate a perceptive account of trauma. Most remarkable is how the text attempts to signify tragedy by manipulating poetic imagery, depicting loss in non-aleatoric terms. In fact, as Susan Gubar notes, poesis provides an adequate vehicle to grasp the vicissitudes of trauma and memory, since it duplicates the aggression of language. As it "abrogates narrative coherence," poetry "denote[s] the psychological and the political, ethical and aesthetic consequences of the calamity without laying claim to experiencing or to comprehending it in its totality" (7).

Accordingly, the rift between the traumatic instant and the moment of writing is best echoed in the poetic. The lyrical denotes the trauma of language, drawing a parallel to the experiential incompleteness that it faces. In order "to signal the impossibility of a sensible story," and to reflect the challenges of narrative logic in the face of the unthinkable, poetic language can supply "spurts of vision, moments of truth, baffling but nevertheless powerful pictures of scenes unassimilated into an explanatory plot" (7). The poetic suggests a self-referential reflection of surfeit – an idiom symptom-matic of the traumatic aftermath, as Gubar notes, whereby the "lyrical utterance often announces itself as an involuntary return to intense feelings" (8). Indeed, resorting to adorned language as a commemorative tool that cannot encompass experience agrees with the Caruthian view of traumatic origin as a *pre*occupying, unattainable scene, whose "unassimilated nature" is hauntingly and constantly retreating (4).

In this light, the text's metaphorical language is required, oddly enough, by its status as code for its own insufficiency. It is the locus of several imperatives. It is a language that reciprocates the extreme nature of the event by mobilizing its tropes to become the site of potentially undecipherable signification. Hence, this project is as much concerned with uncovering elegiac imagery as it is with revealing the inner contra*diction*, the verbal antagonisms belying its supposed constancy. In fact, linguistic impotence is guaranteed by the question of death: meaning is trapped within infinite chains of signification in which terms mirror terms (in a *double entendre*, both idioms and durations).

Reflexive of this anxiety, the elegy at hand seemingly begins from the end, retracing its path backwards. Its first verse (l. 1) is an arresting invocation to "*stop* by the graves and call them." This eruption of the poetic precipitously places one *in situ*, within the dark locus of nothingness. It is an abrupt immersion within the sphere of trauma, promising an "answer" from the tombs. The monologue ponders, albeit equivocally, the possibility of hearing a response from the "inhabitant(s)." The second verse hopes for an exchange between those who remain behind and the unknown: "there," it adds, is a potential didactic outcome from a "moralizing" death (l. 3). Death speaks to anyone discerning: its command is to "repent" (ll. 3–4). Clearly, this is an elegy embracing, from the outset, the idea of meaningful death, part of the grand scheme of things. Death is not pure calamity but a faceless orator, whose teachings are a *quid pro quo*.

The elegy next proceeds by circling around the ideas of the disorderly and the untimely. It seeks equilibrium in the theological by underscoring the fact that death is destiny, an irreversible divine *order*. While negating death as chaos, in a fatalistic move, to exhibit its own passivity: the inescapability of destiny is highlighted via paradox in the third verse: "even when away, fate is nigh" (l. 6). Moreover, death is "ahead of one's *steps*," constantly on the lookout (l. 7). One is reminded of the complexly-layered Derridean statement "*il y va d'un certain pas* – [It involves a certain step/not; he goes along at a certain pace]" ("Aporias" 6). One treads towards nothingness at a certain rate; with a certain negative. The elegiac's subsequent ellipsis heightens the vision of death as beast-like, ambushing one, which underlines the irrevocability of the intervention: "one hopes, but aspiration fails" (l. 8). The verb "to hope" is treated intransitively here, literally and tellingly leaving the object unmentioned.

The oblique tone of the ensuing vocative is also testament to the fact that the poem, thematically and structurally, is attempting to hide its end. Indeed, the objective of addressing death is circuitously delayed by multiple digressions. Allusions to the commonality of dying, and further reflections, are mused upon as natural. Thus, verse five reads: "Our beloved passed away/ Just like snow melting in a day" (ll. 9–10). This hesitating address warrants deciphering, to move past its decoys and reveal what verbal strata embed. Reading becomes a project of uncovering a dis/avowed network of shadows. The self-conscious diction does not divert attention from what it tries to inhume within itself, via continual re-transcriptions – in verse ten, it asserts: "you left … and you did not disappear" (ll. 19–20). Without claiming any closure to the analysis, the poem establishes its boundaries as the crypt where the deceased ultimately rests. In other words, the poem unfolds like a vault. Despite, or because of, its own dynamics of secrecy, it reflects verbal glitches at the moments when it dis/closes itself as a grave: "you reside *here*, so you will not be absent," verse ten continues (l. 21). The question becomes: what if the elegy claimed the departed within, literally?

Before proceeding, a few psychoanalytical concepts that underscore the centrality of textual conflicts and disturbances within the signifying endeavor need to be introduced. It is necessary to mention that the elegy here is read as a cryptonymy, understood *à la* Abraham and Torok. Therefore, the analysis peruses the web of words posturing signification to detect the *uniquely* traumatic language of the elegy. Succinctly put, this "metapsychology of secrets" investigates signifiers attempting to cancel out meaning by operating slippages that divert the attention from their actual intent: *retaining* the love object by reorganizing the psychic structure in "feigned dispossession" thereof (Abraham and Torok 127). This psychic mechanism ingrains the lost object within the ego – firmly engraved as a sign of the ego's narcissistic resistance to loss. Thus, death "affects the psyche by inflicting a *topographical* shift on it" (125). This melancholic disposition unfolds via the elegy's anti-semantic turns, such as "demetaphorization" (126). In a "desperate ploy of filling the mouth with illusory nourishment," this twisting disruption of meaning "has the equally illusory effect of eradicating the idea of a void to be filled with words" (129).

Consequently, the interpretive gesture must take cognizance of "the play of revelation and concealment lodged within" an elegiac that works against itself (Castricano 6). This aporetic act reiterates the difficulties of reading a cipher. The impasse of facing horrendous literality bars any recourse to transcendence or homogenization. Derrida, who mentioned how dying is about "awaiting (one another at) the limits of truth", has also elaborated on the features via which crypts inscribe themselves within an economy of cautious seclusion (Aporias ii). Quartered within the ego, now split and doubled, the lost object of love is buried alive, as it were. Its disappearance is not repressed, for it is not admitted: the unrevealed trauma fractures the linguistic, as its silencing entails an absence of any verbal allusion toward it. Derrida asserts that the crypt is an elaborate project of seclusion:

> No crypt presents itself. The grounds are so disposed as to disguise and to hide … But also to disguise the act of hiding and to hide the disguise: the crypt hides as it holds … [It reveals] an artifice, an architecture, an artifact: of a place comprehended within another but rigorously separate from it, isolated from general space by partitions, an enclosure, an enclave [that] produces a cleft in space … That is the condition, and the stratagem, of the cryptic enclave's ability to isolate, to protect, to shelter from any penetration. ("Fors" xiv)

Abraham and Torok trace cryptic formations back to the function of fantasy in the preservation of the minimization of the psychic agency's efforts (126). Indeed, several verses gesture toward this idea of including the loved other within the (textual) self. Verse eight affirms: "You left without saying goodbye/ As if you're returning after you die" (ll. 15–16). This indicates a symptomatic denial of a rift between the ego and the dead. Still, the text exposes itself: "In the verse your shadow still remains and in-between us" (ll. 21–22). The verse uncannily proclaims itself as the proper haven of the undecidable, which, in Derridean parlance, complicates the "poetico-hermeneutic question" ("Sovereignties" 165). The elegy becomes a secret itself, the place where both the deceased and the aporetic meaning of death belong. Hence, its "overabundance of meanings" and unremitting deflections signal "the very essence of otherness" (165).

This analysis begins with the premise that a crypt is an entombment which exempts the self from facing its powerlessness in loss. It enforces an impossible arrangement of two opposite movements: vocal yet repressive, the crypt undoes and disrupts itself. Accordingly, the elegy postpones access to hidden meanings by structuring a set of enclosed divisions: it acts like "an 'artificial' unconscious lodged like a prothesis" ("Fors" xiii). It is supplementary to itself, a textual appendix that retreats into idiomatic equivocality as a camouflaging stratagem. This cartography of meaning/lessness takes a convoluted path, extending behind unwittingly scattered linguistic slips. The crypt behavds as a proleptically haunted archival record – concurrently preserving and effacing its dweller. Its inner dissonance culminates in its stoppage when the elegy claims: "Words are absent and silence is at its peak" (l. 42). Language masquerades as silence in a poetic impasse. Words are piled upon words to assert the insufficiency of words (l. 43). While confounding the inner-outer, dead-alive, and silent-articulate poles, the verbal crypt avows that "it [speech] is a liar" (l. 44). The elegy's eloquence radiates at the precise moment of its seeming denunciation of expressive breakdown, underlining the traumatic unintelligibility at its core.

The elegy then apologizes, for the letters have tearfully emptied their ink: "[The] letters, while written, cry/ The wound is bleeding" (ll. 51–52). While metaphorically gesturing toward the brutal fracture as the source of overflowing verbalization, the elegy performs a double rendering. First, it confesses that the poetic medium is the spontaneous transcription of pain from the wound, which becomes a narrating mouth. Second, it alludes to the intertwining and disruption of the linguistic and the psychic, in the lament's effort to reach order. It admits, after all, that "regurgitation" or "articulation" is elaborate, like any act of exteriorization or exposure (l. 41). As a final encoding, it adds that one grave, containing "our" hearts, is "rejoicing" (ll. 55–56).

Ultimately, this unsettled elegy asks that one stop by the grave even as it acknowledges the itinerancy of death figures. It laments the absence of a proper farewell, but professes a presence between its lines. It ambiguously introduces a word vault, a repository of the love object. It lyrically stages the incapacity of the lyrical; it displaces the meaning of grave from the world to the word. Encysted within a maze of terms, the love object stands for an unreachable truth, enveloped in contrapuntal references. Unsurprisingly, the elegy becomes disordered enough to mourn properly; for, as will be tackled below, only by failing to stabilize itself does it evoke the memory of the name, which is – literally and otherwise – its last word.

Un/Attainable Mourning

In his treatise on "Mourning and Melancholia," Freud notes that similarity marks the line between the former, denoting a "regular" grief process, and the latter, denoting pathology. Both operations revolve around the "inhibition and circumscription of the ego," as insulating tactics. Both attest the intricacy of relinquishing existing libidinal investment in a love object, even under the pressure of "reality testing" (244). Nonetheless, while both are sequelae of grief, melancholia is a "complex" that "behaves like an *open wound*, drawing to itself cathectic energies … and emptying the ego until it is totally impoverished" (253; my emphasis). Within the protean economy of melancholia, the absurdity is that figuratively attempting to devour the love object does not rhyme with psychcogenic, self-same identificatory cohesion.

In addition to being a disclaimed transition away from the lost object, the melancholic stasis recalls the traumatic inscription itself in its incessant struggle to retrieve prior moments of attachment. The compulsive, libidinal investment in an origin to be recovered is precisely what inhabits the fractures of language and psyche in both cases. By opposition, the work of mourning envisages a redirection of attachment, since the love object has ceased to exist (244). This economical distinction allows Freud to submit that mourning succeeds when the ego prefers to retreat to the safety and gratification of being alive rather than truly face the ultimate consequence of absolute adherence to abolished love objects: death. Libidinal energies find new anchors in mourning, loss is not perceived as impacting the ego. Mourning involves an unhurried eviction of the object from the ego, which becomes "free and uninhibited again" (243–44).

Melancholia is more than a form of resistance to reality. Psychically, it involves a narcissistic regression that reflects a lapse in identification. This fault, in turn, recalls the division within the crypt, which "perpetuates the dividing wall by its very nature" (Abraham and Torok 131). Via a confounding equivocality, blurring the divide between the "I" and the "object" becomes an obstacle denying the distinctness of ego and the world itself, in loss. It mirrors an agency consumed by the perception, or delusion, of being fatally impoverished. Freud hence intimates that, in melancholia, the ego is enslaved, lured into believing that it is an extension of the love object. The ego cannot sever its ties to it, nor face the factuality of its loss. This case is "not the normal one of a withdrawal of the libido from this object and a displacement of it … [Rather,] the free libido was … withdrawn into the ego" (249).

Under these circumstances, one may recognize that the crypt stands at the dense junction of trauma and verbal impotence: it is a gaping wound textualizing traumatic loss. It is, simultaneously, an open mouth burdened by the compulsion of consuming alterity into sameness. Freud summates the process thusly: "an object-loss was *transformed* into an ego-loss and the conflict between the ego and the loved person into a *cleavage* between the critical activity of the ego and the ego as altered by identification (249, emphases added).

Furthering the characteristic inconsistencies of melancholia, the inner psychic rift creates a topographical shift that Abraham and Torok link to the idea of *incorporation.* Also called "nonintrojection," it recuperates and expands the Freudian concept of miscarried mourning by denoting a concoction of the ego that aims to preserve the *status quo*, rather than embark upon a time-consuming, adaptive shift (125).

Accordingly, this fantasy engages in a symbolic ingestion to ward off or resist the hazard of accepting the demands of psychic alterations induced by loss. Abraham and Torok point out that "incorporation is the refusal to acknowledge the full impact of the loss, a loss that, if recognized as such, would effectively transform the [topography of the self]" (127). In other words, the "magic of incorporation" prolongs the love object's psychic existence by reverting to a "feigned dispossession" of the "unnamable" object itself (128). Rather than altering the inner organization of the psychic agency – and "in order not have to "swallow" a loss," the missed object is paradoxically ingurgitated (126–27).

Incorporation indicates the aporia created at the heart of symbolization. Expressing the traumatic loss of a loved object becomes laborious, which highlights the apparent chaotic, half-stated, half-repressed *non-sequiturs* of the elegy at hand. By definition, incorporation implies the helplessness of the verbal in sidestepping the caesura within: in the face of both the urgency and the impossibility of performing one type of mouth-work [a verbalization of sorrow] … another type of mouth-work [ingestive fantasy] is utilized, one that is imaginary and equipped to deny the very existence of the entire problem" (129).

At this juncture, the emerging framework exposes a synchronous faltering of language and psychic agency, itself trapped in a vehement rejection of loss and its concomitant reshuffling of the ego's structural relations. Incorporation, *qua* substitute for a healthy mourning, nullifies the efforts to supplant the love object: one cannot "dispose of it through language" (128). Specifically, the ego fails to translate the factuality of absence into linguistic figuration. It is precisely this annihilation of metaphoricity that this analysis would like to underscore in the elegy. Going against the trope is the common denominator between the intrapsychic interment and the underlying skepticism in representation-as-effacement (that is, the break between the object's presence and the word's evanescence).

Transposed into the world of the elegy itself, the "annulment of figurative language" becomes a mechanism that clouds the possibility of signification (Abraham and Torok 132). It would be remiss, at this level, if the claims of the elegiac – the crypt's arresting power, the non-disappearance of the love object, its specter-like lodging in the verbal, the obfuscating vocabulary, the feigning idiom, the script from the open wound, to the last verse's assertion of the safeguarding in the crypt of the deceased – are not foregrounded as detours. They digress, unflinchingly, so as to "disarray, even to destroy, the expressive or representational power of language" (105). Examining this matrix of designification becomes synonymous with uncovering the perversion, or sabotage, of the message *as* the message. A psychoanalytically-informed hermeneutic mode emerges by locating what Abraham and Torok label *anasemia*, the figure for the breakdown of meaning (85). By moving up the chain of signification, an "anti-semantics" that retraces the repressed discursive potential becomes viable (84). Accordingly, reading line 21 of the elegy ("your shadow, dear departed, is in the verse") becomes a prime example of how "the language of psychoanalysis no longer follows the twists and turns (*tropoi*) of customary speech and writing" (85). As the eerie conflation of melancholia (an agency in the "shadow of the object") and the detritus of disfiguration or demetaphorization keeping watch over the crypt, the elegy doubly enjoins the reader from heeding, and to heed, its dis/order.

Conclusion

An effective mourning, following Freud, entails completely severing the links to the love object. The elegy under scrutiny demonstrates that this is not a painless task. Inhabited by the traces of a past investment, the elegy meanders between conflicting tendencies, markings of unavowed loyalty. It secretly establishes the tomb within as a sign of melancholia, refusing to acquiesce to the fact of separation. For Derrida, this severance borders on the unethical. In fact, he ascribes on successful mourning what Freud reserves for the pathological. "In order to succeed," Derrida states, mourning "would have to *fail*, to fail *well*" ("Work" 144). It has to remain an unfinished business within the ego, which translates to never fully relinquishing the love object. Mourning cannot be teleological; it must center on entanglement. Inasmuch as the elegy fails to demarcate itself, as a sepulcher, from the body it inhumes in its lines, it paradoxically manages to accomplish "its own unproductivity" (144).

In turn, a performative verbal stagnation allows the encryption of the other within the self. If faithful mourning rejects closure, then the elegy at hand manages to suspend grieving as a cryptic fold. Since encoding is ingestion, Derrida adds, "an inclusion intended as a compromise … the cryptic safe can only maintain in a state of repetition the mortal conflict it is impotent to resolve" ("Fors" xvi). In this process, the other is neither subject to a Hegelian assimilation nor molded as undifferentiated self-consciousness. Difference is not subjected to an ethically reductionist, totalitarian move. Rather, the elegy reveals the double gestures of protecting and inhibiting the trace of the other – guarding it "preserved as foreign" ("Fors" xvii). The elegy veils the secret in textual acrobatics. The aborted assimilation becomes an appropriation of alterity that does not homogenize it into sameness. The elegy's bracketing of otherness is a botched mourning, whereby an alien graft ultimately signifies philia: "I cannot complete my mourning for everything I lose, because I want to keep it" ("Points" 152).

Only when coherence recedes before anasemia, as interrupted address or reference, does the poem succeed at deflecting the gaze from its own artifice towards the dead (within). Respecting the other *as* other, the text must engage in a Derridean setting of boundaries, a compassionate antagonism that embraces and delimits. An ethical factor, in this sense, arises primarily out of this very experience of being open to irreducible difference. Thus, the elegiac offers a way of resisting absolute certainty and the will to reduce alterity into a 'graspable' given. It has to ensure that the wound remain open, so as to faithfully memorialize the passing via the staging of an interminable interiorization.

Semantically uprooted and symbolically diffuse, this crypt becomes the problematizing site where otherness disturbs the regimes of meaning. For Derrida, it provides a leeway for loyal remembrance as the repetition of painful exposure to unintegrated loss: "Faithfulness prescribes to me at once the necessity and the impossibility of mourning. It enjoins me to take the other within me, to make him live in me, to idealize him … but it also enjoins me not to succeed in the work of mourning: the other must remain the other" (qtd. in Royle 135). By dis/claiming one's consideration, the elegy foregrounds its core of absent meaning as a moral requirement. It resists amnesia by demanding an anamorphic approach to signification, a self-perpetuating resonance acknowledging its invasive, interminable bouts of inscrutable orientation. The dead, in this fashion, can inhabit the space forced inside the ego and, as Derrida declares, "ventrilocate through the living" (*The Ear of the Other* 58).

Works cited

Abraham, Nicolas, and Maria Torok. *The Shell and the Kernel: Renewals of Psychoanalysis.* London, U of Chicago P, 1994.

Bauman, Zygmunt. *Mortality, Immortality and Other Life Strategies.* Stanford: Stanford UP, 1992.

Caruth, Cathy. *Unclaimed Experience: Trauma, Narrative and History.* Baltimore: Johns Hopkins UP, 1996.

Castricano, Jodey. *Cryptomimesis: The Gothic and Jacques Derrida's Ghost Writing.* Montreal: McGill-Queen's UP, 2001.

Derrida, Jacques. *Of Grammatology.* Translated by Gayatri Spivak. Baltimore: Johns Hopkins UP, 1974.

———. *Aporias.* Translated by Thomas Dutoit. Stanford: Stanford UP, 1993.

———. *The Ear of the Other: Otobiography, Transference, Translation.* Translated by Peggy Kamuf. New York: Shocken Books, 1985.

———. "Fors." Translated by Barbara Johnson. In Nicolas Abraham and Maria Torok. *The Wolfman's Magic Word: A Cryptonymy.* Minneapolis: U of Minnesota P, 1986, pp. xi–xlviii.

———. *Points: Interviews, 1974–1994.* Stanford: Stanford UP, 1995.

———. *Sovereignties in Question: The Poetics of Paul Celan.* New York: Fordham UP, 2005.

———. *The Work of Mourning.* London: U of Chicago P, 2001.

Freud, Sigmund. *Beyond the Pleasure Principle.* Translated by James Strachey. London: W.W. Norton, 1961.

———. "Mourning and Melancholia." 1917. *The Standard Edition of the Complete Psychological Works of Sigmund Freud.* London: Hogarth P, 1957. 237–58.

Gubar, Susan. *Poetry after Auschwitz: Remembering What One Never Knew.* Bloomington: Indiana UP, 2003.

Herman, Judith. *Trauma and Recovery.* New York, Basic Books, 1997.

Laub, Dori. "An Event without a Witness: Truth, Testimony and Survival". In Shoshana Felman and Dori Laub. *Testimony: The Crisis of Witnessing in Literature, Psychoanalysis, and History.* New York: Routledge, 1992. 75–92.

Plato. "The Phaedo". In *The Complete Works of Plato*. Translated by Benjamin Jowett. Indianapolis: Hackett Publishing, 1875. 949–1034.

Royle, Nicholas. *In Memory of Jacques Derrida*. Edinburgh: Edinburgh UP, 2009.

Shakespeare, William. *Hamlet*. London: W.W. Norton, 1996.

Appendix

Stop by the graves and call upon them… There, are replying
In every grave a pulpit and a voice speaking
There, death is moralizing
If you're aware of it, to the Almighty you will be binding
This is Allah's decree, how to object to it and
No matter far away His will is, so close is the end
Death is hastening its steps by surprising
An ambitious person but hopefulness comes to nothing
Our beloved passed away
Just like snow melting in a day
A brave and respected knight
Suddenly, you were blown into a dark and unknown fight
Brother! Is the life for you long?
Or you escape from a path that is wrong
You left without saying goodbye
As if you're returning after you die
Did you know that your road had no return?
In which you will be alone
Remembering you is evidence
You are among us despite your absence
We feel at home the shadow of yours
Like the old days knocking on all the doors
You have smiling eyes
And a voice warbling and wise
Classes after your death
Will find no answering breath
You quit the class, the lesson, the eye
And the hearts deeply cry
You came back stronger than ever
As if you are still closer
Your name's meaning is kindness
And your given name is cleverness
You, death, have exhausted and defeated us
Death is an ailment no doctor can pass

Death an unfair destiny of a brother
Doesn't it have a lover?
You shocked us in our best
As if you choose and test
Shall we open memories' frame?
They are bitter… a flame
The voices confusedly speak
Words are absent and silence is at its peak
Words cannot describe his eminence
Even if truthful words are of evidence
His noble talents are not measurable
Talking about a beloved is pleasurable
You're a militant, struggler, peaceable
Polite, disciplined and respectable
He was always cheerful … and here I am smiling
The aggrieved might laugh though in pain diving
Sorry if the letters, while written, cry
The wound is bleeding and the ink not dry
On that day it rained mournfully
And the clouds wailed tearfully
A grave embraced a jeeb
Rejoicing that the entombed is Najeeb

Translated by Mohamed Anouar Barouni

قف بالقبور ونادِها ..سُتُجيبُ-
في كلّ قبر منبرٌ وخطيبُ
ولسانُ حال الموت فيها واعظ-2
إن كنت تدرك وعظَه ستتوبُ
هذا قضاء الله كيف نردُّهُ-3
وقضاءُ ربّكَ إن نأى ..فقَرِيبُ
والموتُ يسْتبِقُ الخُطى متربِّصًا-4
والمرءُ يأْمَلُ ، والرّجاءُ يَخِيبُ
رحلَ الذين نحبّهم فكأنهم-5
مكثُوا مكوثَ الثلج ثم يذوبُ
يا من ترجَّل عن ركاب جواده-6
وتقاذفتْهُ غياهبٌ وغُيُوبُ
أتعِبْتَ من طول المسافةِ يا أخي ؟-7
أم شئْتَ أن ترتاح منكَ دُرُوبُ؟
فمضيْتَ لم تُلْقِ الوداعَ ولم تقُلْ-8
شيئًا ..كأنكَ في غدٍ ستؤوبُ
هل كنتَ تعرفُ أنّ دربَكَ مُوغِلٌ-9
في اللاّرجوع ..وأنتَ فيه غريبُ
وتركتَ بعدكَ من تركتَ ولم تزلْ-10
أنت المُقيم هنا فلستَ تغيبُ
في البيت ظلُّكَ لا يزال وبيننا-11
كالأمس تخطر ها هنا وتجوبُ
عيناك ضاحكتان في وجه الضنى-12
ولسانُ حالكَ قانعٌ وطرُوبُ
كيف المدارج بعد أن غادرتَها-13
تغدُو ؟ وإن نادتْكَ هل ستُجيبُ؟
غادرت ساحتنا وقاعة درسنا-14
وبكتْكَ منّا أعْيُنٌ وقُلُوبُ
ورجعتَ أقوى ما تكون كأنما-15
لم تبتعد ..بل أنت بعدُ قريبُ
متلقّبٌ بالفضل ..أمّا اسمه-16
فمن النّجابةِ :فاضلٌ ونجيبُ
يا موتُ قد أنهكتنا وهزمتنا-17
والموتُ داءٌ ما شفاهُ طبيبُ
يا موت ما أنصفتَ حين فجعْتَنا-18
بالطّيّبين ..أما لديكَ حبيبُ ؟
ما زلت تفجعنا بأفضل من لنا-19
فكأنما تختارُ ثمّ تُصيبُ
هل نفتح الذكرى على آفاقها ؟-20
للذكرياتِ مرارَةٌ ..ولهيبُ
اللفظُ مُرْتبكٌ يُلمْلِمُ بعضَهُ-21
والصمتُ يحضرُ والكلامُ يغيبُ
إنّ الكلامَ يظلُّ دون مقامه-22
مهما احتذيْتُ الصّدقَ فهو كذوبُ
ماذا أُعدّدُ من نبيل صفاته ؟-23
إنّ الحديثَ عن الحبيبِ يطيبُ
أمناضلٌ ..ومكافحٌ ..ومُسالِمٌ-24
ومُؤَدَّبٌ ..ومُهَذَّبٌ ..ومَهيبٌ ؟
كان الضّحوكَ ..وها أنا مُتبسّمٌ-25
قد يضحكُ المهمومُ وهو كئيبُ
عُذْرًا إذا بكَتِ الحروفُ مدادَها-26
فالجرحُ ينزفُ والمِدادُ خضيبُ
حتّى السّماء بكتْهُ يومَ رحيله-27
فعلى الغُيُومِ مدامِعٌ ..ونُدُوبُ
لكنّ قبرًا ضَمَّ بعضَ قُلُوبِنا-28
مُسْتبْشِرٌ ..إنّ الدَّفِينَ :نجيبُ.
Bessem Cherni ©

In the Name of 'Order' and the Poetics of the Black Marker in Shahriar Mandanipour's *Censoring an Iranian Love Story*[1]

Sihem Arfaoui, I.S.S.H.J., Tunisia

Abstract:
Shahriar Mandanipour's *Censoring an Iranian Love Story: A Novel* (2009) poses the vexed question of literary fertility once literature is usurped by or, in some cases, anticipates and perpetuates censorship as a religiously and politically-encompassed order of things. In this novel, a long legacy of censorship ingrained in a religious and socio-political context struggles for stifling the literary or imaginary realm through apparatuses and tools which have been reconfigured through a Barthesian variation on excluding and mutilating "the very identity of the body writing" (Barthes 142). This article demonstrates that the symbolical surgery of an outlawed love-story is in-depth practiced by the author both consciously and subconsciously to re-emerge in the garb of an intricate superimposition which, in turn, articulates the act of writing in opposition to a despotic regime. In the process of discussing the often-conflicting, albeit inspiring relationship between literature and censorship as an ideological order, I shall explore the ways in which the production of *Censoring* reshapes the imposition of the religious-political power-machine as an occasion for re-creative enrichment, providing the writer with further possibilities, rather than impossibilities.

Keywords: Narrative fragmentation, subversion, superpower, textual surgery.

---

[1] *Censoring an Iranian Love Story* is originally based on "Mandanipour's 1998 short story, Shargh-e Banafsheh (East of Violet), which tells the exact same story only in 30 pages. This short story opposed to the novel functions well as a solid literary work because it is written without the cultural explanations and is definitely aimed at a Persian reader who is no stranger to Persian literature" (Zand 184).

> *It is thus that the late Roland Barthes's theory of the Death of the Author is, in my dear homeland, subconsciously practiced.* (Mandanipour, *Censoring* 57)

Introduction

This paper explores Shahriar Mandanipour's *Censoring an Iranian Love Story: A Novel* (2009) – "a dark comic novel as much about life in contemporary Iran as it is about storytelling" and storywriting (Khakpour 6).[2] It poses the vexed question of literary fertility once literature is usurped by or, in some cases, anticipates and perpetuates censorship as a religiously and politically-encompassed order of things. As the myriad story-lines of *Censoring* suggest, the reader can detect two main entangled domains of order already in conflict with each other. One is mainly religious and socio-political represented by a long legacy of censorship and the other literary or imaginative. These two realms are not naturally in conflict, albeit often incongruent since Plato's time and space, and up to recent times, especially if we remind ourselves of the latest jihadist massacre of the Charlie Hebdo cartoonists on the basis of controversial depictions of Prophet Muhammad (Silva n.p.).

The figurative twist on the Barthesian concept of *the Death of the Author* which is enclosed in the opening citation attempts to highlight the embedded implication of textual surgery. As one possible variation of excluding and mutilating "the very identity of the body writing" (Barthes 142), textual surgery mirrors the complexity of such a value-system as an apparatus practiced by the author both consciously and subconsciously to re-emerge in the garb of an intricate

---

[2] An accomplished writer widely published in Iran, Shahriar Mandanipour "was prohibited from publishing in Iran between 1992 and 1997" (Zand 184). This fact could explain the reason why he has not returned to Iran ever since he came to the U.S. in 2006 as a winner of Brown University's International Writers Project Fellowship; a prize usually awarded to writers who were censured in their homeland (Sethi 44). In the process, Mandanipour contributed "to the brain drain that has continued to afflict the Iranian cultural sphere since the Revolution" (Atwood 41) and participated in creating "a myth about the man behind the work" (Zand 184).

superimposition. In the meantime, the black marker image suggests that the mere choice to set the story of two people who "fall in love through secret messages encoded in in pages of outlawed books" (Thornton 14) in contemporary Iran already poses the question of writing in opposition to a despotic regime. Indeed, any textual engagement with the taboos of sex, politics, and religion remains part and parcel of what Misha Zand describes as "something of a democratic project," securing for Mandanipour "an impressive entry into the English-speaking literary scene" (183).

In the process of discussing the often-conflicting, albeit inspiring relationship between literature and censorship as an ideological order, I shall explore the ways in which the production of *Censoring* reshapes the imposition of the religious and the political as an occasion for re-creative enrichment, providing the writer with further possibilities, rather than impossibilities. To this end, I shall proceed with some comments on the text and its context within the broader parameters of order, disorder, and power. In scrutiny of the religious-political conditions in which Mandanipour's novel was produced, I will emphasize the entanglement of the censorship machine as an external imposition, growing into an internal order which ultimately manifests itself mainly through the fragmentation of complex narrative layers, disordered points of view, and humor as terrains of creative excellence and of subverting a stifling superpower.

1. Text in a context of Order and power

Quite frequently, censorship and art contend against each other, ending in mutilation, visibility or even enrichment. In line with this comment, Mandanipour's work proves that every constriction that strives to stifle literature does not necessarily have everything to do with the imposition of religious, moral, or political order, but could also emanate from the writer's subconscious. As Raha Namy argues: "The novel encourages us to construe censorship broadly, not only as something enforced by government agencies and regulations; different forms of it can also be forced upon one by history, traditions, the general public's or one's family's beliefs and opinions; or they can simply be (un)conscious and/or self-imposed" (n.p.). Equally important is the intricacy of establishing where both main forms of censorship distinguish themselves from each other and the ways in which they, ironically, converge on begetting nothing but further narrative twists and creative excellence, albeit often associated with agony and suffocation.

The following shall delve into a few comments on the generic fluidity of the considered narrative. Akin to multiple genres at a time, *Censoring* unfolds itself on a range of writing modes. For example, it can be classified as "a novel-within-a-novel" (Sethi 44). To this extent, *Censoring* creates "an intriguing postmodern, multifaceted romance steeped in Iranian culture" ("Review" 46). However, the text equally lends itself to "auto-fiction," given the self-referential commentary on the text itself and the conscious play "with the reader's understanding of fact and fiction" (Zand 183). The variety of classifications are further reinforced by the American edition which presents the text as a novel, though its contents are a mixture of a fictional love story and nonfictional aspects deeply ingrained in the ancient and contemporary histories of Iran (Dehghan n.p.).

In the same vein, the title promises a love story but, the latter turns out to be only one major component of the narrative, but not the whole of it, in addition to other sub-stories. According to Atwood, we should decipher at least two narratives in the novel:

> The first, which is indicated in the text with boldface font, is a love story about a young man and woman in Tehran, Dara and Sara. The second account is narrated by the characters' creator, presumably a fictionalized Mandanipour himself. The latter account frequently interrupts the former as the author-narrator clarifies the characters' actions or the veiled language necessary to evade censors. (40)

These different types of narrative suggest a layered structure of a text and a pretext where the pretext often interrupts the text not just to comment on the characters' actions and account for the compulsion for euphemistic references but, also for different other purposes having to do with the story's writing history. Thus, the bulk of the book may be called digressions into the socio-political arena, contemplations on the writer's writerly challenges and printing anxieties.

In addition, Dara and Sara's exploration of "sexual and emotional love in a nation that forbids physical or social interaction between young people of the opposite sex" (Review 46) is in origin "a contemporary re-telling of *Khosrow and Shirin*," a twelfth-century epic poem by Nezami Ganjavi which has been censored two years after the publication of Mandanipour's novel (Atwood 40). What intensifies the characters' relationship is "a love of literature" (Hoffert 85) and resistance to a *status-quo* embedded in the author's trauma of writing under a repressive regime. Suffice it to say that Sara is a student of Iranian literature at Tehran University while Dara is a street peddler "whose illicit wares include not only pornography, new Hollywood releases, and Western brand-name products but also classics of modern Iranian literature such as *The Blind Owl*" (Ostby 87). As such, their attraction is "couched in not only sexual but also intellectual, literary and political terms" (Ostby 82). The whole situation amounts to some kind of a poetic license or excuse. It enables *Censoring* to comment on literature and story production, but also on a larger context revolving around censorship as an order mechanism and the main stratum of superpower.

In the background of the above observation, it should be reminded that order as a pretext for censorship remains imbued with relativity and mutability. Speaking of what can be called a philosophical order, Michel Foucault holds that the "order on the basis of which we think today does not have the same mode of being as that of the Classical thinkers" (Preface xxii). Consequently, they seem cultural, linguistic, or other forms of order. As an example, the moral order according to which we should speak, act, and behave is likely to change not just from classicism to modernity, but also from one culture to another, and so are religious orders and codes. Perhaps, the order which could be the most infinite, unpredictable, and at the same time unstatic is that which pertains to politics. Further unpredictability and fluidity in the shape of order and its modes would arise if the ethical, the religious, and the political ally with one another to enforce order on the higher world of aesthetics, here the literary, and against its intrinsic order, which Russian formalists still tend to think should be free of any extrinsic ideological order.

The understanding of order and its interpretation can easily lapse into its counterpart, the disorderly. By implication, order can even reshape itself as disorder incarnated. Again, Foucault assumes, "there is a worse kind of disorder than that of the incongruous, the linking together of things that are inappropriate; I mean the disorder in which fragments of a large number of possible orders glitter separately in the dimension, without law or geometry" (Foucault, Preface xvii). Disorder does not always wear the garb of incongruity, and can be of different sorts, including the mode of fragmentation or dissemination.

As to the will to set order through censorship, according to Foucault's *Discipline and Punish*, everything originates in and can revert back to power. As a common denominator, the volition to exercise power is behind all rules, either visible or invisible. In fact, Foucault speaks:

> of a certain mechanism of power: of a power that not only did not hesitate to exert itself directly on bodies, but was exalted and strengthened by its visible manifestations; of a power that asserted itself as an armed power whose functions of maintaining order were not entirely unconnected with the functions of war; of a power that presented rules and obligations as personal bonds, a breach of which constituted an offence and called for vengeance; of a power for which disobedience was an act of hostility, the first sign of rebellion, which is not in principle different from civil war; of a power that had to demonstrate not why it enforced its laws, but who were its enemies, and what unleashing of force threatened them. (*Discipline and Punish* 57)

The Foucaultian thesis opens up several avenues for this discussion, among them the insight that the desire for power implicates the maintenance of order as an ultimate procedure which remains indivisible from war-making. It equally underpins the pursuit of legitimating violence or coercion as a tool of order-making.

The same passage has the other advantage of emphasizing rules and duties as being intrinsically connected to the degree that violating the one turns out a triple violation of both and of their bonding altogether. It puts forward a powerful hypothesis which reinforces the possible links that could be established between order and censorship as a cover for "all forms of regulation of the circulation of ideas, spanning from brutal (repressive apparatus: judiciary, police, even army) to softer, more sophisticated models (exclusions, lists of forbidden books or authors, restricted access)" ("Literature and Censorship" n.p.). As a matter of fact, the slippery drift of the state from disobedience into hostility, rebellion, and civil war would cynically transmogrify such an important apparatus of order-making as censorship into a repressive machine no less violent than war-making.

More particularly, the effectiveness of power and repression both as tools and practices seems to be infiltrated with and executed through explicit censorship rather than the implicit.[3] This is because explicit censorship offers "a transparent system of sanctioning the violations" while implicit censorship "deliberately leaves a wide range of openness; it is never completely clear when the border has been transgressed, as well as it is not clear what kind of sanctions can follow" ("Literature and Censorship" n.p.). It is the very openness of implycit censorship which results into the infiniteness and unpredictability of punishments following every disorder or transgression. The amalgam of both modes of censorship can exist in dictatorships as well as so-called democracies in the twentieth-first century, parti-cularly, in periods of national insecurity. Even more, it is unlikely to spare a single field, because censorship would then extend its targets from religious works to philosophy, science, and finally literature ("Literature and Censorship" n.p.). In a literary context, works such as *Censoring an Iranian Love Story* best incarnates imposed and internalized or auto-censorship as a strikingly blurred terrain. This prepares the scene for the ensuing re-examination of *Censoring* as a comment on the ordering/repressive, albeit productive machine of censorship.

2. Nurturing a Culture of Censorship

Censorship thrives mostly in certain particular contexts, mainly of a politico-religious order. To the extent that censorship requires a

[3] Another way to look at the levels of censorship would be by distinguishing between the preliminary/preventive versus the repressive. "While the preliminary censorship guarantees the precursory control of any publication, the repressive censorship takes place after the problematic work is published; if necessary, it seizes the work, prosecutes the authors, etc" ("Literature and Censorship" n.p.). In either case, the preventive versus the repressive aim towards further control and supervision, the level at which *Censoring an Iranian Love Story* gives a view of several writers who have been persecuted and harassed both before and after being published.

certain climate of political oppression and religious conservatism, casting a glance at some cultural aspects as mirrored in *Censoring* proves helpful in understanding the underpinnings of censorship as a superimposed order. In this regard, the novel makes reference to at least two socio-political orders in contemporary Iran, that is, before and after the rule of the Shah. On the one hand, the novel briefly refers to Iran and describes Iranian society during and after the rule of the Shah who tried to rule Iran in a westernized way. The narrator speaks of the latter as a dictator who "banned the Islamic form of dress, or hijab, and ordered Iranian ladies to take off their headscarves and chadors." The Shah followed an oppressive, repressive order of westernization which allowed itself to "stop women who had come out onto the street wearing headscarves and chadors" and even aggress them in public in order to force them to remove their hijab (*Censoring* 108).

On the other hand, irrespective of the above scanty descriptions and references, the examined text is pervasively set in a revolutionary post-Shah Iran. Of special dominance in the novel is a criticism of a revolutionary time in Iran, paradoxically defined by the mandatory veil for women and long sleeves for men, following a regression to an Islamic revolution in the late 1970s (Dehghan n.p.). The text abounds with informative passages commenting on the enforced socio-political codes which reinforce sex segregation in schools, factories, offices, buses, taxis and wedding parties. It unravels a discourse which argues that "any proximity and discourse between a man and a woman who are neither married nor related is a prologue to deadly sin." In addition to retributions in the afterworld, the exposure to "imprisonment, whiplashing, and even death" awaits any such transgressors (*Censoring* 10). Similar statements exemplify a culture steeped in religious fundamentalism which operates on the basis of censorship as a foundational backbone. They reinforce repression by a superpower which casts with its shadow on all aspects of life in Iran and usurps even the literary scene.

In the meantime, re-reading into the censorship machinations as represented through *Censoring*, it is crucial noting that Iran cherished a "censorial culture" throughout its history. As Mandanipour explains it:

> We Iranians, having lived under the dictatorial rule of kings for twenty-five hundred years, have expertly learned that we should never leave any records or documents behind. We are forever fearful that the future will bear even harsher political circumstances, and hence we must be extremely vigilant about our lives and the footprints that linger in our wake. It is for this reason that records of our history are often limited to the travelogues of Westerners and reports by Western spies. (*Censoring* 15)

Accordingly, it is mostly due to a long heritage of dictatorship, even before the rise of Islamism in the region and its neighborhood, that censorship has strikingly developed into a common sense ritual in Iran only to re-emerge as being part and parcel of an Iranian identity.

In a similar line, Persis Karim demonstrates in his article "Writing Beyond Iran Reinvention and the Exilic Iranian Writer" that, particularly,

> under Reza Shah, and then later under his son, Mohammad Reza Shah, the Iranian government sought to control newspapers and writers, particularly those with leftist or Marxist tendencies. Many Iranian writers' works were suppressed, and they were intimidated, arrested, tortured, or killed at the hands of the SAVAK, Iran's state security police, which intervened regularly to regulate and stifle the press and Iran's fledgling book industry. (35)

From here the conventional association between censorship and the Islamic state emerges. In fact, with the rise of the Islamic revolution in 1979 and the appearance of an Islamic constitution, the government has given itself further authority to allow "the printing and publishing of any and all books and journals and strictly prohibits their censorship and inspection." The very suggestion that the constitution "makes no mention of these books and publications being allowed to freely leave the print shop" allows the state unlimited space to exert censorship (*Censoring* 8). It renders censorship "a truly subjective procedure" within a broader system "highly susceptible to current waves in the political ocean" (Atwood 39). By implication, intentional silence is more of a disservice to the freedom of art, since it gives the state the upper hand and further authority to decide which books are to be censored and which ones to be authorized to the publishing industry. As such, even classics could not be exempted from the control of the state and may be subject to censorship.

In order for censorship to be efficient, the state has recourse to the Ministry of Culture and Islamic Guidance which is the governmental agency charged with overseeing and regulating literature in Iran (Atwood 38). Through this executive body, the Islamic state can easily control not just the contents of books, but also their circulation. Mandanipour explains the functioning of the ministry as follows:

> … in the early days following the revolution, after a book had been printed, its publisher had to present three copies of it to the Ministry of Culture and Islamic Guidance to receive a permit for it to be shipped out of the print shop and to be distributed. However, if the ministry deemed the book to be corruptive, the printed copies would remain imprisoned in the print shop's dark storage, and its publisher, in addition to having paid printing costs, either would have to pay storage costs, too, or would have to recycle the books into cardboard. This system had driven many publishers to the brink of bankruptcy. (*Censoring* 8)

As noted, censorship affects not only the readers' access to local literature, but also involves the writer's own survival, by wagering on a controlling spiral that could finally lead to bankruptcy. In addition to the surveillance and filtering of local products, the ministry in question withholds public access to foreign books, since the onset of the Islamic revolution in Iran is associated with banning the imports of foreign books while, also keeping in hindsight some "slight opening in the country's visual and scriptural contact with the world" (*Censoring* 185). In a revealing reference to this aspect, the writer describes an adaptation of *Snow White and the Seven Dwarfs* where "Snow White was wearing a head-scarf and two thick black lines were covering her bare arms" (*Censoring* 13). It is in that sense that the Ministry of Culture and Islamic Guidance acts as the dynamic apparatus of censorship.

Censoring articulates the superpower of the Ministry of Culture and Islamic Guidance through the personhood of Mr. Porfiry Petrovich. This is the name given in origin to the detective magistrate who is in charge of solving Raskolnikov's murders in Dostoyevsky's *Crime and Punishment* (Ostby 88). It is ironic that Mandanipour's text imbues Petrovich with a paternalistic, protective attitude towards the censored Iranian writers. Indeed, Petrovich is responsible for a careful skimming and scanning of "books, in particular novels and short-story collections, and especially love stories" with eyes wide-open to "every word, every sentence, every paragraph, or even every page that is indecent and that endangers public morality and the time-honoured values of society." In such a way, the father-censurer assumes the benefactor's benevolent responsibility of protecting his "sons" against self-disintegration:

> If there are too many such underlines, the book will likely be considered unworthy of print; if there are not that many, the publisher and the writer will be informed that they must simply revise certain words or sentences. For Mr. Petrovich this job is not just a vocation; it is a moral and religious responsibility. In other words, a holy profession. He must not allow immoral and corruptive words and phrases to appear before the eyes of simple and innocent people, especially the youth, and pollute their pure minds. (*Censoring* 9)

The relationship between Petrovich and Mandanipour best embodies censorship "as a gentle paternalism characterized by loving and protective gestures" (Ostby 80). The former intimates to Mandanipour as follows, "I wonder if you realize that I only want what is best for the likes of you ... I honestly feel some sort of friendly intimacy toward you [...] I sense you are thinking of writing things that you shouldn't write, and that if you do, writing them will not have been in your best interest ... Be careful not to kill your innocence by thinking of forbidden things" (*Censoring* 30). In view of the father-figure as a substitute for the super-ego, there is more to paternalizing Petrovich in a way that reinforces Mandanipour's tendency to psychoanalyze auto-censorship. This will be discussed in the coming section.

Throughout the novel, the censurer Petrovich amounts to a ghost who haunts the author during the story production. To this end, Mandanpour would overhear an imagined conversation between himself and the ghost-censurer where the latter suggests: "'The longer Sara and Dara stay together, the greater the danger threatening your story. Find a solution quickly; otherwise, get the fancy of publishing a love story out of your head'" (*Censoring* 293). "Representations of love," Atwood comments, "challenge the government's role as moral compass, and the notion of love threatens the very existence of the Islamic Republic, which established itself on war and violence and continues to maintain itself by remembering and memorializing mistrust and hatred" (38–39). Irrespective of illuminating the extreme extent to which the state can go in order to superimpose its sovereignty, the critique remains outstanding for being impregnated with a neo-conservative, anti-Islamic tone.

In the meantime, the considered articulations of imposed censorship are indivisible from Mandanipour's painfully complex experience as a self-censored writer in Iran. For example, the author-narrator admits the hardships of expressing the rage of a hurt jealous lover, albeit with an eye on the propriety code as the ministry's capital. In similar situations, he affirms:

> Right here, I come face-to-face with another problem in writing my love story. In stories that go to the Ministry of Culture and Islamic Guidance to receive publishing permits, there should be no foul language uttered by the characters, especially popular curse words associated with the primary sexual organs and auxiliary sexual organs. (*Censoring* 146)

On the other hand, Mandanipour grotesquely juxtaposes natural reactions in such decisive moments of anger and jealousy against a very restricted range of reactions being authorized and available to an Iranian writer. As he bitterly ponders:

> characters in Iranian stories, in the most critical moments, in climaxes such as fights and brawls, and even on occasions when they are killing each other, can only go so far as: *Rude idiot ... Snitch ... Jackass ... Cheeky ... I'm going to slap you ...* This is in direct contrast to American films in which during similarly critical climaxes, or even in the course of revelries and romantic interludes, words such as *Shit ... asshole ... son a bitch ... and fuck you ...* fly from the lips of characters to the farthest limits of the movie screen. I know polite American television channels have found an effective method of censoring these foul words even when dealing with rap songs. It is that bleep sound that suddenly pops up in the middle of what the character of the rapper is saying. These bleeps may be effective in movies, and they may render rap songs more acceptable, but they are not a solution for us Iranian writers. How in the world can we put the blare of a bleep in the mouths of characters in our stories? (146–47)

The question-answer structures as well as the successive deletions and juxtapositions mirror the dilemmas of story-writing. These are, in turn, caught between the artist's impulse for naturalness and above all a superimposed order of surgery. By implication, "the intrusions of censorship can consist not only of cutting but also of inserting by obligation, operating in a discourse of violence by deadening the language that is available into clichés" (Otsby 77). In the meantime, by no means is Mandanipour interested in writing a pornographic best seller (*Censoring* 170). Yet he carries on the battle, not of creative writing, but of story-writing while abiding to constrictions of myriad sorts.

Equally showing an outstanding awareness of the gravity of state surveillance exerted on writers, books, publishers, book-sellers, and readers, even Mandanipour's fictional characters share the same haunting as the narrator's own obsessions. As an instance, the protagonist "Sara knows that the circulation system at Tehran University's library is computerized and that any book she borrows can someday be used as evidence against her and she could be expelled" (*Censoring* 15). The facilitating character of the software in the context of censorship clearly points out the state's hold on the printing and distribution of banned books; in such a way that the dividing-line between what is imposed and what is internalized becomes thinner to the extent of indecipherability.

3-Auto-censorship and Monkeying a Haunting Order

In truth, where imposed censorship ends and self-censorship starts is rather circuitous and blurred by the gaps which are likely to emerge between what is meant, what is claimed and what is done. The connection is an intricate dyad which is both unconsciously-loaded as well as largely culturally inculcated. In reinforcement of censorship as an unconscious order, rather than a mere historical imposition, Mandanipour ends up monkeying, in the sense of tricking and toying with, the same order which haunts him all along the story-production process to a stifling degree. As he describes it:

> I too am looking on as my love story is being hung. I am beginning to understand that I have deleted so many scenes and replaced them with new ones, and I have choked and stifled so many sentences, that my novel–the information that I must offer the reader---is no longer coherent. I know I have no right to give in. I have no right to go insane. (*Censoring* 241)

Denying himself the freedom and the authority to spin his yarn according to his own conception of the plot-line, Mandanipour joins the tribe of the sane, the acceptable. However, to do the opposite by giving free will to his own desires turns out a form of insanity or transgression which is ironically illegitimate.

Despite all this, as a complex mirror of state and ego-surveillance, self-censorship is far from being a mere obstacle hampering the narrator's range of artistic expression. Albeit incapable of writing a "story in such a way that it survives the blade of censorship," Mandanipour has an estimate of himself as an experienced writer, with an extended grasp of "Iranian and Islamic symbols and metaphors" and "plenty of other tricks up my sleeve that I will not divulge" (*Censoring* 11–12). In connection to this context, Otsby makes an interesting observation upon emphasizing the use of "clichéd similes that restrict transparent narrative access to the body," arguing that "Iranians now think in poetic simile and cannot invoke the ideological rupture that the act of naming the body would be." According to her, nothing could tell of this disguising poetics than the reliance on euphemistic tropes of "apples, pomegranates, cypress trees, hyacinths and orchids" termed by Mandanipour as 'fruitology'" and used as a descriptive of human sexuality (Otsby 80). Through euphemisms, the considered novel articulates an intrinsic impact of auto-surgery leading to some form of objectifying human desires, in turn, excluded to the mundane. Cultural censorship, in other words, is an occasion to test the writer's survival skills where the writer is to out-excel the censurer or just comply with the pressures of the current market.

At this level, it should be indicated that Mandanipour manifests censorship from within, rather than from without, that is, in ways which embody textual surgery as emanating from the writer's subconscious more than from his environment. In the process, Mandanipour refers to a mechanical process of self-imposed editing through the following figure of love-making which captures the complexity of writing with the knowledge that most of what is written is likely to be shaded:

> I reached a state of mind that I have named "the first lovemaking of writer and words." Every writer has met with his words time and again. They have had frequent conversations. They have even flirted with each other. But

> there are rare moments when the shadows and the naked bodies of the writer and the words, in one time frame of the story, in one setting of the story, are coupled. They become two lovers who have long known each other and who in their clandestine meetings have frequently concealed their longing for one another. And now, for the first time, the writer and the words begin a strange lovemaking, like two ambisexual creatures that have created a new composition. (*Censoring* 68)

Accordingly, it is not uncommon that the writer and the words turn out into lovers longing for each other, yet had to conceal and restrain that longing both in public and in privacy. It is in this sense that Zand pertinently infers that the considered book "is less about censoring an Iranian love story, and rather can be read as, *Censoring: An Iranian Love Story*" (182). The secret love-making between a writer and the words making up the text, in drifting into mystery and nakedness, but also into the familiar and lack of spontaneity could be an image of the stage where the writer and the text being produced remain at some distance from intimacy.

Although *Censoring* hints at certain cultural givens as being productive of censorship, it strongly evokes the notion that there is much about censorship which is unconscious. Mandanipour sets out auto-censorship with the choice of the book cover which, though steeped in Orientalism, demonstrates a complex degree of self-surgery. He opts for a design which hovers between presence and absence, the visible and the invisible, the overt and the covert wherein the second part of the binary is typographically of dominance. Commenting on the cover, Zand asserts the following:

> In three separate printings of the work pictures show a captured woman. The first a young woman in a long black dress, trapped behind a yellow screen of 'Middle Eastern' patterns. In the other, only the eyes of a woman are visible, with partly censured text obscuring the rest of the face and body. One woman is caught behind the beautiful trellis of tradition and religion, whereas the other is blocked by words. (184)

A similar cover yokes the novel to Orientalist interpretations based among other derogations on East/West opposition, the mysterious Orient, and the oppression of women in Islamic cultures.

In line with the above, as Mandanipour endeavors to toy with the censurer, he aims for complexity and evocations through the layered, rather than through what is said explicitly or straightforwardly. The very impulse for monkeying Petrovich lends itself to several techniques which range from the layered narrative to playing out the narrator-observer, by drawing both narrator and characters in the shadow of the censurer, and performing the exonerated censured-narrator to humoring the censurer, in further subversion of the surgery apparatus.

An intricate evasive mechanism of auto-censorship is the compulsion to tell a love story through layers of narration which are often contradictory or complementary. In fact, apart from using pseudonyms for his characters, Mandanipour strongly suggests the uncountable layers of Backlawa (a Middle-Eastern cookie on the basis of almonds or other fruits). Otsby deciphers three typographical layers, including a love story recounted in "an interior bolded text," supplemented to "bolded and struck-through lines," both of which are in turn re-integrated within Mandanipour's "own non-bolded frame story as a frustrated author" (73). Strikingly noticeable about the layered narrative technique is mingling the authorized version of the love-story and the subversive one that the author originally intended to write, but ended up striking it through.

Mandanipour admits, "the crossed-out words in the text are my own doing" (*Censoring* 17). A little further, he explains,

> Just as a pencil can freely write the words of a nauseating love story replete with veiled sexual undertones as a service to a corrupt counter-revolutionary culture, it can also be the instrument with which the sentences of that same story are crossed out. The same way that a pencil in the hands of a corrupt-minded writer or spy or traitor can transfer words that, consciously or subconsciously, carry the viruses of a decadent Western culture, it can also, with the sharpness of its tip, like the needle of a syringe, inject the vaccine against the same antirevolution microbes in the population's veins. (*Censoring* 135)

The excerpt divulges two contrasting desires, one for writing a free, nauseating love story and a second penchant for purifying a corrupt story from all sexual undertones by striking through any trace of western decadence. On the one hand, Mandanipour "did not want to describe a lovemaking scene in a way that would make my story verge on the pornographic and perhaps become a best seller. I believe that any artificial or even trendy element that is added to the tragedy of a story is a betrayal of literature." On the other hand, writing a love-story is not the same as producing a mystery novel; as Mandanipour enquires: "And for how long can we write, 'The man and the woman walked into the room and closed the door …' with no further explanation." In a close context, the writer articulates his dilemma as follows: "I wanted with all my love of words and my love of their explicit and implicit connotations to create sentences in which the words too would make love. I worked for hours on this scene, but whatever I wrote screamed of being denied a publishing permit" (*Censoring* 170). Right here and elsewhere, Mandanipour's is wittily using a double language which ironically invites no less than two interpretations, but afresh tells a lot about the intermeshing dividing-lines between auto-censorship and enforced censorship.

The narrative point of view is affected by the power of censorship to such an extent that the omniscient first-person narrator shifts from a godly-position to that of the narrator-observer. It is assumed that the first-person narrator takes the center stage of the point of view up until toward or after the climax. It is only then that he completely cedes his godly-position to one that does not ironically know even what will happen to his characters nor can he any longer impact their journeys. The vying of the writer's voice with the voice of the censurer and even their unexpected complicity, at certain points in the plot, are crucial in triggering two forms and forces of order and disorder which are by definition antagonistic and aim in opposite directions.

In several episodes, one cannot decode the voice of the narrator from that of the censurer. More than this, both voices are at times undecipherable and can even speak for one another. In fact, the narrator takes on the garb of Mr. Petrovich and, consequently, cannot let his pen sketch the storyline the way he originally sees it. From the perspective that his opening sentences depict "the beauty of spring flowers, the fragrant breeze, and the brilliant sun in the blue sky," there is no scope for Mandanipour to run into any difficulties. However, it heavily bears on his consciousness that the moment he proceeds "to write about the story's man and woman and their actions and conversations, Mr. Petrovich's perspiring, irate, and reprimanding face will appear before [his] eyes" (*Censoring* 10). This constricts him to the superficial level of the mundane because of which the reader misses a lot of the original plot-line. Put this way, Mandanipour has to manage the rules of the self-censorship game of writing in a despotic regime very well. With this degree of internalization, Mandanipour leaves his love-story with very few liberties.

In one example, the narrator-censurer admits his own limits as the creator of the story:

> I cannot include the scene in which Sara takes off her headscarf and the ensuing events in my story and hand it over to Mr. Petrovich. The censorship apparatus will most certainly stamp the scene as provoking and injurious to public chastity. Even worse, there is also the possibility of a political interpretation of the scene. An interpretation that was not in my conscious mind, but now that I put myself in Mr. Petrovich's shoes and read the story from his perspective, I do see it. (*Censoring* 108)

The passage glorifies the powers of the ministry's censurer which can be read into as a witty, catering strategy aiming towards leading the censurer to lose sight of some amorous hints. According to Atwood, "the crossed-out font indicates those areas for which the author anticipates censorship. It is a form of self-censorship, and mechanisms of state control achieve success when individual citizens internalize the procedures and participate in censorship on their own" (40). In the meantime, this very participation is indivisible from being a critique of the whole system through archiving it.

In view of monkeying the censurer, Mandanipour ends up mirroring himself as the censurer's shadow or second-self. He depicts the censurer in conversation with the writer-narrator at all steps of his composition. Consequently, the censurer evolves into an obsession which intervenes in every single scene, image, sequence … and so on. Thus, it is not infrequent that the ministry censor "argues with the author about words and phrases he wants removed from the story on the grounds that they might sexually arouse readers, harm Islamic values, endanger national security or ignite revolution" (Dehghan n.p.). Ironically, nothing best embodies the power of self-censorship than the metamorphosis of the censurer from the writer's shadow into an acting character and, conversely, the drift of the omniscient narrator into narration from the angle of the observer or simple eye-witness.

In this narrative twist, the narrator cedes his power and contents himself with reporting what happens to the characters, without executing any influence whatever. In one particular instance towards the denouement, Mandanipour refers to Dara as his own creator. He surmises,

> all by himself, he has come up with another narrative suspense. He has not sought my advice. Even if he had, I would not have been able to come up with anything. It was therefore his own unadulterated idea to invite Sara to their home at ten o'clock at night when his parents are asleep and to quietly sit with her here in this yard, and perhaps to even sneak her up to his room. (*Censoring* 211)

In this sense, the narrative detachment and withdrawal of the omniscient narrator play out a passing trick hinting at the writer's deep rejection of Dara's scheme. The fact that the writer admits his incapacity to come up with anything in facing this scheme can be interpreted in several ways; among them the hint that the writer cannot devise a better plot-line, or possibly the suggestion that the fictive narrator and his views are and should be seen as separate from those of the writer. In one sense, the writer draws himself as being innocent of claiming equality with Dara in his improvised plans, stating "I have been no match for him" (*Censoring* 230).

Self-exoneration is another outstanding garb for auto-censorship which somehow involves the reader into sympathizing with a writer whose story is on the verge of collapse and ruin. Addressing the imagined censurer, Mandanipour wonders: "You call this a love story? Or a …? Look at what has become of my hopes and dreams. Every single bone in this story is broken. Every single one of its chapters has gone to a wasteland around Tehran, those same places where they burn garbage. Perhaps I should have just strangled Sara like Desdemona at the very start and put us all out of our misery"" (*Censoring* 293). In short, auto-censorship in art proves nothing more than a form of self-mutilation, culminating but into despair and frustration.

More than that, this strategic catharsis could trap the censurer into pitying a writer whose love story is taking another direction different from the one he originally intended: "The story is falling apart. The characters are each playing a different tune without being able to collectively create symphonic harmony" (*Censoring* 230). The writer's vain attempts to change the mind of his character and deter his devilish ideas, as he feverishly walks around Sara's house, stands out as an integral component of self-exoneration. Consider the following address: "Dara, go home! You are ruining everything. I am a censored writer. I can easily delete you from my novel if I choose. I'll send you down a street, and suddenly a truck will crash into you and you will die" (*Censoring* 240). In reminding Dara of being a censured writer, Mandanipour ironically threatens of taking up his full creative powers and privileges of taking this character's life in the very same way that he made it up. This articulates the author-narrator's "sense of emotional trauma implicit in [the] critique" (Atwood 40) as much as it is an instance where the voice of the writer and that of the censurer merge together to an extent of similitude.

In line with strategic narrative self-exoneration and in another surprising twist, Mandanipour coercively allocates Dara some space for freedom of expression. Right here, Dara's censured voice is redeemed from effacement and disempowerment to regain the center stage of the narration, at least for a while:

> Dara grabs my throat. He shoves me back and slams me against the wall of his room. For the first time I realize how strong his right arm has become as a result of painting walls and ceilings. In my face he shouts:
>
> "You shouldn't have written me like this. You shouldn't have written me as browbeaten and pathetic. You wrote me as an earthworm. You wrote me so that no matter what they do to me, all I can do is squirm and bear the pain. You wrote me like this to pass your story through censorship. I don't want to be written as an earthworm that even when they cut it in two turns into two earthworms. You are my murderer too for having written me as so utterly miserable. All the torment and misery there is you have written for me. You are no different than the torturer who would flog me so that I would concede there is a God. I want to write my own murder." (*Censoring* 231)

As Dara insinuates, turning into a censurer of his own characters, Mandanipour becomes no more different from a torturer, for both use the same tools of suppression in order to serve their own ends. If Dara were to be murdered, then better for him spin his own murder in the process of usurping the narrator's sphere as the only creator of the characters and, thus, die as a hero. Similar admissions remove Dara from a pathetic position to one of admiration and heroism for daring to speak out his mind, against all odds. In this passage, Dara comes to share much with the narrator, for both being harassed, end up speaking up their mind at all costs, albeit using slightly different poetics.

Humoring is one more effective gesture towards a critical monkeying of the censurer. In one funny instance, Mandanipour describes the impact of the censorship apparatus on the movie industry by mockingly referring to one of the sexiest scenes he has ever seen in a movie made in Iran after the Islamic revolution. It is about a man and woman who take a fallen sparrow to a café and while the "woman begins caressing the sparrow [...] the man reaches out from across the table and, ever so carefully, so that his fingers do not come into contact with the woman's hand, caresses the sparrow's head and neck" (*Censoring* 91). In this eternal exchange of caressing the sparrow, Mandanipour seems to humour the censurer through an explicit allusion to the victory of noble human emotions over any scissors. In another example, he considers the impossibility of a love story "in which the abandoned and tormented lover who has learned of the presence of a wealthy suitor in his beloved's life does not knock back a few drinks to console himself." Mandanipour contrasts such an inconceivable alternative in the current mindset to "those characters in dubbed foreign films screened in Iran who only order milk or orange juice in bars," only to be served by bartenders "gold-colored milk or burgundy orange juice" (*Censoring* 149).

In another humoring act, Mandanipour goes a step further, showing that the censurer is wagering on a lost battle against artists. In fact, he argues that self-censorship particularly represented by the three dots can have an inciting effect on the reader's imagination, that is, opposite to what is ordained. According to him, their effect is similar to building a nuclear bomb. Indeed,

> the moment a reader, especially an Iranian one, sees these three villainous dots, a reaction similar to the chain reaction triggered by nuclear fission of the uranium atom takes place in his mind, and it results in the release of terrifying nuclear energy. When readers see these three dots, control of their

> imagination is no longer in the hands of the writer, nor is it in the hands of Mr. Petrovich. (*Censoring* 147)

A movie-maker, who can come up with scenes which, though acceptable from the outside, can be very amorous from the inside, is much like a story-writer who can devise different strategies to trick the censurer. "Because the scenes and sentences that I cannot publish in my book," Mandanipour asserts, "I will write in my mind, and given that until now no one has been able to read my thoughts and fantasies to punish me for them, I will make love to these words in the same way that Dara lives for the magic of cinema and falls in love and for his beloved he dreams up romantic novelties ..." (*Censoring* 69). Comments and running dots are more of a direct challenge to the censurer who is more of a disempowered reader as long as he can control what is said, but never the unsaid.

In endeavoring to trick the censurer, the writer ends up tricking the reader. To borrow Sara's words, a "writer who can trick the censorship apparatus can trick his readers, too" (*Censoring* 63). In spite of the fact that many "love stories, in maneuvering their way through the Ministry of Culture and Islamic Guidance either are wounded, lose certain limbs, or are with finality put to death" (*Censoring* 10) as well as the writer's initial admission that the involved version of his novel explains why he has not become a great writer and gives a view of "just another young man with *Great Expectations* of [his] future as a writer" (*Censoring* 14), Mandani-pour's text attests to his excellence against all odds. Even the number of digressions in the novel and the unanswered questions could not lead us to underestimate the writer's imaginative skills in mirroring the intricacy of the impact of censorship on literature and its superpower as an internal and external force in a certain historical context.

> Mandanipour has considerably nuanced the concept, writing about the existence of a culture self-censorship before the 1979 regime change in Iran, before the Pahlavi dynasty (1925–1979) and even before the constitutional revolution in 1906–1911. The work mixes the political elements of censorship with its cultural footprints centuries back in Persian literature. He leaves the question about whether censorship has been imposed on the people by the government, or if the people have contributed to the maintenance of the walls of censorship in society as well. (Zand 182–83)

Neither should we consider Mandanipour as an accomplice of the revolutionary fundamentalist value-system which is of dominance.

The closure of the novel twists a super-imposed order of censorship in different ways, mainly by questioning the repressive and suppressive powers of a censuring state. In a particular instance, Mandanipour targets the state for driving its own people into insanity and, gradually, leading the country into mutiny:

> I can understand that after years of tolerating oppression, humiliation and pain, and suffocation, now, like an infected cyst, rage has burst open in Dara's soul and leaked its poison into his blood, driving him insane. This is just the point dictators fail to understand, and even if they do, they have no alternative but to increase the ranks of their torturers and censors, until the day when the insanity of revolution floods the streets and burns and kills. (*Censoring* 231)

The citation uses catharsis as a way of conjuring a pathetic portrayal of Dara as a figure worthy of our empathy and sympathy, even through his insane attempts to pursue his beloved. In the meantime, it confirms the compulsion of despotic states to control its subjects and censure its writers to a harassing degree, verging towards rebellion. Ironically, Mandanipour reflects: "Imagine you live in a country where you are not even free to be insane. It's frightening" (*Censoring* 240). This is ironic, because even to go insane requires a state permit. Similar statements take part in cementing the author's status as an Iranian writer exiled since 2006, the year Mandanipour left Iran to the U.S. (Ostby 74).

Even with the different cuts here and there, Mandanipour seems to be set from the start that his memoir will not have the chance of publication in predominantly self-censured culture. For one thing, despite the fact that the book in question was initially written in Persian and in the U.S., and was later translated by Sara Khalili into English, it is far from being meant for local Iranian readers. It was obviously meant for a foreign audience, "for the Other who doesn't know Iran, who doesn't read Persian" (Atwood 40; Namy n.p.). The novel "recurrently addresses itself to readers who are not familiar with Iranian culture, history, and literature," in a way, pandering to "its dominantly western readers" (Namy n.p.). To this end, we often encounter transliterated words, general explanations of symbols, digressions into cultural specifications ... and so forth. This particular process of familiarizing the contents of the text is termed as "proverbialization," which according to Marie Ostby, "takes the form of necessary over-explanation of cultural terms geared toward a non-Iranian, though not always American, audience" (85). Having been "written in Persian with the intention of translation into English," the story "points to a more recent trend whereby Iranian authors generate English-language texts that seek to reach broader audiences and to stretch beyond the limitations of the state-controlled publishing industry" (Atwood 41). "While the narrator is busy telling the love story," Zand comments, "the text seeks to translate/interpret Iranian culture—more specifically to translate the culture of Iranian censorship" (182). Thus, *Censoring* is intent on dealing with censorship as a primary entangled order/disorder.

Conclusion

Reading *Censoring an Iranian Love Story* is undoubtedly an exercise in forging the skill of re-reading and dismembering the literary text. The appreciation of its multi-layered complexity requires an active reader much like Sara who

> reads the white between the lines, and wherever a sentence is left incomplete and ends with three dots like this "...," her mind grows very active and begins to imagine what the eliminated words may be. At times, her imagination goes further and grows more naked than the words the writer had in mind. (*Censoring* 14)

Mandanipour has devised a story-line wherein the narrator experiences a genuine fervent struggle between two conflicting orders, vying with each other for survival and even dominance during the story-writing experiment. In this process, the reader is never lost sight of. The latter is to a great extent responsible for making sense of the unsaid, unmasking the erased, and savoring the layers of Backlawa.

In addition to this, if the discussion above attests to anything, it is to the force of both culture and the system in power in inculcating certain orders such as censorship in the unconscious till they become engraved as common-sense practices. It mirrors the "collective trauma that censorship has inflicted on Iranian society," ranging from ordinary people to the elite and their imaginary world (Atwood 41). In a similar line, the analysis opens the reader's eyes to the fact that "[a]lthough Iran is historically a land of poets and poetry, and embodies a culture steeped in the rich exchange of language, ideas, and writing, it has also had a long history of persecuting and driving out many of its finest writers and artists" (Karim 35). Thus, it remains quite constricting to surmise that *Censoring* only "illuminates the labyrinth of paradoxes entrapping the politically repressed, and celebrates the liberating powers of literature and love" (Seaman *22*).

One fails to appreciate the considered novel if he/she fails to grasp that "censorship is not only a matter of political repression, but can also be part of a long tradition of indirect expression. The implicit narrator thus tells a story of Iranian culture's long-lasting love affair with the concept of censorship" (Zand 182). In turn, this expands our understanding of censorship as a system larger than governmental suppression. Speaking of censorship, we should rather speak of "the hegemony of censored lives—whether it is characters' lives censored by authors, authors' lives censored by a government, or books' lives censored by the demands of the literary marketplace" (Ostby 93). Redefined, censorship is rather part and parcel of hegemonic thinking.

The only re-creative asset to all of this, as Mandanipour suggests, is driving the "writer to abstain from superficiality and to instead delve into the layers and depths of love and relationships and achieve a level of creativity that Western poets and writers cannot even dream of" (*Censoring* 140). In the same context, the writer comments:

> It is thus that Iranian writers have become the most polite, the most impolite, the most romantic, the most pornographic, the most political, the most socialist realist, and the most postmodern writers in the world. I just don't know in which school of story writing I should categorize Iranian stories in which thugs, similar to the gravedigger in *Hamlet*, speak literary and philosophical words. (*Censoring* 148)

In further subversion of the censorship machine, Mandanipour goes to the point as to assume:

> I think if we Iranian writers continue such exhausting exercises, at long last our syphilis-stricken dream of winning a Nobel Prize might become reality.

> I should remember to tell that fortunate writer, or unfortunate writer, because in Iran he or she will surely be accused of collaborating with Western intelligence services, to make sure and thank Mr. Petrovich when addressing the Nobel Committee. (*Censoring* 44–45)

As such, the censurer becomes, probably unknowingly, of disservice to the censored text. The very same apparatus, we should remember, has bestowed us with great works such as *Animal Farm* and *Lolita*, among other masterpieces.

As a broader inference, the above discussion illustrates in part the ways in which order and disorder necessarily evoke each other to the extent that the borderline between them can easily turn out a common, intermeshed terrain, particularly in times of social, economic and political unrest. Order and disorder could be made to intermingle with each other, to culminate in a state of endless contradictions, incongruities, grotesqueries, and complex haziness which would affect even the essential meanings, interpretations and representations of both ends. In the midst of such an orderly (dis)-order, literature could be both a loser and a winner in the sense that a writer would witness pains which are inseparable from pleasures, failures indecipherable from achievements, pressures inseparable possibilities. Particularly when politicized, literature could divulge that what constitutes order and dis-order can be misunderstood and misinterpreted and the dividing-lines get intermeshed. More than this, such power discourses when applied to literature either consciously or subconsciously could beget suppressions, oppressions, complicities, and traumas, albeit allowing for opposition, creativity, and excellence to arise.

Works Cited

Atwood, Blake. "Sense and Censorship in the Islamic Republic of Iran." *World Literature Today* (May–June 2012): 38–41.

Barthes, Roland. "The Death of the Author" *Image, Music, Text.* Trans. by Stephen Heath. Hammersmith: Fontana Press, 1977. 142–48.

Dehghan, Saeed Kamali. "On Love and the Censor." A review of *Censoring an Iranian Love Story. The Guardian.* Saturday 15 August 2009.

http://www.theguardian.com/books/2009 /aug/15/censoring-iranian-love-story. Accessed October 2013. N.p.

Foucault, Michel. *Discipline and Punish: The Birth of the Prison.* 1977. Translated by Alan Sheridan. New York: Random House Inc., 1995.

---. Preface. *The Order of Things: An Archaeology of the Human Sciences.* Trans. *Les Mots et les Choses.* New York: Vintage Books, 1994. xv–xxiv

Hoffert, Barbara. "Review of *Censoring an Iranian Love Story*, Shahriar Mandanipour." Knopf. May 2009. c.304p. tr. from Farsi by Sara Khalili. *Library Journal* (April 15, 2009).

Karim, Persis. "Writing Beyond Iran Reinvention and the Exilic Iranian Writer." Worldliteraturetoday.org. March/April 2015: 35–7.

Khakpour, Porochista. "What to read now: Unlikely Works of Iranian Origin." WLT November/December 2015.

"Literature and Censorship: Who is Afraid of the Truth of Literature? (5th International Comparative Literature Colloquium." http://www.encls.net/?q=event/literature-and-censorship-who-afraid-truth-literature-5th-international-comparative-literature. Accessed January 2015. N.p.

Mandanipour, Shahriar. *Censoring an Iranian Love Story: A Novel.* Trans. Sara Khalili. 2011, Routledge: Taylor and Francis Books, 2009.

---. *East of Violet*. 1999. Tehran: Nashr-e Markaz Publishing, 2009.

Namy, Raha. "De-Censoring an Iranian Love Story." *The Quarterly Conversation*. Iss. 28. (June 4, 2012): http://quarterlyconversation.com/de-censoring-an-iranian-love-story. Accessed November 2013. N.p.

Ostby, Marie. "De-censoring an Iranian-American "Memoir": Authorship and Synchronicity in Shahriar Mandanipour's *Censoring an Iranian Love Story*." *Iranian Studies* 46,1, (January 2013): 73–93.

"Review of *Censoring an Iranian Love Story*," Shahriar Mandanipour. Knopf. May 2009. c.304p. tr. from Farsi by Sara Khalili. *Publishers Weekly* March 23, 2009: 46.

Seaman, Donna. "Review of *Censoring an Iranian Love Story*," Shahriar Mandanipour. Knopf. May 2009." 22 *Booklist* April 15, 2009.

Sethi, Anita. "Review of *Censoring an Iranian Love Story*," Shahriar Mandanipour. Knopf. May 2009." *New Statesman* (31 August 2009): 44.

Silva, Cristina. "Charlie Hebdo Attack: The Prophet Muhammad Cartoons." *International Business Times* (01/07/15). http://www.ibtimes.com/charlie-hebdo-attack-prophet-muhammad-cartoons-may-have-caused-paris-magazine-1775898. Accessed May 2017. N.p.

Thornton, Matthew. Mandanipour to Knopf: Review of *Censoring an Iranian Love Story*, Shahriar Mandanipour. Knopf. May 2009. *Publishers Weekly* January 28, 2008: 14.

Zand, Misha. *Review of Censoring an Iranian Love Story: A Novel* Shariar Mandanipour, Translated into English by Sara Khalili London, Abacus, 2011, ISBN 978-0349121451. *Book Review. Middle Eastern Literatures*, Vol. 15, No. 2, August 2012: 181–5.

The Apollonian and the Dionysian in *The Great God Brown*: A Nietzschean reading of O'Neill's Order and Disorder

Welid Hmeissia, I.S.E.A.H.Z, University of Tunis

Abstract

This paper provides a reading of order and disorder as Apollonianism and Dionysianism in Eugene O'Neill's *The Great God Brown* by exploring their use in literary analysis and studying the evolution of these concepts from Greek mythology to Nietzschean philosophy. Dionysus can be synonymous with disorder in terms of instability, formlessness and limitlessness as he is the god of metamorphoses and excess, which inspires Nietzsche's Dionysian chaotic artistic drive. O'Neill's Dion Anthony depicts this disordered impulse. Phoebus, however, teaches 'Know thyself' and 'Nothing in excess'. He is the god of measure and symmetry. Apollo is order. Hence, Nietzsche's Apollonian highlights the *Principium Individuationis* and numbs the Will. O'Neill depicts it through William Brown, a lifeless architect. This paper illustrates how the drives and characters of order and disorder are at the same time antagonistic and yet complementary after accounting for their mythological and philosophical origins. We will see how order and disorder merge, diverge, complement and stimulate each other for new births without failing to highlight the risks inherent in them.

Keywords: Dionysian, Apollonian, drives, antagonistic and complementary.

Eugene O'Neill's *The Great God Brown* is a puzzling play that permits different readings varying from a fight between an economic materialist and a sensitive artist to a sheer struggle between good and evil. However, a Nietzschean reading appears most needed to take the literary text into the philosophical and psychoanalytical realms. Moreover, the play permits such an analysis considering that it is full of dichotomies and dualities. Nietzsche's Dionysian and Apollonian philosophies, which are in accordance with earlier theories like Kant's 'phenomenon' and 'thing-in-itself', Schopenhauer's 'representation' and 'Will' and Edmund Burke's 'beautiful' and 'sublime' or which adhere to more recent theories such as Derrida's 'structure' and 'force' or 'formal containment' and 'dynamic transgression' and Kristeva's 'symbolic' and 'semiotic', could be extended to an analogy of order and disorder. The aforementioned concepts are united by the fact of encompassing intricate conceptual relationships based on both divergence and complementarity, which is the case of the theme of order and disorder. The analysis stems from a philosophical reading that is steeped in a mythological one. Thus, this paper suggests a theoretical informative background to introduce mythological references to be related to order and disorder, then to study how they have been transformed into Nietzschean philosophical concepts that are impersonated by the two major protagonists of *The Great God Brown*, William Brown and Dion Anthony, who are the incarnation of Apollonian order and Dionysian disorder, and eventually to examine the reasons underlying their self-destruction.

Before dealing with philosophical and literary order and disorder, we have to refer to the mythological symbols that are at the origin of the key appellations used in this paper. In Greek mythology, Dionysus is mainly known as the god of wine, ecstasy and intoxication. However, his relationship with death is also important. He is the emblem of defiance of death, which is the constant element in life-cycles. As to Dionysus' relevant features, we shall mention formlessness, limitlessness and excess. He is the antithesis of stability and physical order through his multiple births as each one of them takes place in a different *location*: from his mother's womb to Zeus' thigh and to reconstruction from pieces by Rhea. Secondly, we can say that Dionysus is a god who deconstructs the notion of limits, hence another form of order. His mythology is centered on his superiority to death, as he is "the god who is destroyed, who disappears, who relinquishes life and then is born again" (*Larousse* 160), and he is also the god who saves his mother from the world of Hades – a disturbance of the order of the two realms. Besides, he is definitely the god of excess and intemperance through his cult of intoxication. His unrestrained life-celebration is equated with disorder, as this extreme elation exceeds the boundaries of sanity. He is synonymous with stirring instincts through wine, dance and music which are the components of the Dionysian dithyramb as represented by the Bacchae, the Maenads, the satyrs, Pan and Silenus. On the other hand, the Apollonian order is reflected through his physical description, actions and mottos. Apollo is the symbol of male beauty – despite the relativity of the latter – and could be linked to aesthetic order. The classical idea that beauty is part of order is relevant especially that his physical representation tends to meet an aesthetic ideal. As to his significant deeds, Apollo is both a colonizer and a builder. The latter is more highlighted in myths and is more consistent with his depiction as a symbol of order. In fact, it is recorded that he "delights in the constructions of towns of which he himself lays the foundations" (*Larousse* 116). At the same time, Apollo is the god of symmetry, which could be defined as an architectural and a geometrical order. The celestial archer's mythology is marked by numerous conquests to restore order such as his fights against titans as well as being synonymous with the recorded mottos 'Know thyself' and 'Nothing in excess'. Above all, he is the depiction of anti-barbarism and moderation *par excellence*. In brief, Apollo is order.

Relying on the symbolism of these two gods, Nietzsche has taken part in the philosophical tradition of the two-fold division of the world as being a mutable force called *Will* and represented by the Dionysian impulse, constituting the drive of life and underlying the apparent life forms or the Veil of Maya dubbed Apollonian. The "initiate and disciple of [Dionysus]" (Nietzsche 6) uses mythology to create the Dionysian. He introduces it as "a spirit with unfamiliar needs, as yet unnamed, a memory bursting with questions, experiences [and] hidden reaches" (6) and if one asks: "'What is the Dionysian?' the answer will come: 'it is "unknown and unimaginable"'" (6). In simpler terms, the Dionysian is an impulse and a drive. It is the very image of the god Dionysus who destroys limits. It is not a force of anarchy, but one of *positive nihilism*, as he – who is driven by this impulse – deconstructs the surface-level order and common surface values, then rebuilds *theirs*. The Dionysian fights against dismemberment (physically endured by Dionysus) by announcing the "breakdown of the *principium individuationis*" (Nietzsche 22) and aiming at universal oneness. This "thoughtless and amoral artist-god" (Nietzsche 8) *creates* through reconciliation with internal disorder. The "essence of the Dionysian [can be read in an] analogy of intoxication" (Nietzsche 22) the goal of which is to liberate instincts. It is a "magic potion of life" (Nietzsche 27) that removes death from its central position in Man's concerns and disturbs natural order with a death-transcending joy by restoring natural disorder to the center.

As to Apollo, Nietzsche invests in symmetry, form, beauty, limits, and mainly in excess in measure to draw a Dionysian alter ego. In Nietzschean philosophy, Apollo is the symbol of form. Construction, symmetry and beauty are pivotal terms in the Apollonian framework of order. Apollo is "the God of all plastic energies [and the] master of the beautiful" (Nietzsche 21). Apollonian architectural symbolism teaches us that "redemption in appearance can be attained" (Nietzsche 86). However, this observation comes with Nietzsche's negative assessment, as symmetry and form remind him of "Egyptian inflexibility and coldness" (58). Architecture is the art of order but also the art of lifeless forms and the exultation of the latter means rejoicing in limits and boundaries. The goal of Apollonianism is to draw boundaries and limits between individuals. We could say as well that Apollo wants to bring individuals to *order*. Life is experienced through measure, restraint and divorce from wild impulses, which means numbing all that is Dionysian or natural. Finally, being a principled and ethical god, he maintains moderation and self-knowledge as well as repudiation of instincts. For this, the Apollonian artist is deemed *naïve*, as he has mythologically and figuratively killed the demons and Titans, symbols and bringers of disorder, which has removed him further from the defiers and breachers of the Olympian order.

Such impulses and concepts have been used by Eugene O'Neill to create *The Great God Brown.* His protagonist Dion Anthony is the representative of Dionysianism. O'Neill has intended to conceive this incomplete incarnation of the Greek god and of the Nietzschean concept through the first name: Dion foe Dionysus. Of course, Dion holds criteria that are reminiscent of the god – and Pan due to the closeness and almost interchangeable characteristics of both divinities. In this part of the analysis, we will attempt to uncover the pertinent instances of analogy between the character and the god-concept. First, let us say that Dion was born in the dithyramb. He first makes his appearance on stage amid a mood of festivities. There are sounds of music, dancing and drinking in the background coming from a casino. Even though there is no real analogy of Dionysus' Thiasus, the element of the maenads is present. Margaret is not a maenad *per se* but her obsession with Dion's ways of life or simple being is striking. The way she speaks about him makes her appear as an intoxicated follower. She is almost disconnected or insulated from her surroundings and she speaks as if she were in trance, ignoring then William Brown's words. For instance, she looks up to the moon and says: "Dion is so wonderful" (O'Neill 312). A simple look from Dion makes her "feel so crazy" (313). Her adoration confirms Dion's closeness to the image of Dionysus or mostly of Pan as she says: "Dion's so different from all the others. He can paint beautifully and write poetry and he plays and sings and dances so marvelously" (313). He is held in veneration by Margaret who considers him a god on whom the meaning of her life depends. The reference to natural metaphors, such as "Dion is the moon and I'm the sea" (314), and her transcendent devotion to him confirm the image of a maenad which, by extension, substantiates Dion's representation of Dionysus and Pan.

Intoxication is another characteristic that is found in the personification of Dionysus. Dion is a drunkard. Beside his description in fits (which are not clearly caused by alcohol or masks), Margaret clearly blames him for "the hard drinking" (322) he indulges in. In addition to intoxication, limitlessness through the absence of measure in drinking can be inferred. Furthermore, Dion is against forms and conformity, which can be seen in the way he dresses in public. He is socially on the margin, as Pan is. When it comes to forms, Dion reiterates his hate for architecture throughout the play. When his father obliges him to study it, he gives him a sarcastic answer: "(*mockingly – to the air*) It's difficult to choose – but architecture is less laborious" (311). We can infer the penchant for what is formless and fluid through the numerous reminders of Dion's innate and *natural* talent of drawing – here, of course, we must oppose the lines of drawing to the *learnt* mathematical lines of architecture. We can also see fluidity in poetic musicality. "Dion can recite lots of Shelley's poems by heart" (312), Margaret says before adding: "Dion's so different from all the others. He can paint beautifully and write poetry and he plays and sings and dances so marvelously. But he's sad and shy…" (313). Dion stands for art and beauty indeed.

Dion brings us closer to Pan's incarnation in the play. The horned god's playfulness comes in addition to other important features. Pan is the marginalized Greek divinity *par excellence*. He is even despised for his lack of pomp, an idea we can identify by analogy in Dion's description by Mr. Brown: "Did you see young Anthony strutting around the ballroom in dirty flannel pants?" (308) Dion and Pan are strangers looked at with "carelessness" (310) first and with envy later. We may as well note that O'Neill did not let a lot to infer with the description of Dion's mask as a "*mocking reckless, defiant, gaily, scoffing and sensual young Pan*" (310). Carnal gratification, which is an element of Dionysus' Thiasus and the main label of Pan, is also present. Margaret recounts the scene of Dion kissing her: "That one time he kissed me – I can't forget it! He was only joking – but I felt – and he saw and just laughed!" (313). Later, Dion exclaims: "I love, thou lovest, he loves, she loves! […] Now I can make love – to anyone" (316). Another instance of Dion's erotic nature is his ambiguous relationship with the – apparent – prostitute Cybel, as he spends most of his time at her place. Finally, Dion utters a word that is proper to Nietzsche's Dionysus: "Pride! Pride without which the Gods are worms!" (323) – which brings us to Nietzsche's description of the Dionysian artist. Being close to nature and conscious of the Veil, this artist refuses to act at the surface for he is not an artist of appearance. Yet, as aforementioned, he is obliged to refer to the surface of things in order to transmit their essence. The Dionysian artist sees himself as a superior and more authentic creator than the Apollonian. It is a dimension where arrogance is praised. All this is almost a replica of Dion's refusal to work for the Apollonian William Brown. Actually, Dion represents the "severe pride of the artist" (*Tragedy*, 56).

O'Neill is rather faithful to the mythological description of Apollo in order to create a literary incarnation.[1] Billy Brown is a "handsome, tall and athletic boy of nearly eighteen. He is blond and blue-eyed, with a likeable smile and a frank good-humored face, its expression already indicating a disciplined restraint. His manner has the easy self-assurance of a normal intelligence" (325). He is a fair elegant young man who remains so all along the play. Seven years after the former description, Billy is still portrayed as "a fine-looking, well-dressed, capable, college-bred American business man, boyish still and the same engagim personality" (325). A slightly more mature William Brown keeps the same appearance. "He is the ideal of the still youthful, good-looking, well-groomed, successful provincial American of forty" (339). Even when he starts to have a look of suffering, he puts on a mask that is almost a replica of the former depiction of his face. "He is now wearing a mask which is an exact likeness of his face as it was in the last scene – the self-assured success" (347). William has the immutable orderly surface perfection that is related to Nietzsche's Apollo. Beside the physical analogies set with the god of symmetry, let us mention architectufe as a feature that confirms the similarity. Apollo is a successful architect god, which matches William's profession. The success of the latter in the business of architecture and his economic prosperity can be linked to the victories and achievements of the Greek god who is prosperous in his

[1] He was depicted as a young man of idealized beauty, with a vigorous body, a broad chest and slim hips. His beardless face with its delicate features is surmounted by a high forehead and thick, long hair which sometimes falls freely behind him, sometimes is knotted on top or at the nape of his neck so that only a few curls fall to his shoulders (*Larousse* 116).

endeavors. The expression 'disciplined restraint' is also relevant as it reminds us of 'Nothing in excess' and 'Know thy limits'. He is "Perfect Brown" (O'Neill 347).

However, in order to perceive clearly the Apollonian in Billy Brown, he must be studied in terms of his relationship with Dion. For instance, Apollo admires Dionysus'/ Pan's naturalness. We must keep in mind that the former has stolen the art of prophecy and music from the chthonian, hence inferior, Silenus and Pan. These acts go against the usual direction of stealing: here, the disciplined superior takes from the unrefined inferior so it is not a matter of need but one of envy. In the play, Billy wonders at Dion's freedom from and nonchalance *vis-à-vis* the surface order and social behavioral norms and recommendations. In the prologue, Dion is first described to us through Billy's eyes. He says: "(*admiringly*) Dion came in his old clothes on a bet with me. He's a real sport. He wouldn't have been afraid to appear in his pajamas! (*He grins with appreciation*)" (308). Billy's feelings towards Dion turn to awe as he appears embarrassed and uneasy while talking to him. Dionysus' presence "annihilates, cancels and absorbs Apollo" (Nietzsche 32). The "Apollonian harp [is outshined by] the Dionysian scream of excess" (32). What is studied is surpassed by the natural and impulsive. Besides, towards his death, Billy screams: "I don't want justice. I want love" (O'Neill 374). This rejection of the rational for what is sensuous echoes Nietzsche's idea of how the Dionysian shows the Apollonian that his life is one of "suffering and knowledge" (32) and reminds him of the true facet or essence of life, a fact known by Dion who says: "Brown will still need me – to reassure him he's alive" (374). Entangled in the shackles of social success, William the Apollonian loses the pleasure of what is natural. He has grown too artificial or as Dion puts it, "too fat now" (374) to enjoy the simple and innate facets of life or "to learn to walk, let alone to dance or run" (374). Another proof of the existing Dionysian-Apollonian relationship can be seen in Billy's failure to draw a satisfying blue-print of a house. His work is rejected by the client and described as "too cold, too spare, too like a tomb [...] for a livable home" (358). On the contrary, Dion's work is cherished. The Apollonian symmetry is too removed from Life.

Finally, let us consider this equation: on the one hand, we have Apollo's recurrent failure with women and his jealous nature; on the other hand, Pan's approved and promoted carnal and uncouth nature, added to Dionysus' entourage of maenads. This allows us to deduce a direct relationship of jealousy between the "master of the beautiful" (Nietzsche 21) and the earthly god, and the god of wine. By analogy, William Brown loses to Dion in terms of love. His efforts to charm Margaret are thwarted by Dion's simple presence in name and not even in body. In the prologue, Billy tells Margaret "I love you" (313) whereas, as if not hearing his voice, she wonders about Dion's feelings and whereabouts. He is indeed cancelled by Dion so he tries to understand the reason of his ragged friend's success with Margaret. He asks the other contended woman Cybel for Dion's secret of superiority:

> Tell me – I've always been curious – what is it that makes Dion so attractive to women – especially certain types of women, if you'll pardon me? He always has been and yet I never could see exactly what they saw in him. Is it his looks – or because he's such a violent sensualist – or because he poses as artistic and temperamental – or because he's so wild or just what is it? (340)

He begs her through this vigorous speculation to be able to compete with Dion who appears superior through violence, sensuality, wildness or a chaotic yet natural life-style as opposed to Billy's disciplined unsatisfying behavior. He keeps imploring Cybel not to meet Dion anymore: "At least – I'll give you anything you ask! – please promise me you won't see Dion Anthony again! [...] (*Jubilantly, kissing her hand – politely*) Thank you! Thank you! I'm exceedingly grateful" (341). He begs to find a place in women's hearts next to the innately dominating Dion. All this confirms William Brown as Apollo's incarnation who is described by Robert Graves as follows: "Apollo was not invariably successful in love" (78).

However, despite this apparent superiority of the chaotic impulse, their relationship remains one of mutual dependency, be it philosophically or dramatically. Dionysian disorder needs measure, refinement and beauty. Artificial order, hence, is an accepted simulacrum of genuine disorder. Nietzsche writes that "the Apollonian qualities of the mask are the necessary results of a glance into the terrifying inner world of nature. [They are] bright spots […] to heal the eyes" (53). It is the means to have a safe look at the Dionysian disorder without being entangled into its permanent chaos. Thus, the relation with the "innermost [chaotic] ground of the world" is presented to us as an "*allegorical dream-image*" (Nietzsche 24) of order. The Dionysian also provides a service to the Apollonian. According to Nietzsche, measure, boundaries, beauty and form are not sufficient for the Apollonian cult of order to create life. To survive the ordeal of the substratum of order, the Apollonian needs the Dionysian pleasure of excess and disorder. "And look! Apollo was unable to live without the Dionysian" (32), Nietzsche confirms. Order and measure appear as pale when compared to life of excess or to the frightening chaotic but truthful demoniacal hymn of nature. The Apollonian needs the Dionysian to remind him of his faint color of appearance. As the twin-drives, Dion and Billy appear as canceling each other while they are in need of each other's presence. Dion and Billy are friends and they remain so despite jealousy or contempt. Dion lacks the order represented by employment, income and stability which are the realm of Billy. The latter needs the relaxing natural disorder that allows a break from suffocating measure, restraint and discipline.

Due to the failure to admit this inter-dependency, the two impulses appear distorted in O'Neill's dramatization of Nietzschean philosophy. In the play, through the "exercise in unmasking" (Bigsby 68), the Dionysian struggles to attenuate or alleviate his disorder by the antithetical ideology of asceticism and the Apollonian attempts to balance his excess of order by vanishing and becoming a distorted Dionysian version. They are both blind to the accurate complementary impulse. To announce the beginning of the protagonists' self-destruction, we need to refer to Nietzsche's Dionysian bargain where the follower loses the elements that define his individuality and enters through trance the dimension of the united great all, and where trouble, pain, sorrow and death are neither fled nor fought against with Herculean might. The Dionysian simply teaches to cohabit with these elements, accept them as parts of nature and tame them with Apollonian decorum. In exchange of these comforting beliefs, the

Dionysian needs to be separated from all that goes against instincts and life, as it does not cohabit with antithetical drives. If so, the person's psyche ends suffering from the destructive unbound chaos of impulse.

Dion Anthony appears in the play as a dual character. He is both a young man with a pure face, announcing "*religious faith in life*" (O'Neill 310) and one with a mask of a "*defiant [...] scoffing and sensual young Pan*" (310). The observation of the transition from one personality to the other is not a complicated process in the play. When mask-less, Dion is sensitive, fragile and religious. When masked, he is provocative, sarcastic and playful. Dion is aware of his antithetical impulses: Dionysus and Pan, on the one hand and Saint Anthony, on the other. *Carpe Diem* meets asceticism. In his bewilderment, he wonders:

> Why am I afraid to dance I who love music and rhythm and grace and song and laughter? Why am I afraid to live, I who love life and the beauty of flesh and the living colors of earth and sky and sea? Why am I afraid to love, I who love love? Why am I afraid, I who am not afraid? (315)

The terms music, rhythm, song, laughter, beauty, flesh and natural elements touch upon a life-celebratory mood that reminds us of Pan's pastoral debauchery. However, the presence of fear in this celebration signals sickness. He values self-contempt and weakness which are the traces of Saint Anthony and of Christian asceticism. Dion turns to the inherited wrong form of order to quench his natural Dionysian disorder and end up torn in between. He fails to sublimate the impulse that comes with it. There is an anomaly in Dion's taming of the Dionysian. His sickness is spotted in his wrong choice of an ally. However, not being recognized without his mask leaves Dion with no illusion of life without disorder. He does not exist without the mask of disorder.

As prophesized by Nietzsche, Dionysus becomes an impulse of bitterness and evil. Dion sums up this shift through a divided speech. He first describes his experience with Pan: "Now! Be born! Awake! Live! Dissolve into dew – into silence – into night – into earth – into space – into peace – into meaning – into joy – into God – into the Great God Pan" (318). However, he announces the short-lived Dionysian experience as a change occurs. His voice is no longer the same as he exclaims: "Time to exist! […] Learn to pretend! […] Learn to lie" (318). He becomes the harbinger of death. In the role of a portentous preacher, he screams: "Join the procession! Great Pan is dead! Be ashamed" (318). It is the last speech of the Dionysian through the lens of Apollonianism in him before shifting. Dionysian natural chaos is no more and Mephistophelean destruction appears. The birth of the latter results from a murder. Pan is smothered by the antithesis of life: Saint Anthony. Dion describes it perfectly: "When Pan was forbidden the light and warmth of the sun he grew sensitive and self-conscious and proud and revengeful and became Prince of Darkness" (348). The mask will torture the person wearing it for *inside* an antagonist drive exists. Smothering the original drive aborts the bargain and the individual is caught in a death trap that is the mask. "The cup of Dionysus has become the chalice of hemlock" (LaBelle 442), in this case, the mask.

However, the natural disorder that is the Dionysian is eternally reborn as a god is. The impulse is finally transmitted to the lifeless William Brown. Dion says while dying: "(*Mockingly*) My last will and testament. I leave Dion Anthony to William Brown" (350). Smothering the Dionysian disorder in William Brown is not as clear as it is in Dion's case. We may theorize that Brown has received the mask in a dangerous level of perversion so he is presented as a passive victim. Still, he also smothers the Dionysian in his own way. It is true that Billy is Apollonian but this impulse, when studied from a Nietzschean point of view, appears classical in its relation to Dionysus. Billy's flaw also resides in his religiosity. He fails to fathom and tame the Dionysian he has inherited from the mask. Thus, he experiences the same cycle of events Dion goes through. In fear of the irreligious self he becomes on wearing the mask, William's personality also ends up becoming dual. His face, which before this instance remains Apollonian as his original mask, grows ascetic and dying while the inherited mask remains the same. In fact, the masked Brown goes in his irreligiosity more than Dion does. He is both Apollo and Dionysus here and totally anti-religious. Brown's problem is one of not fathoming the Dionysian bargain. His torture and loss are due to the wrong management of the Dionysian philosophy.

Dionysianism, despite its chaotic promise, is a life-affirming concept. Its enmity towards the limiting / limited *form* and the restricting surface makes it safe to promote it as an anthropomorphic concept. This is, of course, from a Nietzschean point of view, as the philosopher classifies it as a natural drive. However, it does not cohabit with other impulses and drives, which makes it an intricate and dangerous ideology nonetheless. Dionysianism comes with the punishment of the one who smothers it with another antithetical impulse. The Dionysian frenzy is a risk taken in the bargain. The latter itself is a risky step to take as the follower gives up his life to extend the existence of the god / ideology. The equation is individuality for Will, that is *I* for the universal essence. The Apollonian, the other Nietzschean drive, is secondary to the Dionysian. Apollo is a life necessity as it teaches another way to look at it: life as / is form and form brings redemption. The teaching of this drive is one of salvation in individuality and beauty. There is no terrifying sublime and the burden of belonging to the universe does not exist. Instead, there is the light nature of the personal I and of the assimilated self. However, this drive remains limited and enslaved to form and surface. The Apollonian has no insight into the eternal essence. The dependent god fails to inspire its follower with a sense of completeness. The natural and the spontaneous are missing in this drive. An Apollonian will always crave for such elements. Form will never be satiating and gratifying. Nonetheless, a merging of both is the only way to master one's order and disorder and hence to be able to understand life and endure it. This problematic combination remains, of course, the alternative to the religious solution since we are working within the framework of Antichristian (to say anti-religious) philosophy.

The dichotomies that are impersonated respectively by Billy and Dion, and Apollo versus Dionysus provide a pertinent and rich representation of the theme of order and disorder. What is common to O'Neill's play and Nietzschean philosophy is their demonstration of other forms of the antagonistic yet complementary nature of order and disorder. The depiction of concepts, despite its imbalance, remains faithful to the gist of Nietzschean philosophy and to O'Neill dramatization. The superiority of the frightening yet praised Dionysian disorder is matched by a display of its need of Apollonian order. Besides, despite the inferiority of the latter as represented by Billy's jealousy of Dion's lively disorder, this paper has highlighted how absolute disorder cannot exist. In the play, the maskless Dion is not only non-recognizable to his family but he appears terrifying. He is obliged to live and love by proxy that is by borrowing part of Billy's way of life. As aforementioned, Dionysian reality is so horrifying and chaotic that it needs the Apollonian order with its theatrical icon, which is the mask, to become bearable and graspable. This is also shown by the need of professional success and stability – a form of order that Dion lacks and eventually seeks from the Apollonian character who himself remains too removed from life and whose pleasures are inhibited. Thus, reciprocal dependency has come full circle. However, the play's main theme could be described as a crisis of choice of a way of living and mainly of balancing drives. Both characters representing order and disorder perish because they are incapable of harmonizing their impulses and of including an ideology of death into their equations. However, what could be described as intriguing and worth looking into, is the aforementioned order of preference that Nietzsche has for the Dionysian and O'Neill's identification with Dion. How appealing disorder is and to which extent the philosopher and the playwright detach themselves from reality remain interesting questions to be answered through biographical studies.

Works cited

Bigsby, C.W.E. "Eugene O'Neill." *A Critical Introduction to Twentieth-Century American Drama 1: 1990-1940*. Cambridge: Cambridge UP, 1985.

Graves, Robert. *The Greek Myths: Volume I*. London: Penguin Books, 1990.

LaBelle, Maurice M. "Dionysus and Despair: The Influence of Nietzsche upon O'Neill's Drama." *Educational Theatre Journal* Vol. 25.No. 4 (1973): 436–42.

New Larousse Encyclopedia of Mythology. London: Hamlyn, 1989.

Nietzsche, Friedrich. *The Birth of Tragedy*. Trans. Douglas Smith. Oxford: Oxford University Press, 2008.

O'Neill, Eugene. "The Great God Brown." O'Neill, Eugene. *Nine Plays*. New York: The Modern Library, 1959. 307–77.

Aesthetic readings of order and disorder

"Now they shake hands without hearts:" Order and Disorder in Gabriel Okara's "Once Upon a Time"

Asma Dhouioui, I.S.L.T., University of Carthage

Abstract

In this article, I will study the contrast between the past and its simplicities (order) and the present and its complexities (disorder) in "Once Upon a Time," a poem in free verse by the Nigerian postcolonial and modernist poet Gabriel Okara. The past is depicted as coherent and harmonious and as a moment when people, especially Nigerians, sincerely loved each other and commonly lived as a unity. Alternatively, the present is represented as corrupted and chaotic, a period in which people are careless about each other and dishonest with each other; and this creates disorder in their lives. In a serious and critical tone, the speaker expresses his nostalgia for the past and his criticism of the present. As he moves from innocence to experience, he loses his virtues (innocence, spontaneity, honesty, for example …), and feels a bitter sense of alienation from the self and the other due to the chaos of modern culture infected by materialist Western values. In a dramatic monologue highlighting the value of the African oral tradition, the adult speaker, seeks for inspiration from an innocent child; therefore, roles are reversed. Indeed, the speaker embarks on a journey of self-discovery, and because of a genuine search for an alternative social order, he regretfully laments the loss of an authentic Nigerian identity and condemns the hypocrisy of adults. Hence, this paper draws attention to the importance of cultural consciousness in forging individual identity, and foregrounds the fundamental questioning of disorder brought by colonization and its aftermath. To illustrate my purpose, I shall apply a close reading in parallel with a social and historical contextualization of the poem.

Keywords: The past, The present, Postcolonial, Nostalgia, Identity

Introduction

In this article, I will pursue the themes of "Order and Disorder" in the light of a comparison between past and present in "Once Upon a Time", a poem written by the Nigerian postcolonial and modernist poet and novelist Gabriel Okara who incorporates African thought, folklore and imagery in his poetics.[1] "Once Upon a Time" is a satirical lyric structured as a dramatic monologue. It consists of seven stanzas of irregular length, with no definite rhyming scheme which emphasizes the fact that it is a monologue from a father to his son for the addressee never responds to the speaker. Consequently, one cannot trace call-and-response in this poem. Irregular lines and stanzas and the lack of rhyme replicate the speaker's anguish and the chaotic state of modern culture. Although the poem is in free verse, it offers a lot of musicality and harmony (as in "like dresses-homeface, / officeface, streetface, hostface, / cocktailface" (S. 4, ll. 3–5)) that are missing in contemporary real life but sought for in poetry and this makes the poem sound authentic. The tone throughout is serious, nostalgic, regretful; the mood is negative and bitter.

1 The Choice of Language as a Means of Resistance

This poem, ironically written in English which is a kind of colonial legacy, presents a critical standpoint to the legacies of colonialism. In Nigeria, where so many languages and dialects are spoken, English, the colonizer's language, paradoxically becomes the unifying tool for communication. "In multilingual postcolonial societies, such as Nigeria," to quote Ismail S. Talib, "English is quite often regarded as a neutral language" (105). More than that, learning the language of the colonizer was a means to integrate in the social and cultural spheres of the British even after independence; and this, in itself, is a form of disorder. Moreover, Talib states that "It has been argued that it is through the continued use of the English language, and the values encoded in it, that British colonialism is perpetuated" (105). Nevertheless, English, which was responsible for cultural imperialism, has been used in the struggle against colonialism. Language, Talib

[1] Taken from *Gabriel Okara: Collected Poems*, ed. Brenda Marie Osbey (Nebraska: Nebraska University Press, 2016), p. 4.

argues, "plays an important role in the aesthetic realization of postcolonial literatures" (155). Nigeria is still influenced by modern Western culture, attitudes and values, even after its independence in 1960. Edward Said explains that "Though for the most part the colonies won their independence, many of the imperial attitudes underlying colonial conquest continue" (17). In fact, it seems that the problem is more cultural than linguistic for Okara. Like Chinua Achebe, Okara uses the English language to criticize the negative effects of cultural colonization. However, as he writes in English and not in Ijaw or Ijo, does it mean that he sacrifices his African self-affirmation?

The poem is particularly embedded in postcolonial discourse; it is a sort of counter-discourse. It lays emphasis on the issue of identity and how it is constructed in a pre-colonial time and how it is manipulated by a colonized/ postcolonial society. The speaker's late recognition that colonization has destroyed his sense of personal identity or selfhood is the poem's gist, a critical perspective on colonization. In this vein, Bill Ashcroft and all comment that postcolonialism "deals with the effects of colonization on cultures and societies" (168). Actually, colonialism has ended, but its effects on economy, politics, language and culture have not. In *Culture and Imperialism*, Said argues that "direct colonialism has largely ended; imperialism [...] lingers where it has always been, in a kind of general cultural sphere as well as in specific political, ideological, economic and social practices" (8). Hence comes the role of postcolonial literature to uncover the noxious and lasting effects of colonization.

Equally important to this linguistic choice is a preference for orality which stands as a writing strategy in Okara's creative works. Orality or "orature", a term used by the Kenyan writer Ngũgĩ wa Thiong'o, refers to the use of oral elements in a more literary context to create a hybrid form. Throughout Okara's "Once Upon a Time," repetition, improvi-sation, and storytelling are obvious. Likewise, colloquial expressions are employed in the poem under study such as "Feel at home," "come again," and "Good-riddance." Katherine Williams argues that:

> Okara's linguistic experiment attempts to universalize language by

> replacing it the *energia* of English with the *energia* of Ijo, thus reconstituting the flawed body of one language with the living soul of another and creating an amalgam that overcomes cultural particularity. In this way, Okara tries to resolve the language/ audience opposition that bedevils every African writer. (58)

Indeed, "Once Upon a Time" reads so naturally, so spontaneous, and so inspiring. Even so, the memorable quality of the text does not hide its worth as an act of cultural resistance. Ato Quayson asks the following questions: "Do contemporary African poets view orality as the repository of a retrievable African ontology and aesthetic? [...] Is the *turn towards* orality always a *turn away* from alien poetic traditions?" (155; emphasis in the original). Indeed, it is orality that offers the poet a sense of identity and the poem a notable touch of musicality. In this vein, Obi Maduakor asserts that: "Okara is reputed to be the only poet among his peers to have mastered his rhythms sufficiently to sing. He achieves this feat through the magic of repetition, manipulating the repetition of words, parallel structures, or similar cadences for their sound effects" (42). The reading process inspires the reader, demands their attention, and exposes Okara's individual talent and traces his poetic identity.

2 Duality

Duality foregrounds cultural differences and historical changes. It makes use of some poetic devices, particularly, repetition and parallelism which are both functional in building a sort of balance and in creating contrast and highlighting paradoxes and challenges. Besides, similes and metaphors run throughout the text to compare the African warm past with its moral values to the cold present influenced by European codes of morality. "Once Upon a Time" describes the clash between the values of ancient Africa and the culture of modern Europe and depicts how this clash affects people's lives and psychologies and ends in generating fragmented subjectivities. Literally, the dichotomy of order and disorder forms many possibilities in the poem. While the traditional African (pre-colonial) lifestyle values innocence, sincerity, hospitality and simplicity, modern Western lifestyle gives much importance to the world of adult experience marked by hypocrisy, inhospitality and sophistication.

Central to all these dualisms is the significance of cultural recognition. The poet moves from a mythical depiction of the past to a critical representation of the present. Furthermore, one can summarize this dichotomy as one between the same and the other; the speaker in the past/ as a child is the same and the speaker as an adult is the other.

3 Comparison between the Past and the Present

Similar to the attractive title through which the poet tries to achieve a strong and positive effect, the poem opens with the storytelling phrase: "Once Upon a Time," used in the beginning of fairy tales. This phrase reflects the sense of a distant past; as if the poem itself were a fairy tale; it leads the reader to expect a story to be told. Africans are natural storytellers; hence comes the significance of the title and the narrative quality of the poem which is also lyrical, descriptive and reflective. The poem is directed to "son," highlighting the importance of kin relations for Africans and the feeling of fatherhood for those who are younger; a boy is everybody's son. The addressee is the speaker's son, or more generally the implied audience is Africans, Nigerians. It is an open message not only from a father to his son but from a poet to all readers, to every reader. But the addressee may be just an abstraction.

As the speaker contemplates the past, he remembers that actions were genuine and symbolic of good intentions and sincerity: "they used to shake hands with their hearts" (S. 1, l. 2). The first three lines of the first stanza positively deal with the past while the second three lines, which begin with "but", pejoratively depict the present. Once upon a time, people used to laugh with their hearts and eyes. They "used to" is an expression that conveys a habit in the past; "to laugh with their hearts" (S. 1, l. 2) is a transliteration from Ijo idiom. To be sure, laughter is an expression of great happiness because the real authentic laughter comes from the heart. When happiness comes from the depths of the self, it is noticeable in the eyes that reflect the psychological state of the individual.

But now, they "laugh with their teeth" (S. 1, l. 4) which suggests to predators ready to pounce, or attack.[1] Besides, Okara uses a direct

[1] "[T]hey" is an impersonal pronoun which implies otherness, difference and indifference.

metaphor: “ice-block-cold eyes” (S. 1, l. 5), a compound to show the frigidity of feelings, the lack of warmth, the non-identification with others’ sorrows, but also to underline the (post)colonial gaze toward the other. Accordingly, “block” reflects rigidity and distance, barriers that stand between people who look for anything that can be used against each other: “search behind my shadow” (S. 1, l. 6). There is no longer cordiality, nor respect, but rather distance and disrespect. In addition to that, people now “shake hands without hearts” (S. 2, l. 4), without feeling, without sincerity, for they are materialist and looking for their personal interests. In brief, there are no more social bonds. Therefore, the excessive use of run-on lines in the second stanza as well as throughout the text exposes the poet’s genuine desire to recreate these bonds, even verbally. The use of alliteration in “hands” and “hearts,” on the other hand, puts forward the speaker’s affliction away from cordiality. In this respect, the insistence on the word “heart” draws attention to the significance of emotions in constructing the individual’s sincerity or lack of it.

Indeed, the past is distorted when hand-shaking (a cultural symbol) becomes a gesture with negative connotations. Although the speaker’s people shake hands with the right hand, the symbol of strength and manhood, their left hand, the symbol of awful deeds and evil, looks for benefits: “while their left hands search/ my empty pockets” (S. 2, l. 5, 6). These metaphorical expressions are quite functional in exhibiting untrustworthiness, deceitfulness, and more generally social corruption. “[T]hey” (S. 2, l. 4) can similarly refer to greedy British or corrupt Nigerians. People are now dishonest; for while shaking hands, they use the free hand to look into “empty pockets” symbolizing poverty and a modernist sense of emptiness and triviality; “empty pockets” may as well be an allusion to colonial exploitation in general. This phrase illustrates that all good intentions have unfortunately gone. Thus, the metaphor emphasizes how there is lack of trust, as everybody is trying to use others for personal benefits. The concession “but” comes in the third line (S. 2, l. 3) to mark division between the past and the present while “used to,” “gone” stand in contrast with “[n]ow” emphasizing this separation between past and present, order and disorder.

In *The Wretched of the Earth*, Frantz Fanon, one of the pioneers of postcolonial theory, indicates that one of the most important values the colonized learned from the colonizer is individualism. He argues: "The colonized intellectual learned from his masters that the individual must assert him self. The colonialist bourgeoisie hammered into the colonized mind the notion of a society of individuals where each is locked in his subjectivity, where wealth lies in thought". Therefore, and according to Fanon, "'Brother,' 'sister,' 'comrade' are words outlawed by the colonialist bourgeoisie because in their thinking my brother is my wallet and my comrade, my scheming" (11). In this, Fanon combines the sociological with the psychological. In view of that, one can foreground the functionality of African poetry in drawing comparisons, criticizing social ills, and condemning (post)colonial troubles.

Unfortunately, a new set of values is established by colonization. Shift occurs in hospitality, from a warm welcome in "Feel at home" (S. 3, l. 1) to rejection, refusal in "shut on me" (S. 3, l. 6). So guests are no longer received with hospitality. Even the short lines of the third stanza translate the fact that the social value of hospitality is shrinking. Here the tone becomes mocking and ironical. Equally suggestive in this sense is the use of consonance and internal rhyme in "twice" and "thrice" which are not only used to highlight musicality and harmony (although they reflect the African passion for music and rhythm), but rather to mock hypocrisy and to criticize unfaithful relations. The negative image of the closed doors particularly symbolizes the absent or limited opportunities for sociability and for a better future. Therefore, the speaker is disappointed with the values of his new society. On this, Chukwuma Azuonye says: "Comparing the present postcolonial time with the past, the speaker expresses the feeling that people have lost the innocence and openness of their indigenous pre-colonial culture and etiquette" (2). Hence, Okara openly condemns the corruption of his society and the hypocrisy of adults owing to colonization, and implicitly invites his people to pay more attention to the relationship between the individual and the collective.

4 Lessons Learnt by the Speaker

By the fourth stanza, the tone becomes more lyrical and more ironical at once to mirror the speaker's personal experiences in a distinctively critical manner. This stanza begins with "So" indicating transition or result, particularly with regards to the use of the present perfect tense: "So I have learned many things, son" (S. 4, l. 1). This implies that the speaker has now gained experience. He too has learnt to be false and to change faces for different spaces and occasions: "homeface" (S. 4, l. 3), "officeface," "streetface," "hostface" (S. 4, l. 3); but finding comfort in none. Each face has "its conforming smile" (S. 4, l. 5); the outcome is "cocktailface" (S. 4, l. 5) suitable for all circumstances "like a fixed portrait smile" (S. 4, l. 6), a negative image for conformity, indeed. People change their identities as easily as they change their clothes, "like dresses" (S. 4, l. 3). The ironic use of simile comes stronger in "homeface" (S. 4, l. 3), for even at home one needs some mask. Besides, the simile that closes the stanza: "like a fixed portrait smile" (S. 4, l. 6) with all its contextual associations of passivity, rigidity and sophistication dictated by social rules and roles, implies the depiction of an unnatural smile. Indeed, simile associates the smile with a mixture of enigmatic expressions for the adjective "fixed" may allude to passivity, melancholy, or mystery; and this evokes the world's famous smile of Mona Lisa with her mysterious facial expression.

The speaker then recognizes that he has to follow social conventions and to pursue social expectations; that is social order which proves to be mere chaos. Hence, his current identity is inauthentic; and he feels responsible for that. The father admits to his son that he too has adapted to live amidst such false people; that he too learnt to 'wear' different smiles for different occasions; unfortunately, none is authentic. Thus, the speaker criticizes the fact that people adapt to changes that can entirely change their lives. Therefore, the question of agency, a concept of great importance in postcolonial studies, calls for the speaker's responsibility in defying society's strict rules and in resisting British culture by trying to eschew the burden of colonial history. One can easily observe the anecdotal pattern of the poem.

Indeed, the lessons which the speaker gained in his life are quite revealing. Through a close examination of the poem, one notices the predominance of the first-person singular (I). The speaker lyrically portrays his life experiences. Like in the fourth stanza, the speaker/ father still enlists what he has learnt from society in the fifth (the longest stanza, 8 lines of verse): "I have learnt too" (l. 1) and avows that he has fallen prey to the negative influence of a changing society contaminated by Western values. Similar to a narrative, the stanza starts with "And" to proceed with the story; the power of narration captures the reader and induces him/her to complete reading the poem or the story. The speaker is like everyone else; he learnt superficial laughter with no emotion "to laugh with my teeth" (l. 2) and coldness to "shake hands without my heart" (l. 3) (metaphorical expressions) and hypocrisy by saying "Glad to meet you/ Without being glad; and to say 'It's been/ nice talking to you' after being bored" and to say 'Goodbye' (ll. 6–8) where he means 'Good-riddance" (l. 5). This stanza is built upon a number of paradoxes, for instance, "being glad" and "bored" to underline hypocrisy again and again. Besides, the preposition "without" suggests absence and negation implying that there is no longer warmth. The poet is dejected because of hypocrite people and also because of his acquired hypocrisy, as he is obliged to conform to expected social norms.

It is the mirror that urges the speaker to question his identity. The mirror is transformed into an enemy that reflects "only [his] teeth like a snake's bare fangs" (S. 6, l. 7). Fangs suggest not only insincere laugh but rather hostility and the probability of poisonous attack and menacing danger. This is harsh self-criticism: the snake, a dangerous and poisonous creature, bears negative symbols (treachery, betrayal) in most cultures. Here, the tone becomes increasingly angry, critical, and ironic all at once. This also explains the use of negative poetic diction in phrases like "good riddance," nouns like "fangs," adjectives like "muting," and verbs like "unlearn." A powerful sense of irony is employed to reveal the speaker's anxiety over the negative change he underwent and his criticism of social hypocrisy. Like the mirror, the speaker is cruel, and, in a way, penalizing. Looking at the mirror has become a negative experience, not to see beauty but insincerity, disgust, contempt. It is a self-critical, self-reflexive approach. Simile, used recurrently in the poem, turns into a line of attack against the self that is contaminated by the awful habits of the other. Simile is, then, a figurative approach to advocate, through rich pictorial imagery, the negativity of "selling" oneself to a contemporary state of affairs. In addition, the use of alliteration in the repetition of the sad "w" sound in "want," and "what" (S. 6, l. 2) and in "when" and "was" (S. 6, l. 3) alludes to the pain, the sorrow, the regret of the speaker owing to what he has learnt in such a material society, to the point that he does not know himself in the mirror, for his identity is a false one. Like so many other Nigerians, the speaker has lost his authentic Nigerian (cultural) identity and he feels alienated in his own society, for he is westernized. This pessimism is more explicit in Okara's novel *The Voice* (1964), which presents a gloomy prediction of a politically corrupt Nigeria. Likewise, "Once Upon a Time" is a satirical comment on the speaker's society and a perpetual questioning of his social identity.

5 Nostalgia vs. Regret

Undoubtedly, the speaker is nostalgic to the past, childhood, spontaneity, his 'true' African self; he is also and critical of the present, modern society. Nostalgia and memory replicate a central and thematic role in the poem; both are linked to the past; and display his deep relations to his culture. It is nostalgia that establishes his return to the past that defines his memory, a source of inspiration and a mode of resistance to the obliteration of his cultural identity, that serves him for personal growth. According to Mary Carruthers, memory is "a storehouse" (14), "a mental picture" (16); "the 'art of memory' is actually the 'art of recollection'" (20) that is a much valued faculty in oral cultures. Indeed, memory reflects the individual's life and subjectivity and creates a version of (personal) history. Memory embedded with nostalgia make the speaker recall the African past, the good old days when Africans lived in tribes. Henceforth, names in the first stanza are plural, for instance, "hearts," "eyes," "teeth;" only "shadow" (dark imagery) is singular, for happiness lies in group life. Thus, "Once Upon a time" is a sort of elegy and eulogy dedicated to the past. It is for this reason that the second stanza begins as well with a storytelling expression: "There was a time indeed" (l. 1). "[I]ndeed" stresses that honesty, to the best of his memory, was a reality in the past. One of the services this poem could bestow is providing the poet or the speaker with the tools of revising his own life and highlighting his attempts at reconciling with the past thanks to memory to which he pays so much heed. Another service could be an appeal to revive the cultural memory of modern societies.

Indeed, the poem's deepest aspirations are expressed in a highly emotional language in the last two stanzas. The speaker, who emphasizes that he has rigorously revised himself, wants to get rid of his hostile and insincere laugh. He wishes to unlearn whatever he has learnt, for he reaches a state of self-hatred and self-rejection. He loathes looking at himself in the mirror for all he sees is what he dislikes; thus, he abhors himself as well. Therefore, things fall apart for him, to borrow the title of Chinua Achebe's novel.[1] The speaker laments the loss of innocence as though it were a requisite of growing up. Nonetheless, he requests his "son," or the implied audience behind him, to "believe" in his strong will to return to his raw state, to purity. In a particularly strong affirmation: "But believe me son" (S. 6, l. 1), he candidly and regretfully expresses his desire to go back to childhood and to forget all the "muting things," or whatever has silenced him. Because of his self-identification, he will be away from self-denial and close to a momentous decision to look for remedies.

6 Longing For Change

Shift in tone from the negative "unlearn" to the positive "relearn" foreshadows the potential for makeover, for correcting mistakes which necessitates a whole process: learn—unlearn—relearn. Both unlearning and relearning are useful strategies to decolonize the speaker's mind, for the speaker ends by discovering and acknowledging that he has become like the colonizer. In this vein, Frantz Fanon asserts that: "The colonized subject thus discovers that his life, his breathing and his hearbeats are the same as the colonist's" (10). Shift in the tone of the poem is accompanied by shift in tenses

[1] The title *Things Fall Apart* is actually taken from a line from the poem "The Second Coming" by W. B. Yeats.

from the simple past to the simple present, then to the present perfect tense, the in-between space between past and present, or the movement from, to borrow the concepts put by Frantz Fanon, assimilation to unease towards rejection. The speaker then confesses: "I want to be what I used to be" (S. 6, l. 2), showing instant regret about the choices he previously made. But, although the poem seems conversational, the listener/ addressee does not answer back; henceforth, he represents everyone who ignores the reality of society. And it is this point, in particular, that predicts the difficulty of change.

As the poem approaches its end, the speaker reaches a conclusion of his own. His longing for a lost past is stronger. The seventh stanza, the final and the shortest stanza, is a quatrain that stands for the conclusion of the text. It starts with the conjunction "so" which brings about the third transition or change in the text. The alliterative repetition of "how" hints at the unbroken sorrow of the speaker who, albeit looking for lessons from his son, is still desperate about the potential of real change; and, it is for this reason that "once upon a time" of the title and the first line of the poem are used again to allude to the fact that going back to innocence and honesty is only a fairy tale that will never take place in the real world, or simply a utopia.

However, it is time to make changes. The adult speaker is ripe for change and renewal. He expresses his critical need for the younger addressee's help and guidance. He firmly wishes to go back to the old ways, to pretty good habits when he was a child like his son; and he keeps reminding the reader of the addressee "son," a word charged with particular warmth. He begs his child to teach him how to express his true feelings, how to be a coherent self again. Therefore, adults can learn from children in their coming into being. "The child is the father of man," to borrow Wordsworth's statement. This is only a wish, but the dynamics of change will certainly be complicated, lingering. This is an interesting and ironic reversal, for the speaker needs directives. Unlike other fathers, the speaker does not want his son to follow his example. Indeed, it is a moral obligation to draw the attention of younger generations to the dangers of cultural contamination. Hence, the final stanza is a plea, an urgent emotional appeal for a romantic return to the warm past. And this is the only remedy to his unrest, to what he hates in his demeanor. Thus, the poem ends with a moral lesson; in that case, it is serious and didactic. There is, however, a hint of hope in it for it ends on a positive note or tone clear in the imperative: "show me" (S. 7, l. 2) used by the adult persona looking for advice.

The speaker is no longer torn between two cultures. Now he is beyond the divide; at least he recognizes that he aspires to his previous life. He exhibits no sign of inertia whatsoever. He gains a sort of cultural consciousness or historical awareness in due course. In brief, he is now ardently determined to reconstruct the past, to restore a lost balance, a much needed balance, indeed. And this, in particular, explains why the speaker goes into rhapsody in the closing stanza. Henceforth, the tone shifts to happiness, optimism and enthusiasm promising a new beginning.

The poet, as in other modernist poems, depicts the search for identity, or the question of "self" that is always fragmented and alienated from the world around. Most importantly, the poem exhibits a subjective perception of reality and a critical attitude towards individualism. The reader, as a result, will automatically feel loss and alienation. Technically speaking, modernism here is observable in the newness of the subject matter or at least of its presentation, the immediacy of telling the story and illustrating the emotions coming with it. Modernism is also noticeable in the poet's experimentation with form, genre and style, insistence on new properties of musicality without a necessary adherence to metric regularity, and finally a breaking away from established rules, traditions and conventions. "Once Upon a Time" becomes a different text.

This text is written between the borders of a tale, the story of (de)colonization. It begins and ends with "Once Upon a time," mirroring a sort of circularity, or a vicious circle that the former colonized native turns within and around. So the poem proves to be an ironic parody of fairy tales. The poem here shifts from a modernist into a postmodernist text and this highlights "the intersection of postmodern and postcolonial discourses [...] in their concern with marginality, ambiguity, disintegrating binaries," to quote Elleke Boehmer (2005 237). More than that, it is a poem that displays the image of fragmented modern societies and reflects the complexity of identity that is no longer stable or complete. Individual identity is given more importance than collective identity; and this creates a dilemma between the speaker's two conflicting identities. Hence postmodernist techniques such as self-reference, paradox, allusion and irony (a recurring device) are employed in the text.

Conclusion

"Once Upon a Time," albeit an ironic parody of fairy tales, is straightforward. Its message is clear, for nothing seems arcane. What matters, we learn from the poem, is a vital redefinition of the self, a sincere attempt at rediscovering a lost African identity and at reasserting a lost sense of dignity. This implies a call for a return to origins and a search for identity. But it seems that identity depends on memory. This text, because of its lyrical power, reveals the speaker's fuller understanding of himself; not a bad goal at all: self-realization. He wants to go back to himself, to his former self, to the innocence of childhood, a major theme in the poem, reminding us of William Blake's *Songs of Innocence and Songs of Experience* (1798). It is only in this return that he will be able to reach a sort of panacea. In a word, the poem is an open message not from a father to his son but rather from a poet to all readers, to every reader. Indeed, the poem has a dramatic effect on the reader. Genuine emotion is the best order of feeling, of nature, of human life. Fake smile is disorder! Honesty is order; dishonesty is disorder! Truth is order; lie is disorder! Hypocrisy is disorder! Be yourself, be authentic, be sincere, discover your true self and keep in touch with the world of childhood.

Works Cited

Ashcroft, Bill et al. *Post-Colonial Studies: The Key Concepts.* London: Routledge, 2007.

Azuonye, Chukwuma. "'The White Man Laughs': Commentary on the Satiric Dramatic Monologues of Gabriel Okara," in *Africana Studies*, January 2011. 1–17.

Boehmer, Elleke. *Colonial and Poscolonial Literature: Migrant Metaphors.* Oxford: Oxford University Press, 2005.

Carruthers, Mary. The Book of Memory: *A Study of Memory in Medieval Culture*. Cambridge: Cambridge University Press, 1990.

Fanon, Frantz. *The Wretched of the Earth.* (1961) Trans. Richard Philcox. New York: Grove Press, 2004.

Maduakor, Obi. "Gabriel Okara: Poet of the Mystic Inside," in *World Literature Today*, Volume 61, Number 1, pp. 41–45, Winter, 1987.

Osbey, Brenda Marie (ed.) *Gabriel Okara: Collected Poems.* Nebraska: Nebraska University Press, 2016.

Quayson, Ato (ed.) *The Cambridge History of Postcolonial Literature,* 2 vols. Cambridge: Cambridge University Press, 2012.

Said, Edward W. *Culture and Imperialism*. London: Chatto and Windus, 1993.

Talib, Ismail S. *The Language of Postcolonial Literatures: An Introduction.* London: Routledge, 2002.

Williams, Katherine. "Decolonizing the Word: Language, Culture, and Self in the Works of Ngũgĩwa Thiong'o and Gabriel Okara," in *Research in African Literatures*, Volume 22, Number 4. Winter, 1991. 53–61.

Metamorphoses in John Keats's Narrative Poem *Lamia*: Between the Ethics of Order and the Aesthetics of Disorder

Farhat Ben Amor, Faculty of Arts and Humanities of Kairouan

Abstract

In Keats's narrative poem *Lamia* (1819), the idea of metamorphosis pertains to the malleability of the structure of the chain of being to fit different orders. In this way, Lamia could experiment with the orders of womanhood and godhood despite her beastly condition as a serpent. Her series of metamorphoses does not, however, linger, for she ends up vanishing during the marriage festivities with her ensnared lover, Lycuis, on confronting the eyes of the philosopher, Apollonius, the emblem of reason, rather than magic.

The aim of this paper is to stand on Keats's underlying methods of presenting his characters in *Lamia* and to discuss the nature of the catharsis the denouement of the story yields. Essentially, the main focus of this study is to unravel the despicable dissonance built between the ethical dimension of the story envisaged in redressing the orderly nature of the chain of being, on the one hand, and the aesthetic side of Lamia's magical world which keeps intensifying its immersion in such a creative poetic imagination that makes her 'vanishing' by the end of the poem hardly bearable emotionally, on the other hand.

Keywords: (dis)order, chain of being, imagination, magic, metamorphosis, reason

The inscription of *Lamia*'s materials in Greek mythology does not seem to hinder Keats from elaborating his own 'touch' in building the story of Lamia's metamorphoses. While also highlighting the centrality of Robert Burton's *The Anatomy of Melancholy* (1621) as an important source for Keats's *Lamia* (1819), Jane Chambers points to the space of freedom Keats allowed himself to entertain while reverting to the myth of Lamia. In this process, Chambers begins by claiming that "a myth is fundamentally a narrative that creates moral boundaries only to test, challenge or overstep them the minute they are fixed. This brings about a constant questioning of those morals which in its turn results in ambiguity and lack of resolution" (588).

Certainly, this 'ambiguity and lack of resolution' with respect to the set of 'morals' which myths abound with are ascribed to perpetual changes and development in man's intellectual and aesthetic life across eras, so that the 'moral boundaries' are kept forever 'tested, challenged and overstepped' at any time. Actually, Chambers cites Keats's *Lamia* as an example of such flexibility wrought to approaching myths, holding that "Keats created space to transform the ambiguities to his liking. He certainly does so in *Lamia*" (588). What might be mostly 'ambiguous' in *Lamia*, which Keats 'transforms to his liking,' is related to "such a moiré pattern set into the fabric of *Lamia* that each time the poem has been turned in the critic's hands, it reflects different colors" (Twitchell 49). Essentially, the poem's possession of "different colors" pertains to the duality governing the structure of its characters: Lamia, Lycius and Apollonius.

I. Lamia: the appealing transgressor

To delineate Lamia's transgression of order demands tracing the path that her magic enables her to follow as well as showing the effect her magic brings to characters who are hit by its wand, involving Lycius and indirectly all the Corinthians, except Apollonius, the philosopher. As a sinner of transgressing the orderly nature of the chain of being, Lamia begins with weaving her magic plot of enthrallment whereby to blind people from an adequate apprehension of reality. Anne Wilson presents the distinctive features of the magical plot as follows: "A magical plot is distinguished by its use of magical devices, in a distinct ritual structure. A magical hero does not use stratagems which would work; instead, he uses a ritual" (8). Lamia's 'magical devices' and 'ritual' seem to be efficient enough to bring about changes, whether to her order of being or to other characters. The first time she appears in the poem is in the following shape: "a palpitating snake, / Bright, and cirque-couchant in a dusky brake" (Part I. 46).

The ominous effect that image of Lamia's first appearance induces is sustained by her dialogue with Hermes, "the god whose attributes are intimately connected with magic and enchantment" (Ricks 734), which shows her overpowering him. Although he is the god of magic, Hermes remains unable to find his lost nymph, and only thanks to the intervention of Lamia's magic can he achieve his will. However, the price Hermes is asked to pay, in return for winning his nymph, consists in granting Lamia a lovely woman shape that allows her to entice Lycius. Explaining her will to Hermes, Lamia says: "Give me my woman's form, and place me where he is. / Stoop, Hermes, let me breathe upon thy brow, / And thou shalt see thy sweet nymph even now" (Part I. 120–2). Hermes 'stoops' to her demand without the slightest hesitation, since he seems to find no space to give an answer to Lamia. He contents himself with expressing his acceptance of her terms through sinking into "serenity" (Part I. 123). So, Lamia's infringement of the orderly nature of the chain of being succeeds, with regard to her ability to barter with the god for the fulfillment of her desire. It is as if her demand to metamorphose into a woman were a recompense she deserves from the god: "Left to herself, the serpent now began / To change" (Part I. 146–7).

Certainly, this moment of 'change' is a turning point in the plot of the poem, for it marks the instigation of Lamia's implementation of her plan to seduce Lycius. Being metamorphosed into a woman, she is introduced as "a lady bright with, / A full-born beauty new and exquisite" (Part I. 171–2). With that 'full-born beauty,' Lamia could ensnare Lycius' admiration. More than that, she manages to further disrupt the order of the chain of being through playing the role of a goddess to Lycius. Coyly, she pretends that being a goddess impedes her from acceding to his demand to be united with her, under the pretext of her superiority over him (she is a goddess and he is a man).

She scoffs at him, haughtily, saying: "Thou art a scholar, Lycius, and must know / That finer spirits cannot breathe below / In human climes, and live" (Part I. 279-81). In saying so, Lamia seems to contradict her own self, inasmuch as she presents the 'human climes' as denied to her since she *allegedly* belongs to the higher order of 'finer spirits.' However, she continues to play with the order of being through succumbing to Lycius, afterwards, when she notices his helpless infatuation with her. The poet tells us how she easily "threw the goddess off, and won his heart / More pleasantly by playing woman's part, / With no more awe than what her beauty gave" (Part I. 336–8).

What is being articulated, then, is the ability of Lamia's magic to allow her to experiment with different orders of the chain of being. These series of experimentation result in the suspension of the conventional norms of the logic of being through the poet's granting Lamia's magical fabrications entries whereby to invade all the orders of being without exception. Yet that suspension of logic seems to be confined to the subjective repertoire of Lamia and those who are hit by her magic, like Lycius. In the objective world of reality, Lamia remains deprived of a woman-like body that could allow her to prove her actual metamorphosis into a woman, which explains the massive trouble she faces during her marriage festivities. Through her magic, she keeps clinging to blind Lycius and the Corinthian attendants from apprehending her truth. In other words, she works to dissimulate reality in order to perpetuate her magical plot. "Dissimulation aims at hiding the real by masking which makes it invisible, repackaging by disguising it, modifying its appearance and dazzling by confusing it, reducing certainty about the nature of things" (Galasinski 84).

Lamia does well in dissimulating reality even when she is led to marry Lycius. During the marriage festivities, she relies heavily on her "subtle servitors" (Part II. 118) who are qualified as "viewless servants," devoted specifically "to enrich / The fretted splendor of each nook and niche" (Part II. 126–7). As a consequence, Lamia manages to appear to Lycius and all the Corinthian attendants as a "regal" bride bathing in luxury (Part II. 133). Actually, the poet expatiates on the amazement of the attendants at the stupendous castle in which the marriage takes place. We see them, for example "with busy brain / Arriving at the portal, gaz'd amain / And enter'd marveling" and "ne'er before had seen / That royal porch, that high-built fair demesne" (Part II. 150–4). Equally, the superabundant feast provided to the guests suggests opulence and gorgeousness that makes it resemble "the Dionysian frenzy" in its excess (Wille 22). Dionysus, to whom Lamia is implicitly likened, is "the mythical Olympian god of metamorphosis and the indefinable and is associated with love and wine, spilling over with life and energy" (Brunel 298). In Lamia's Dionysian-like feast, too, the excessive effect of wine on the attendants is underlined: "discoursing low / At first, for scarcely was the wine at flow; / But when the happy vintage touch'd their brains, / Louder they talk" (Part II. 201–4).

The Corinthian attendants to the marriage festivities of Lycius and Lamia evince, then, their fall in the embrace of a Dionysian-like excess of 'life and energy.' They seem to get rid of all sorts of restrictions and established regulations of order "when the wine has done its rosy deed, / And every soul from human trammels freed" (Part II. 209–10). This ecstatic rapture, which Lamia's magic succeeds in weaving during the marriage festivities, may bear much affinity to "the cult of Dionysus in ancient Greece which had a cathartic function. It temporarily delivered people from their civic tradition, and at the same time gave them free rein to their cruel instincts" (Brunel 313). The implied association of Lamia's magical plot with 'catharsis' and 'deliverance' causes it to be linked metaphorically with emancipation and freedom, which entails the poet's tacit idealization of it. By implication, all the disorder Lamia's magic could install is aesthetically tinged with conventionally-considered to be ethically-laudable moments of gleeful rapture created by deliverance from a bondage-like order. Moreover, the 'spilling over with life and energy' which Lamia's magic provides to the Corinthians may bring about a symbolic metamorphosis of Lamia's image: from a fearful duplicitous Satanic-like monster, in the beginning of the narrative, to a heroic leader of emancipation from a tyrannical-like despicable order. Actually, this kind of emotional excess of happiness is identified by Denise Gigante as the new concept of 'monster' that arose in the late eighteenth and early nineteenth centuries and found expression in the literature of the romantic period. This change was "from a concept of deformity to a notion of monstrosity as too much life" (438).

II. Apollonius: the dream-fighter moralist

The precipitation of Lamia's magic into Dionysian-like exhilarating moments of breaking order that are brimming with 'too much life' is countered by the force of reason embodied in Apollonius, the only guest who remains immune from her snare. Being "a philosopher and well-skilled in the secret arts of magic" (Ricks 723), Apollonius succeeds adeptly in redressing order and defeating Lamia's magic. Thus, his presence in the poem is delayed as to appear only in the end of each part of the poem, just to abort the project of Lamia's magic and, with it, to deflate the momentousness of the disorder that is about to be actualized after inflating it for a while. However, his redressing of order does not hide the ominous tone through which he is introduced, as if he were the only loathsome antagonist who stains a historic romance between Lycius and Lamia, as a man and a woman who is originally a goddess (as the news is spread among the Corinthians and Lycius himself thinks it to be). This ominous tone can be detected from his first appearance to Lycius and Lamia: "Slow-stepp'd, and robed in philosophic gown: / Lycius shrank closer, as they met and past, / Into his mantle, adding wings to haste" (Part I. 365–7).

As an object of fear, Apollonius, despite the formal pose his 'philosophic gown' suggests, acquires a Gothic-like image of the ghostly ravisher whe often shows much inhuman proportion against his prey. Actually, when asked by the equally bewildered Lamia, Lycius seems to confirm the Gothic inscription of Apollonius: "'Tis Apollonius sage, my trusty guide / And good instructor; but tonight he seems / The ghost of folly haunting my sweet dreams" (Part I. 375–7). Implicitly, Apollonius undergoes a metaphorical metamorphosing process of being: from the emblem of goodness and wisdom to a 'ghost' disrupting Lycius' happiness. This dramatic degeneration of the image of Apollonius, in Lycius' eyes, into a Gothic-like ghost is translated in the disruption he causes to the order of the marriage festivities of Lycius and Lamia, in the second part of the poem. He is going to be the sole agent of transforming the elixir of happiness and the Dionysian-like frenetic excess of rapture all the Corinthian attendants fully live out into a tenebrous funeral-like context. Symbolically, then, he becomes an agent of disorder while intending to redress order; he is "a philosopher who, in the end, brings about destruction, despite holding the 'truth'" (Rita 173).

The prevailing ominous tone surrounding the appearance of Apollonius in the scene keeps presenting him in Gothic-like terms, as if to undermine the size of the 'truth' which he possesses. His tracking of Lamia's magic, rather than introducing him as someone in quest for truth, presents him as a Gothic-like pursuer of her and, thus, making the image of Lamia conform to the pursued victim in a typically Gothic context. As Allyson Vaughan maintains, "Lamia's magical powers do not entirely protect her from the kind of control and violence other Gothic female characters are subjected to" (25). Actually, the recurrent reference to Apollonius' 'eyes' and his penetrative fixation of them on Lamia seems to become a motif in the poem and serve to highlight the Gothic-like context of pursuance. When Lamia is sitting with her bridegroom Lycius in a magnificent sofa, Apollonius "fix'd his eye, without a twinkle or stir / Full on the alarmed beauty of the bride, / Brow-beating her fair form, and troubling her sweet pride" (Part II. 246–8). The brow-beating aspect of his look is enough to put an end to Lamia's existence and, therefore, is inscribed in a typically Gothic victimization of the pursued prey. Indeed, Lycius ascribes the dissipation of Lamia to Apollonius' eyes: "Shut, shut those juggling eyes, thou ruthless man! / Turn them aside wretch!" (Part II. 277–8).

Eventually, Lycius makes explicit the demonizing aspect of Apollonius' eyes while bemoaning to the Corinthian attendants the loss of his bride. Addressing them in a highly emotive diction, Lycius complains: "Corinthians! look upon that grey-beard wretch! / Mark how, possess'd, his lashless eyelids stretch / Around his demon eyes! Corinthians, see! / My sweet bride withers at their potency" (Part II. 287–90). Being 'possessed' and having 'demon eyes,' Apollonius is made to typify evil with all its respects, as if he were the one, rather than Lamia, who uses magic to incur others in misfortune. In the words of Mark Sandy, Apollonius is presented as moved by the gluttonous "desire to contain happiness into what seems to Lycius as his evil schemes of revenge" (7). It is with his penetrative eyes that Apollonius 'contains' the couple, Lycius and Lamia, and carries out his 'revenge.' In fact, Apollonius' "eyes still / Relented not, nor mov'd" (Part II. 295–6) while defending himself against the attack of his disciple. Equally, on his first uttering of the word 'serpent' which causes Lamia to "breathe death breath," the poet tells us how "the sophist's eye, / Like a sharp spar, went through her utterly, / Keen, cruel, perceant, stinging" (Part II. 299–301). The reiteration of "look'd and look'd again" (Part II. 304) emphasizes the lethal 'spar-like' potency of Apollonius' eyes, for it culminates in Lamia's vanishing and Lycius' death, which seals the narrative of the poem.

Still, the shattering impact of Apollonius on the seamy order of events in the poem remains, in essence, a reassertion of order in the chain of being. There might grow a puzzle over how the poem's plot would have ended if there had not been a character like Apollonius among the Corinthians. Certainly disorder would have prevailed in that case. So, even though his intervention in the story disrupts the dreamy order of the Dionysian-like feast and rapture which the Corinthian attendants experiment with during the marriage festivities of Lycius and Lamia, Apollonius' presence may serve to redress the balance through imposing the wakeful order of reality. Symbolically speaking, the anti-Dionysian wakeful order of reality to which the plot of the narrative moves may bring to mind the contrast that exists between the Olympian gods, Apollo and Dionysus, in Greek mythology. (The derivation of Apollonius in the poem might have to do with Apollo.) As a god, Apollo "presides over the universal system of physical harmony. He presides over the ripening of human intellect and brings it to comparable fruition in a harvest of harmonious expression. He emblemizes order, form, everything that is fixed in a place" (Brunel 56).

In *Lamia*, Apollonius seems to be utterly motivated by these Apollo-like features that share one chief aspect which is 'order.' The order to which Apollonius tightly clings is deemed to be generative of the idealized qualities of 'harmony' and 'ripening of human intellect.' The manifestation of order in Apollonius' character can be shown in:

his behavior, his method of defending himself against the heavy slur his disciple, Lycius, casts against him, and the power which Apollonius manages to get thanks to that method. As far as his behavior is concerned, Apollonius reveals moral decency and well-posed character. For instance, he apologizes to Lycius for coming while not being invited to the marriage, which is emotively loaded, for it includes a mild reproach mingled with compassionate feeling of duty towards him. Adeptly, Apollonius begins with emphasizing his awareness of the etiquette of hospitality as an order that has to be respected: "'Tis no common rule, / Lycius,' said he, 'for uninvited / To force himself upon you" (Part II. 164–6). Then, he reveals the necessity he finds himself in to break this 'rule' with respect to the marriage of his disciple to Lamia: "'yet must I do this wrong, / And you forgive me'" (Part II. 167–8). It is true that Apollonius does not seem to succeed in making Lycius aware of the critical situation he is in, for the latter contents himself with "blushing" and "leading / The old man through the inner doors" where the marriage festivities continue (Part II. 169). Yet, the poet foreshadows Apollonius' success in mission. This is carried out metaphorically through personifying philosophy which is associated with Apollonius: "Philosophy will conquer all mysteries by rule and line" (Part II. 235).

The 'rule' and 'line' may metonymically emblemize the strict mathematical 'order' governing the world which philosophy, as the mother of sciences, seeks to decipher. Thus, the foreshadowing of the supremacy of philosophy over 'mysteries,' in addition to presaging the nearness of the end of Lamia's magical world, anticipate the power of Apollonius' arguments while defending himself against the attacks of Lycius. This power may help reduce Lycius' assaults and make them appear as "an illogical reaction to the sight of Apollonius as a 'trusty guide'" (Wille 14). As a sober philosopher, Apollonius reveals a well-poised calmness while retorting to the highly impulsive derogatory speech of Lycius. Apollonius contents himself with affirming his duty of protecting his life-long disciple against all sources of evil. In an emotively loaded statement, he says: "from every ill / Of life have I preserv'd thee to this day, / And shall I see thee made a serpent's prey" (Part II. 296–8) Apollonius' rhetorical proficiency can be unraveled in his ability to condense his own affective relationship with his disciple as to cover the three matrices of time (the past, the present and the future) to underline his never-ending faithfulness to Lycius. Indeed, his statement summarizes the past as being devoted to teach Lycius how to shun 'every ill' in order to evade a moment like what is happening in the present of the narrative in which an 'ill' is taking place. It is the 'ill' of infringing the order of being through choosing to marry Lamia who is but a 'serpent.' In choosing to enlighten Lycius to this truth, Apollonius deems that he is saving his disciple from a dark future that he is about to incur himself in and, thus, may remain 'a serpent's prey' forever.

III. Lycius: the blind lover

Lycius' love story begins with presenting him as a 'prey' to the magical charm of Lamia. His epiphanic encounter with Lamia is conveyed in a context of beguilement whose fatality seems to bear ill-omens that he remains unable to decipher till the end of his life. Moreover, there is a quick process of anesthetization, or what Roland Barthes calls in his book *A Lover's Discourse*, "hypnosis" (189) that characterizes the sharpness of Lycius' succumbing to the snares of Lamia's magic. Actually, the poet makes an explicit contrast between Lycius' states, prior to his sight of Lamia and after it. Lycius' "indifference," qualified by Lamia as "drear" (Part I. 238) turns abruptly into his being wholeheartedly captured by her, just on hearing her first words. This happens when Lycius passes near Lamia (who has just been narrated to be metamorphosed from a serpent into a woman). It is as if Lycius, too, underwent a symbolic metamorphosis whereby his 'indifference' is transformed into a mesmerized captivation in the snares of Lamia's magical world. The first words of Lamia generate this metamorphosis with respect to Lycius: "For so delicious were the words she sung, / It seemed he had loved them a whole summer long" (Part I. 249–50). Lycius' ensnarement in Lamia's words is suggested to be so omnipotent that it effaces the state of 'indifference' characterizing him before these 'words' from his memory.

The implied effacement of Lycius' indifference to Lamia's magic entails the instigation of a totally different state that he fatally steps in. In other words, Lycius undergoes a brainwashing-like situation that cuts all ties with previous ones so that he is suggested to grow no longer a disciple of Apollonius' philosophy, on his being severely hit by Lamia's magical wand. As Sean Wille observes, "before Lamia came, Lycius too was a philosopher. But his exaggerated infatuation with the sensuous Lamia makes him renounce rationality, thereby pushing and overstepping the boundary of the morally accepted" (18). What puts Lycius into a prey-like situation, then, is his transgression of the 'moral boundary' that consists in his 'renouncement of rationality' at the expense of his blind succumbing to Lamia' magical world. This will lead him to overlook the order of the chain of being when he keeps the same eagerness to be united with Lamia, despite her being a goddess as she alleges to be. In reality, Lycius' embrace of Lamia's magic can be revelatory of "Lamia's position as the beauty which attracts the young philosopher away from what he seems to consider it to be as 'cold philosophy' that he has learnt from Apollonius" (Rita 173).

Such a latent aesthetic appeal of Lamia's magical world to Lycius is suggested to outweigh his taking into consideration of the moral side of infringing the order of the chain of being. After the charm of Lamia's 'delicious words,' there comes now her beauty which causes Lycius to appear as if he were drunk. As the poet narrates, "And soon his eyes had drunk her beauty up, / Leaving no drop in the bewildering cup, / And still the cup was full" (Part I. 250–2). Lamia's beauty is made to represent a perfect embodiment of an idealized 'whole' that never retrenches its generosity. Actually, the verb 'to drink up' is juxtaposed by the indication that 'still the cup is full.' Lamia's 'beauty,' then, is associated metaphorically with wine which is being excessively offered so that Lycius, who is drinking from it, appears as if he were drinking from a fountain, rather than a 'cup.' The intoxicating wine-like beauty Lamia bestows on Lycius is inferred to 'bewilder' him so much that he finds in her the essence of his being. Thus, he contents himself with looking at her, considering her to define the whole order of the world. Imploringly addressing what he considers it to be his goddess Lamia, Lycius says: "Ah, Goddess, see

/ Whether my eyes can ever turn from thee" (Part I. 257–8). In saying so, Lycius affirms his ultimate heedlessness to the order of the world without and his total succumbing to Lamia's magical world that he mistakenly considers it to be, nevertheless, of a divine order.

From this irritable state that binds excessive love and magical intrigue within the same canon, Lycius is made an incarnation of a tragic lover. Thus, the poet dwells on Lycius' first sight of Lamia, while preparing us to see it as a fatal mistake whose enormousness equals that of Orpheus in classical mythology. Orpheus' tragic error consists in breaching the promise given to Pluto – the god of the infernal region. Pluto accepts to "release Eurydice (Orpheus' wife) from death, on the condition that Orpheus would not look back until they (Orpheus and Eurydice) reached the earth. He was just about to put his foot on earth when he looked back. Eurydice vanished" (Ricks 737). Keats's allusion to the tragic aspect of Orpheus' looking back, while dramatizing Lycius' first sight of Lamia, is revealed through using this mythical tale as a simile to what happens to Lycius when Lamia pleads him to heed her call. The poet tells us how Lamia tries to win Lycius' compassion: "Ah, Lycius bright, / And will you leave me on the hills alone? / Lycius, look back! And be some pity shown" (Part I. 244–6). Then, the poet proceeds to comment on the manner through which Lycius looks back: "He did – not with cold wonder fearingly, / But *Orpheus-like* at an Eurydice" (Part I. 247–8, italics mine).

By extension, Lycius' looking back to Lamia amounts to the tragedy which Orpheus is inferred to face, on the vanishing of his beloved, Eurydice, after reaching a state in which the likelihood of winning her is about to be fulfilled. (Lamia, too, will be 'vanished' during the marriage festivities, echoing, thus, Eurydice's own.) Ironically, Lycius' insurmountable fear that Lamia could 'vanish' from his sight starts to haunt him from his first encounter with her. While being 'drunk' with her beauty, Lycius goes far as to consider Lamia's sight to be the sole source of life: "For pity do not this sad heart belie – / Even as thou vanisheth so I shall die" (Part I. 259). Equally, he alludes to the absurd end that would await him if he were to be severed from her: "if thou shouldst fade / Thy memory will waste me to shade" (Part I. 269–70). Much suspense is nourished by the background the reader has already accumulated in the poem about Lamia as originally a beastly serpent whose possession of magic enables her to metamorphose into a woman. Namely, this suspense pertains to Lycius' being put as the pawn of Lamia's magic, with regard to his expectation of being cast to 'death' and 'waste' if ever Lamia may vanish from his sight. Thus, "the death of Lycius at the close of the poem is a macabre representation of the illusory dream mode disclosing its realistic counterpart" (Sandy 11).

Still, Lycius makes many attempts to confront this 'realistic counterpart' of his 'dream' that he keeps refusing to consider it 'illusory,' which proves the potency of the fervor of his love for Lamia. Despite his mistaken belief that Lamia is a goddess and, only under his stipulation is she transformed into a woman, Lycius works on mating the two orders of 'dream' and 'reality' through making them complement each other. This attempt is translated through his decision to let his private love for Lamia be known publicly among all the Corinthians. Mark Sandy reads this urge to move a love story from the private to the public sphere within a common Keatsian tendency: "The lovers in Keats's narrative poems cannot remain within the interior safety of their own illusory and private fictions, as they must legitimize their identities and existence in the public sphere, if their love is not to become sterile and suffocating" (23). Indeed, Lycius deems that Lamia's agitation cannot be calmed down without propagating it among the Corinthians – a matter which he dares to do through planning magnificent marriage festivities. Lovingly addressing Lamia, he says triumphantly: "Let my foes choke, and my friends shout afar, / While through the thronged streets your bridal car / Wheels round its dazzling spokes" (Part II. 62–4). Equally, he seems to take Lamia's preservation to his intention (which is, in reality, due to her double alienation both from the Corinthians and from the order of womanhood) lightly and ascribe them to her coyness. Lycius "took delight / Luxurious in her sorrows, soft and new" (Part II. 73–4).

Lycius succeeds in leading his 'coy' Lamia to accede to his demand and invites all the Corinthians to his marriage. As a bridegroom, he is introduced in the elixir of happiness, "sitting, in chief place, / Scarce saw in all the room another face, / Till, checking his love trance, a cup he took / Full brimm'd" (Part II. 239–42). Amid that supreme joy, there comes, however, one of his 'foes' who does not 'choke' as Lycius has promised Lamia before the marriage festivities take place, but rather manages to disrupt the celebration and turn it into a funeral-like setting. It is Apollonius, the supposedly life-long guide of Lycius. As an envious lover, Lycius cannot bear the looks of this man to his bride, especially that he sensually apprehends a change in Lamia's hand: "'Twas icy, and the cold ran through his veins; / Then sudden it grew hot, and all the pains / Of an unnatural heat shot to his heart" (Part II. 251–3). To his misfortunate luck, this 'unnatural heat' is but an abortive announcement not only of his marriage but also of his existence altogether. Soon, Lamia vanishes from sight, on Apollonius' words 'serpent,' and Lycius dies in his "marriage robe" (II. 311). Yet, before dying, Lycius' faithful love for Lamia equips him with enough power to launch his attack against Apollonius whom he deems to possess "impious proud-heart sophistries, / Unlawful magic, and enticing lies" (Part II. 285–6). Elliot Gilbert gathers that "the fact that it is Lycius, and not Lamia, who tries to silence Apollonius depicts the young man as himself very much involved in fostering the illusion under which he labors" 60). The 'illusion' Lycius 'fosters' testifies, nevertheless, to its being animated by a genuine love towards a woman whom he thinks to have belonged to a higher order in the chain of being as a goddess.

Conclusion

This study gears towards presenting the trio that people the text of Keats's narrative poem *Lamia* as being quintessentially good despite the moral and aesthetic flaws they exhibit at first. All the while, the poet underlines his eagerness to extend humanistic traits, including such emotive impulses as pity, love and care, to humans (Lycius and Apollonius) and non-humans (Lamia) alike. By virtue of that exhaustiveness of dealing with different orders of being on equal foot, the poet manages to foreground the humanistic pull motivating all his characters towards noble goals. Hence, the main meta-morphosis Lamia, as a beastly serpent, undergoes remains chiefly "a psychological rather than physical one" and is "brought about by her excess of love" (Rita 169). Nevertheless, there still lurk tragic aspects in the overall structure of *Lamia*, whether in the death of Lycius while festively celebrating his own marriage with Lamia, in the vanishing of Lamia after being cornered pitilessly by Apollonius' eyes, or in the implied crime committed by Apollonius while intend-ing to illumine his disciple of the true origin of his bride Lamia.

In brief, the deep-seated void that keeps irritatingly delineating the whole structure of *Lamia* and its denouement pertains chiefly to the absence of sound dialogue between different modes, despite their being derived from the same humanistic impetus. Ultimately, the awkwardness of the antagonism between Apollonius and Lamia seems to get that negative quality due to the symbolic implication of their respective 'mode' of apprehending objects in philosophy and poetry which ought to complement each other, rather than to constitute warring forces in the way they are dramatized in *Lamia*. Thus, the latent appeal of the poem may revolve around the necessity to mate ethics with aesthetics and, by implication, the order which philosophy seeks to envisage with the disordered fabrics of imagination from which poetry imbibes. Read in more symbolic terms, the poem may represent an authoritative example that shows what we might call 'the romantic agony' Keats works to express, where the voice of imagination is often relegated, if not muffled, by the louder voice of science and reason.

Works cited

Barthes, Roland. *The Lover's Discourse. Fragments.* Trans. Richard Howard. London: Penguin Books Ltd., 1991. Print.

Brunel, Pierre, ed. *Companion to Literary Myths, Heroes and Archetypes.* Trans. Wendy Allaston. London: Routledge, 1978. Print.

Chambers, Jane. "For Love's Sake: Lamia and Burton's Love Melancholy." *Studies in English Literature, 1500–1900.* Vol 22. No 4. Autumn. 1982. 583–600. Print.

Galasinki, Dariuz. *The Language of Deception. A Discourse Analytical Study.* London: Sage Publications, Inc. 2000. Print.

Gigante, Denise. "The Monster in the Rainbow." *PMLA.* Vol 17. No 3.

2002.433–48. Print.

Gilbert, Elliot. *The Poetry of John Keats.* New York: Monarch Press. 1995. Print.

Keats, John. Ed. Paul Wright. ''Lamia.'' The Compete Poems of John Keats. Hertfordshire: Wordsworth Editions Ltd. 2001. 171–89. Print.

Ricks, Christopher. "Dictionary of Classical Names." *John Keats. The Complete Poems*. 3rd ed. London: Penguin Group Ltd. 1988. 721–42. Print.

Rita, Maria. "From 'A Serpent, a Lamia' to a Rainbow-Sided Creature: Keats's *Lamia* and the Metamorphosis of the Monster." Revista Letras, Curitiba. No 80, 2010. 165–7. Print.

Sandy, Mark. "Dream Lovers and Tragic Romance: Negative Fictions in Keats's *Lamia*, *The Eve of St. Agnes* and *Isabella*." *Romanticism on the Net.* No 20. 1–24. November. Durham University. 2000. Print.

Twitchell, James B. *The Living Dead: A Study of the Vampire in Romantic Literature.* North Carolina: Duke University Press. 1984. Print.

Vaughan, Allyson. "The Woman Pursued – Keats's *Lamia.*" *ENG 481 – Gothic Literature.* Spring. 2015. Print.

Wille, Sean. *Ambiguity in the Works of John Keats: A Comparative Study of the Setting, the Characters and the Female in La Belle Dame sans Merci and Lamia*. Ph. D. Dissertation. Ghent University: Faculty of Arts and Philosophy. 2011.

Problematics of order and disorder in language

Tunisian Students' Conception of Structural Order in the English Argumentative Essay

Ons Abdi, Faculty of Letters and Human Sciences, Kairouan, Tunisia

Abstract

This article sets out to investigate third-year Tunisian students' beliefs about structural order in English argumentative essays. A questionnaire was presented to 48 Tunisian third-year students. The questionnaire probes the students' conception of the structure of argumentative texts. In the process, it also examines their awareness of the different constituents of the essay and their order within the more general organization of: introduction, body and conclusion. To describe what they write in each of these parts, the respondents chose three out of seven possible options and ranked them in an order of importance. The options were carefully chosen from previous studies on Arabs' argumentative writing. The findings show that the majority of participants do not have a clear conception of the general macro-structure of the argumentative essay.

Keywords: conceptions, structural order, argumentation, contrastive rhetoric, EFL writing.

Introduction

The notions of order, structure and organization are central to the production and processing of language, be it spoken or written. Language is governed by a finite number of rules that generate ordered patterns observable at the word, phrase, clause and sentence levels (Brinton and Brinton 5). Grammatical rules are responsible for the generation of sentence structures, as they determine which units co-occur and their order. Words making up sentences are thus not chained together in a linear internal order, but are rather structured in units called "constituents" (Brinton and Brinton 185). Noam Chomsky, in his book *Syntactic Structures*, makes a distinction between the sentence's surface structure and its deep structure. He argues that the former describes the constituents' linear order while the latter reveals the hierarchical relations that group words in a sentence. This hierarchical order is not only specific to sentences, but also characterizes larger chunks of discourse. In this sense, Hatim describes a text as follows:

> When we first approach a text, we identify a series of *elements* (words, phrases, clauses) in the order in which they appear. But this progression does not tell the whole story, and the sequence of the various elements is not, as is widely believed, solely linear. Rather, it is essentially hierarchic, with some elements enjoying a higher communicative status than others. (55)

This description of the text's structure underlines the hierarchal order joining the different components of the text into an overall structure wherein these components realize various communicative functions. According to Hatim, "to appreciate the structural organization of texts is one way of imposing order on how the various elements of a text concatenate to serve a given rhetorical purpose" (54). Halimah believes that, in the teaching of composition, the "mechanics of writing," such as "syntactic structures," "vocabulary," and "grammar," are highlighted at the expense of general rhetorical patterns that contribute to the realization of the essay's rhetorical aim (47–8). He maintains that writing is not tantamount to solely using these mechanics but, also to thinking and organizing one's thoughts. This idea is adopted by Raimes who emphasizes the importance of structural organization and effectively ordering one's thoughts and ideas.

This article explores Tunisian students' conceptualization of the structural organization of argimentative texts. In the next section, Kaplan's much-cited contrastive rhetoric study on essays' structural order is presented, and other studies on Arabs' argumentative writing are reviewed with a special focus on texts' rhetorical organization. Some theoretical models used to analyze argumentative writing are then presented. These models are among the options used in the questionnaire.

Contrastive rhetoric and structural order

Contrastive rhetoric (CR) is the label Kaplan endowed his research inquiry with. He initiated his research by studying paragraph development in the English expository writing of 600 students from different cultural backgrounds as compared to the typical English expository essay ("Cultural Thought Patterns"). He concluded that "each language and each culture has a paragraph order unique to itself" (14). Kaplan classified the students' writing into five "rhetorics" or "cultural thought patterns," namely English, Romance, Russian, Oriental, and Semitic (15). He based his categorization on differences in paragraph development. The following "doodles" are visual representations of his findings on cross-cultural variation in logical order and writing (Figure 1).

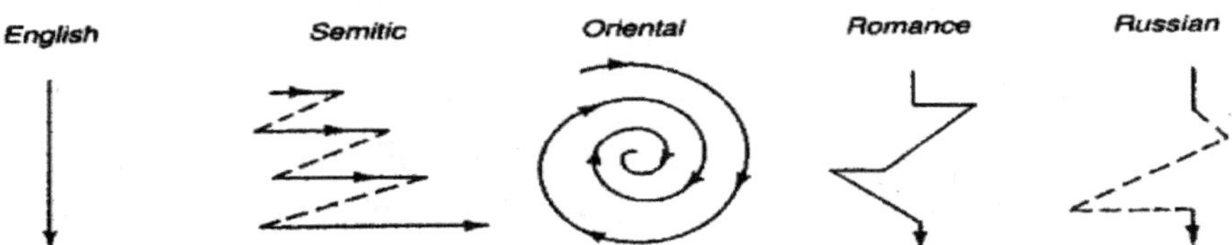

Figure 1: Kaplan's visual representations of rhetorical patterns.

Kaplan asserts that English rhetoric is affected to a great extent by Anglo-European culture and Platonic Aristotelian thought patterns (3). He argues that English native speakers prefer a direct/linear paragraph development. This orgqnizational order corresponds to a deductive approach to writing (Liu and Furneaux 75). The other thought patterns, as can be seen from the "doodles" above, are, consecutively: parallel constructions, indirect/spiral, quasi-linear digressions and partial parallelism. Kaplan ascribes the differences in rhetorical organizational order between English and other languages to cultural differences ("Contrastive Rhetoric and Teaching" 15). Indeed, CR is founded upon the hypothesis that ESL learners from different cultural backgrounds transfer rhetorical order from their first language to their ESL writing. This transfer produces a "persistently un-English 'feel'" (Doushaq 28) and a taste of "peculiar strangeness" in the essays (Koch 2). Kaplan contends that rhetorical patterns are cultural and thus, what might appear as a logical argument in one culture can be viewed as sophistical or illogical in another ("Cultural Thought Patterns" 2).

Order and structure in CR studies on Arabs' argumentative writing

Since Kaplan's study about paragraph development in the expository writing of EFL students considered as the foundation of the field of CR, studies contrasting the writing of EFL learners, in general, and EFL Arab learners, in specific, to that of native speakers abounded. Kaplan claims that Arabs' argumentative writing is different from the rhetorical norms of English writing (Ismail 108). The initial CR hypothesis as advanced by Kaplan has been improved, expanded upon, and even challenged by other scholars (Connor, *Contrastive Rhetoric*; Kubota; Selinker; Zamel).

In CR studies on Arabs' EFL writing, differences between English native speakers' writing and Arabs' English writing were reported. These differences were spotted at both the micro-discourse and macro-discourse levels. Although CR's general assumption is that the text's general organizational order and rhetorical strategies vary from culture to culture, linguistic local features were also studied, for they were believed to impact the general structure of the text (Mohamed-Sayidina).

CR scholars did not limit their analyses to Arabs' EFL writing. They also described the linguistic and rhetorical features of the Arabic language itself, believed to be transferred to the learners' English writing (Connor, "New Directions"). In this regard, Reid describes Arabic as "an immensely poetic language, filled with coordinate clauses and a tendency towards generality and analogy; use of detail or supporting data is not essential" (449). Reid's view of Arabic writing implies lack of a clear underlying structural order while the overuse of coordination was echoed in other papers as well (Thompson-Panos and Thomas-Ružić's; Yorkey). Shouby's account of Arabic, which predates the birth of CR, highlights this structural disorder hinted at by Reid. She particularly points out a "repetitive over attention to minute details, but without reintegrating these details into a composite and well-organized whole" (299). Johnstone's comments on the structure of Arabic argumentation also point toward the organizational weakness of Arabic writing as she maintains that an Arabic text "proceeds horizontally rather than vertically, in which ideas of equal importance for an argument are chained together" (230). She also states that it "is structured by the notion that it is the presentation of an idea – the linguistic forms and the very words that are used to describe it – that is persuasive, not the logical structure of proof which Westerners see behind words" (Koch 195). Kaplan's subsequent publication is reminiscent of this statement. He affirms that "the primary focus of writing in Arabic rests on the language of the text, not on its propositional structure" ("Contrastive Rhetoric and Learning" 289–90). In this respect, both Kaplan and Koch highlight the idea that Arab writers are more concerned about local linguistic choices than the global structural order of essays.

In another study about expository writing, Ostler shows that the difference between Anglo-American and Arab writers' rhetorical choices is a matter of location. She observes that unlike English native speakers who develop most of their ideas in the introduction, Arabs do not develop their ideas until after the introduction. And whereas the former write well-developed summarizing conclusions the latter produce general conclusions that feature proverbs. Similar observations have been made about Arabs' argumentative writing in English. In her review of some CR studies, Bacha argues that some of these studies show that the claim in L1 Arabic argumentative texts is located most of the time towards the end of the text and that these texts are often "descriptive" and "anecdocal" (230).[1] Baratta contends that,

[1] The claim is defined, according to Toulmin's model as "the central proposition or opinion of the writer" which could be "used interchangeably with thesis" (Bacha 231).

according to previous studies, certain cultures, namely Arabic, encouraged postponing the writer's position until the conclusion. The tendency in writing, described by Ostler, Bacha and Baratta, could be viewed as part of the inductive structural order wherein the writer starts with a general statement "and then narrows it down to specific idea(s) at the end of the essay" (Alotaibi 234). The deductive linear rhetorical order believed to be preferred by English native speakers is the opposite: the writer starts with a precise claim that is expounded upon throughout the rest of the essay (234).

Models describing the structure of argumentative essays

The focus of this article is on argumentative writing as described by Connor and Lauer who state that the reader conceives of argumentative texts as a problem-solving process. This conception is encapsulated in their argument superstructure model. According to Connor, superstructure is "the organizational plan of any text and refers to the linear progression of the text" ("Linguistic/Rhetorical Measures" 74). Connor and Lauer used the argument superstructure model to analyze argumentative essays based on Kummer's problem-solution theory, which was demonstrated to be empirically linked to argumentative essays (Tirkkonen-Condit, *Argumentative Text Structure*; Tirkkonen-Condit, "Text Type Markers"). This structure is made up of four main sections: Situation, problem, solution and evaluation. The situation slot is devoted to "background material, that is, facts and views intended for orientation" (Connor 74). Then, the problem is raised. The following section is reserved to presenting the steps needed to solve the problem. And finally, the solution(s) are evaluated (Ismail 152).

Toulmin's paradigm is also appropriate for the rhetorical analysis of argumentative texts. It is split up into three major parts along with three other optional sections. The three main sections of an argument are: claim, data and warrant. Toulmin defines the claim as "assertions put forward publicly for general acceptance" (Connor 74). The data corroborate the claim and justify it while warrants serve to link the data to the claim.

Another theoretical paradigm used in accounting for argumentation is Swales' move analysis (*Genre Analysis*). This framework is applicable to all genres, including research articles, abstracts and dissertations (Yang). Unlike the other theories which investigate the organizational structure of texts in terms of rhetorical sections, this theory defines the move as a "functional unit, used for some identifiable rhetorical purpose" (Connor and Mauranen 51). Thus, any section of the argumentative essay is composed of a number of moves. Examples of moves used in argumentative essays include: "establishing an issue," located in the introductory section, "justifying the thesis" in the body of the essay and "calling to an action" in the conclusion (Yang 2). In his study on argumentative essays by L2 college writers from different backgrounds, Yang based his essay analysis on Swales' framework and identified six moves distributed evenly in the introduction, body and conclusion. These moves are: "informing the reader about the issue," "stating the writer's position," "explaining the writer's position by providing reasons," "reinforcing the reasons with evidence," "reminding the reader of the writer's position" and "relating the writer's position to real life and the future" (3).

It is noteworthy that the afore-mentioned theories are used to account for the English argumentative writing of both English native speakers and speakers of other languages. The different sections and moves are structured to serve the global rhetorical purpose of changing the audience's original stance and convincing them. It has been shown, however, in the previous sections of this article that many claims have been made about Arabs' argumentative essays as lacking appropriate organizational order. Arab writers are portrayed "as confused, coming to the same point two or three times from different angles, and so on" (Hatim 161). Their written productions were described as characterized by a "lack of self-awareness in the writing process, and simplicity of thematic structure" (Sa'Adeddin 38).

Overview of the study

The term beliefs is used to "refer to learners' conceptions and/or understanding as a set of mental constructions or representations, which guides, or creates and maintains, a disposition towards their specific learning and/or classroom practices" (Wan 53). Accordingly, this notion is used to refer to what the students already know as opposed to what "they need to know" (Barcelos 10). Students' beliefs have also been defined as metacognitive knowledge or the "stable, statable although sometimes incorrect knowledge that learners have acquired about language, learning and the language learning process" (Wenden 163). Victori describes metacognitive knowledge as mental representations and maintains that questionnaires represent an appropriate instrument to explore learners' beliefs. Understanding the learners' conceptualizations about the structure and contents of argumentative essays could contribute to understanding the difficulties they face when writing. Indeed, according to Wingate, "many of the problems they [learners] encounter are caused by their lack of knowledge of what an argumentative essay requires, particularly the need to develop their own position in an academic debate" (145). This study investigates Tunisian third-year students' beliefs about the structural organization of argumentative essays. It has the following objectives:

1. Explore the students' conception of the macro-level structure of the argumentative essay.
2. Discuss the findings in relation to their previous writing experience.

The questionnaire

A questionnaire comprising rating and ranking questions has been administered to 48 Tunisian third-year students of English at university level (eight male and 40 female), aged between 21 and 27 years old. The questionnaire is divided into three sections (see Appendix). Section one elicits background information. Section two is about the students' writing experience and section three is about their conception of the different components of the argumentative essay. The questions in sections two are rating questions and serve to contextualize the findings of the study. In section three, the students were given three ranking questions about the contents of the three main parts of the argumentative essay, namely, introduction, body and conclusion. To describe what they write in each of these parts, the students were presented with seven choices for each part, then asked to choose the three most appropriate options and rank them in order of importance (see appendix). Limiting the selection and ranking process to three options was meant to reduce the cognitive stress of ranking all seven options.

The components of Connor and Lauer's argument superstructure measure are among the options. Another option consists of the moves identified in Yang's study mentioned in a previous section of the article. The rest of the choices are not specifically related to argumentative writing. For instance, the option "in the introduction of my argumentative essay, I write about the context of the topic" is suggestive of Bamberg's four-point coherence scale. According to Bamberg, successful writers "provided an introduction that oriented the reader to the situation and placed the subject in context by identifying time, place and circumstance" (422). Another example is the option "in the introduction of my argumentative essay in English, I turn the topic into questions," inspired from Swales' CARS model (Create a Research Space) which involves asking questions in the introduction that are answered throughout the essay (*Research Genres*).

Findings and discussion

Students' answers to the sentence completion task in section three were quantified in terms of frequency and rank. The first sentence completion question starts as follows: "In the introduction of my argumentative essay in English, I…." The most frequently selected alternatives in a descending rank order are: "1. explain the topic", "4. write about the context of the topic" and "3. use a quotation I know or a famous person's opinion to introduce the topic" (Figure 2, a). Some of the other options were frequently selected, but have a lower rank. It is worth noting that the two most frequently chosen options are not specifically related to argumentative writing which is generally understood as convincing the audience of the writer's opinion. These options are very generic in nature and do not offer any descriptions of the different components or moves to be found in the introduction.

The most frequently chosen options for the second sentence completion question in a descending order of rank are: "2. answer the questions asked in the introduction", "5. develop the ideas mentioned in the introduction" and "3. discuss the topic in more depth" (Figure 2, b). As with the first ranking question, the options selected for the second question do not describe the contents of the essay's body and are not specific to argumentative writing. The answers are too vague and indicate a movement from the general to the specific, reminiscent of the inductive order said to be preferred by Arab writers.

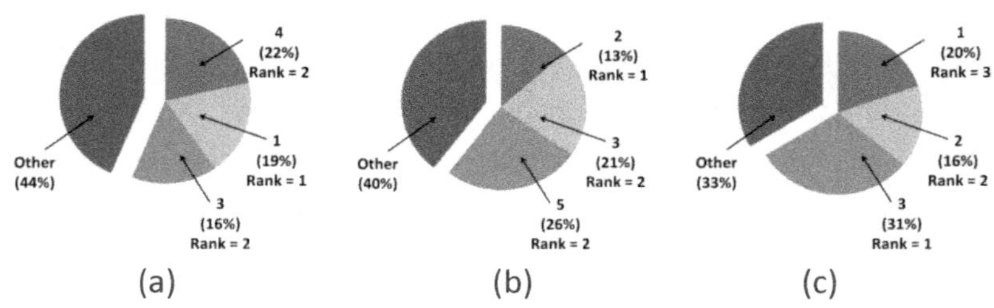

Figure 2: Most frequently chosen options and their ranks for (a) question 1, part 3, (b) question 2, part 3 and (c) question 3, part 3.

The most frequently selected options in a descending rank order for the third ranking question are: "3. remind the reader of the ideas I talked about in the body," "2. conclude by adding new ideas to the topic" and "1. open new horizons" (Figure 2, c). Just like the possibilities chosen in the first and second sentence completion questions, these choices are also generic and not specifically related to argumentation. They are not revealing of the components of the conclusion, unlike the fourth and fifth options adapted, respectively, from Connor and Lauer's model and Swales' move analysis theory (*Genre Analysis*). Not only did the students opt for the most general descriptions of the conclusion section, but also seemed to agree that, in the conclusion, it is possible for the writer to add new ideas not mentioned before. Adding new ideas in the last section of the essay corresponds to neither the deductive nor the inductive order of writing. As for the option "open new horizons," it is suggestive of a discourse move related to Arabic argumentative writing, whereby the writer concludes the essay by asking thought-provoking questions that encourage the audience to think about new ideas related to the topic.

It is also worth mentioning that although the majority of students (74%) claim to have been trained in argumentative writing, they do not seem aware of the persuasive nature of this particular genre whose rhetorical purpose is "to take a position on some issue and justify it" (Derewianka 75). In fact, when answering the three rating questions, the students favoured general answers to answers delineating the structure of the argumentative essay, even though the latter contained key words such as "position" (to mean opinion), "problem," "solution" explicitly linked to argumentation while the former comprised indefinite terms such as "ideas," "context" and "topic".

Those findings show that the majority of respondents do not have a clear idea of the general macro-structure of the argumentative essay. Although presented with options that represent different persuasive moves, students opted for generic answers. This does not reflect any awareness on their part of the components and rhetorical order of argumentative texts. More importantly, they do not seem to be aware that this genre involves adopting a position and defending it.

Conclusion

This article is part of a broader contrastive study that investigates Tunisian students' argumentative written productions. Studying the students' writing captures the difficulties they face not only at the local linguistic level, but also with ordering their ideas at the macro-level of discourse. On the other hand, studying their beliefs about argumentative writing can determine their needs and help in designing appropriate teaching materials that suit those needs. The findings of the present study suggest that the students do not have a well-defined conceptualization of the general structure of the argumentative essay and the order of its different components. The students' vague conceptions signal the need to focus on the general structural order in the teaching of argumentation. It is important, however, to look at the learners' essays to determine whether those conceptualizations are predictive of their writing performance.

Works cited

Alotaibi, Hmoud. "Thesis Statement in English Argumentative Essays by Arab Students: A Study of Contrastive Rhetoric." *Arab World English Journal Vol. 5 no. 3* (2014): 230–47.

Bacha, Nahla Nola. "Teaching the academic argument in a university EFL environment." *Journal of English for Academic Purposes Vol. 9 no. 3* (2010): 229–41.

Baratta, Alex. "How to make a good argument: Teaching the thesis statement to university students." U of Manchester, 2011.

Bamberg, Betty. "What makes a text coherent?" *College Composition and Communication Vol.34 no*. 4 (1983): 417–29.

Barcelos, Ana Maria Ferreira. "Researching beliefs about SLA: A critical review." *Beliefs about SLA*. Springer (2003): 7–33.

Brinton, Laurel J., and Donna Brinton. *The Linguistic Structure of Modern English*. John Benjamins Publishing, 2010.

Chomsky, Noam. *Syntactic structures*. Walter de Gruyter, 2002.

Connor, Ulla. *Contrastive Rhetoric: Cross-cultural aspects of second language writing*. Cambridge University Press. 1996.

---. "Linguistic/rhetorical measures for international persuasive student writing." *Research in the Teaching of English* (1990): 67–87.

---. "New directions in contrastive rhetoric." *Tesol Quarterly, Vol.36 no. 4* (2002): 493–510.

Connor, Ulla and Janice Lauer. "Cross-cultural variation in persuasive student writing." *Writing across languages and cultures: Issues in contrastive rhetoric, Vol. 2* (1988): 138–59.

Connor, Ulla and Anna Mauranen. "Linguistic analysis of grant proposals: European Union research grants." *English for specific purposes, Vol. 18 no. 1* (1999): 47–62.

Derewianka, Beverly. Exploring how texts work. Primary English Teaching Association. *Newtown, Australia*. 1990.

Doushaq, Hufeeq H. "An investigation into stylistic errors of Arab students learning English for academic purposes." *English for Specific Purposes Vol.* 5 *no.* 1 (1986): 27–39.

Halimah, Ahmad Mustafa. *EST writing: rhetorically processed and produced; a case study of Kuwaiti learners*. Diss. University of Essex, 1991.

Hatim, Basil. *Communication across cultures: Translation theory and contrastive text linguistics*. Vol. 20. U of Exeter Press, 1997.

Ismail, Soliman. *Arabic and English persuasive writing of Arabs from a contrastive rhetoric perspective*. Diss. Indiana U of Pennsylvania, 2010.

Johnstone, Barbara. "'Orality' and discourse structrure in Modern Standard Arabic." *New perspectives on Arabic linguistics, Vol. 1* (1990): 215–33.

Kaplan, Robert B. Cultural thought patterns in inter-cultural education. *Language, Vol. 16* (1966): 1–20.

---. "Contrastive rhetoric and the teaching of composition." *TESOL quarterly, Vol. 1 no. 4* (1967): 10–16.

---. "Contrastive rhetoric and second language learning: Notes toward a theory of contrastive rhetoric." *Writing across languages and cultures: Issues in contrastive rhetoric, Vol. 2* (1988): 275–304.

Koch, Barbara Johnstone. *Repetition in Discourse: Cohesion and Persuasion In Arabic Argumentative Prose*. Diss. University of Michigan. 1981.

Kubota, Ryuko. "Discursive construction of the images of US classrooms." *TESOL Quarterly.* Vol. 35 no.1 (2001): 9–38.

Kummer, W. (1972). Aspects of a theory of argumentation. *Textsorten,* 25–49.

Liu, Xinghua, and Clare Furneaux. "A multidimensional comparison of discourse organization in English and Chinese university students' argumentative writing." *International Journal of Applied Linguistics.* Vol. 24 no.1 (2014): 74–96.

Mohamed-Sayidina, Aisha. "Transfer of L1 cohesive devices and transition words into L2 academic texts: The case of Arab students." *RELC Journal.* Vol.41 no.3 (2010): 253–66.

Ostler, Shirley E. "English in parallels: A comparison of English and Arabic prose." *Writing across languages: Analysis of L2 text* (1987): 169–85.

Raimes, Ann. *Techniques in Teaching Writing.* Oxford University Press,1983.

Reid, Joy M. "ESL composition: The linear product of American thought." *College Composition and Communication Vol.35 no. 4* (1984): 449–52.

Sa'Adeddin, Mohammed Akram AM. "Text development and Arabic-English negative interference." *Applied linguistics Vol. 10 no. 1* (1989): 36–51.

Shouby, Eleanor. "The influence of the Arabic language on the psychology of the Arabs." *The Middle East Journal* (1951): 284–302.

Selinker, Larry. "Interlanguage." *IRAL-International Review of Applied Linguistics in Language Teaching.* Vol. 10 no. 4 (1972): 209–32.

Swales, John. *Genre Analysis: English in academic and research settings*. Cambridge UP, 1990.

---. *Research genres: Explorations and applications*. Ernst Klett Sprachen, 2004.

Thompson-Panos, Karyn, and Thomas-Ružić, Maria. "The least you should know about Arabic: Implications for the ESL writing instructor." *TESOL Quarterly* (1983): 609–23.

Tirkkonen-Condit, Sonja. *Argumentative text structure and translation. Vol. 18*. University of Jyväskylä, 1985.

---. "Text type markers and translation equivalence." *Interlingual and Intercultural Communication: Discourse and Cognition in Translation and Second Language Acquisition Studies. Tubingen: Gunter Narr*, 1986.

Toulmin, Stephen E. *The Uses of Argument*. Cambridge UP, 2003.

Victori, Mia. "Methodological issues in research on learners' beliefs about language learning." The 12th World Congress of Applied Linguistics (AILA 99). Tokyo, Japan. 1-6 August 1999. Presentation.

Wan, Wan. "Constructing and developing ESL students' beliefs about writing through metaphor: An exploratory study." *Journal of Second Language Writing.* Vol.23 (2014): 53–73.

Wenden, Anita. "What do second-language learners know about their language learning? A second look at retrospective accounts." *Applied linguistics.* Vol. 7 (1986): 186–205.

Wingate, Ursula. "'Argument!' helping students understand what essay writing is about." *Journal of English for Academic Purposes.* Vol.11 no. 2 (2012): 145–54.

Yang, Hae Sung. "Rhetorical Patterns in L2 Writers' Argumentative Essays." Fall TESOL Conference. San Francisco State University. 4 December 2009. Presentation.

Yorkey, Richard. "Practical EFL techniques for teaching Arabic-speaking students." *The Human Factors in ESL* (1977): 57–85.

Zamel, Vivian. "Toward a model of transculturation." *TESOL Quarterly.* Vol.31 no. 2 (1997): 341–52.

Appendix

Questionnaire:

Please put a cross ☒ in the appropriate box.

Part One: Background Information

1. Name and Surname: ______________________________
2. Sex: Female ☐ Male ☐
3. Age: ______________________________

Part Two:

1. I practice writing essays in English:

   Every week ☐ Every month ☐ Every semester ☐ Annually ☐ Never ☐

2. I consider my writing in English:

   Poor ☐ Average ☐ Good ☐ Very Good ☐ Excellent ☐

3. My teacher evaluates my essays in English as being:

   Poor ☐ Average ☐ Good ☐ Very Good ☐ Excellent ☐

4. Did you have composition lessons in English on argumentative writing?

   Yes ☐ No ☐ I don't know ☐

Part Three:

Choose the **three most appropriate options** and rank them from 1 to 3 in order of importance.

1. In the introduction of my argumentative essay in English, I …

   explain the topic ☐

   turn the topic into questions ☐

   use a quotation I know or a famous person's opinion to introduce the topic ☐

   write about the context of the topic ☐

   inform the reader about the issue and state my position ☐

   describe the situation and state the problem ☐

   Other ☐

   Specify:

   ____

Choose the **three most appropriate options** and rank them from 1 to 3 in order of importance.

2. In the body of my argumentative essay in English, I …

   move from the context to details ☐

   answer the questions asked in the introduction ☐

   discuss the topic in more depth ☐

   explain my position by providing reasons and reinforcing them with evidence ☐

   develop the ideas mentioned in the introduction ☐

   suggest steps or actions to solve the problem ☐

   Other ☐

   Specify:

   ____

Choose the **three most appropriate options** and rank them from 1 to 3 in order of importance.

3. In the conclusion of my argumentative essay in English, I …

   open new horizons ☐

   conclude by adding new ideas related to the topic ☐

   remind the reader of the ideas I talked about in the body ☐

   evaluate the outcome of the steps suggested to solve the problem ☐

   remind the reader of my position and relate it to real life and the future ☐

   move back to the context to conclude ☐

   Other ☐

   Specify:

   ____

Constraints on the order of final consonants in Tunisian Arabic

Mounir Jouini, Higher Institute of Languages, Nabeul.

Abstract

The paper studies the constraints on the order of final consonants in Tunisian Arabic (TA) within the framework of Optimality Theory (OT). TA allows a maximum of two consonants at the right edge of the syllable while initial as well as final triconsonantal clusters are broken by an epenthetic [ɪ] (Jouini, 2014). Accordingly, the type of syllable that the paper studies is the rightmost superheavy syllable of the shape CVCC (where C is a consonant and V is a vowel). Specifically, this paper focuses on the order of the final CC sequence as governed by the Sonority Sequencing Principle (SSP), which requires that final consonants exhibit a falling sonority. Yet, SSP is commonly violated and sonority reversals are frequently observed in TA. Most approaches to sonority reversals consist in discarding the final consonant (that is CVCC=CVC+C) and considering the superheavy syllable CVCC as an ordinary heavy syllable of the shape CVC. Tempting as they look, however, none of these approaches represents a satisfactory analysis of the TA CVCC syllable. The approach presented in this paper adopts mora-sharing (where two segments of the rhyme share a mora) and interprets SSP as a constraint family that comprises a constraint governing the mora and another one governing the syllable. This allows an exhaustive tautosyllabic analysis of the syllable with no violation of the bimoraic maximum weight.

Keywords: Optimality Theory, mora-sharing, SSP, superheavy syllables, exhaustive parsing, Tunisian Arabic

1 Introduction

Cross-linguistically, the unmarked syllable types are the light monomoraic and the heavy bimoraic syllables. When CVVC and CVCC exist as a separate syllable type in a language, they force a three-way distinction between light, heavy and superheavy syllables. Within moraic theory, Weight-by-Position (Hayes, 1989) may force the final consonant in these hypercharacterized structures to be dominated by a third mora, thus yielding a trimoraic syllable. Languages that have trimoraic syllables include Hindi (Broselow et al. 1997; Hayes, 1989), Estonian (Prillop, 2013), English (Hammond, 1999), German (Hall, 2002), and Finnish (Sherer, 1994). Arabic exhibits this type of syllables in the majority of its related dialects, with cross-dialectal differences concerning mainly distributional restrictions (that is whether the dialect allows superheavy syllables word-initially, medially, and/or finally). However, the literature since Selkirk (1981) and McCarthy and Prince (1990) has long argued that the final consonant in these superheavy syllables plays no major role in Arabic phonology, and that it is best considered as extrametrical. This is in addition to the fact that trimoraic syllables are disfavored and generally avoided by means of phonological repair operations such as vowel epenthesis. Thus, a trimoraic analysis of these syllables in Arabic is not motivated; they are to be interpreted as bimoraic.

The observation, that superheavy syllables are quite similar to ordinary heavy syllables with regard to phonological processes such as stress assignment, leads to drawing the following equivalencies: CVVC = CVV and CVCC = CVC. In both cases, the final consonant is set as extrametrical and the remaining sequence is bimoraic. This final C has triggered a variety of representations. For instance, it may be considered as a *degenerate syllable* (Selkirk, 1981). In other words, the final consonant is licensed by a syllable node and interpreted as the onset of a syllable with an empty nucleus. Slightly different is Boudlal's (2001) notion of *minor syllable* where the final consonant is dominated by a mora for minimal weight requirement. Still, another alternative is the representation of the final C as an *appendix* (Vaux and Wolfe, 2009), in which case it is interpreted as a non-moraic consonant that is directly adjoined to the syllable node. Kiparsky's

(2003) interpretation of *semisyllables* as unlicensed moras further enriches the representation by allowing a mora to dominate the final C and affiliate with the prosodic word node following Itô and Mester's (1992) *Weak Layering Hypothesis*. The adjunction to the prosodic word node is motivated by two main reasons: the maximum weight restriction on syllables and feet (therefore, it has to adjoin to a higher node) and OT's minimal violation principle (thus, it should not adjoin to a category higher than the Prosodic Word).

In addition to all of these interpretations of the final C in CVVC and CVCC syllables, there is still another approach, which will be followed and further extended in this paper. It is the mora-sharing view (Broselow, 1992; Broselow et al. 1995; Broselow et al. 1997; and Watson, 2002, 2007). The distinctiveness of this approach is that it considers the final C as a coda consonant (i.e. tautosyllabic) that contributes to weight without incurring a violation of the bimoraic maximal weight. This is realized by allowing the final two segments in CV$\widehat{VC}$ to share a mora in violation of the NoBranchingMora (NBM) constraint.

However, mora-sharing has been applied to CVVC syllables but not to CVCC ones because of an apparent asymmetry between the two types. This asymmetry emerges from two observations. First, in many Arabic dialects, CVCC syllables are only attested word-finally while CVVC ones may occur word-finally or word-internally. Second, there are languages that allow CVVC but not CVCC syllables, yet no language with superheavy syllables would allow CVCC but not CVVC. These observations have led to considering CVCC syllables as trimoraic.

Although the distributional argument above is sound, there is much to say about the phonological one. In fact, one of the reasons for not allowing mora-sharing in CVCC syllables is the order of final consonants. That is, following the SSP, sonority starts falling after the nucleus of the syllable. For example, a word such as 'dark' respects the SSP as [r] is more sonorous than [k]. [rk] is a possible coda in English, but its reversal [kr] is not. Interestingly, these sonority reversals are allowed in TA, so that there are words such as 'sukr' (*sugar*) and 'fikr' (*thought*). This order of the final consonants with respect to sonority is quite crucial to an analysis that adopts mora-sharing. A CC sequence in a CVCC syllable shares a mora when the first C is more sonorous than the second one. Yet, when the order of the final consonants is reversed and the first C is less sonorous than the rightmost one, then an alternative analysis has to be presented.

In this article, I argue that mora-sharing in TA final CVCC syllables is possible through a careful manipulation of SSP and a few other OT constraints. Exhaustive parsing is maximized through a high ranking of PARSE-μ (a constraint requiring moras to be parsed into syllables). All the segments in the syllable are tautosyllabic with no incurred violation of the maximal size of two moras. CVCC syllables are quite similar to CVVC in TA, but they involve different constraint interactions (cf. Mahfoudhi, 2005). They take into consideration the sonority distance between the first and the second consonant in a final cluster. In fact, the order of the final consonants in a CVCC syllable is crucial in this sense: if the first consonant is more sonorous than the second, then the cluster shares a mora (CVCC = $CV_{\mu}\widehat{CC}_{\mu}$), but if the final consonant is more sonorous, then the head mora is shared (CVCC = $C\widehat{VC}_{\mu}C_{\mu}$). It is the relative ranking of two constraints on mora-sharing and two others on SSP that determines whether the branching mora is the first one or the second one.

The following sections present an overview of previous approaches to superheavy syllables, an argument in favor of mora-sharing and a construction of a constraint hierarchy that governs mora-sharing in CVCC in such a way that the order of final consonants triggers one of two different constraint interactions.

2 Previous approaches to the CVCC syllable

Given that the superheavy CVCC syllable has an extra consonant to the right of the universal heavy syllable CVC, there have been two broad ways to dealing with it. Either the final C is considered extrasyllabic (that is CVCC=CVC+<C>) or it is considered as tautosyllabic. In the latter case, the result is either a trimoraic syllable or a bimoraic syllable with two segments sharing a single mora. In a subsequent section, I will show that mora-sharing is the most adequate approach to adopt in the study of TA final consonants.

2.1 Extrasyllabicity

Considering the final C in CVCC as extrasyllabic seems to be a straightforward way to treating the syllable as an ordinary heavy syllable. The final C is consequently considered invisible to phonological rules. This is further motivated by the status of the final C as a segment that meets the different requirements for extra-metricality (Hayes, 1991). Within OT, the final C can easily be accounted for in terms of universal constraints on syllable structure. It is possible, for instance, to rank *COMPLEX$_{CODA}$ high, so that CVCC is rendered into CVC<C>. An alternative way would be to interpret NOCODA as a gradient constraint in order to allow it to have access to the number of violations, thus, minimizing the number of coda consonants.

Setting the final C in CVCC as extrasyllabic is an easy job within OT. It raises, however, some representational and theoretical issues. Extrasyllabicity does not say anything about the status of the final C, except that it is extrasyllabic. Yet, is it moraic or not? To which node in the prosodic hierarchy does it attach; the syllable, the foot or the prosodic word? Is it a stray segment or is it an onset of a potential syllable? Attempts to answer these questions vary among those who call the final C an appendix or a degenerate syllable.

2.1.1 The appendix

The traditional view of the syllable holds that the number of syllables in a word is determined by the number of sonority peaks. A sonorous segment, typically a vowel, forms a syllable along with the consonants on its left and right edges, extending until the boundary of a word or until another sonority peak is met. This view entails that a single vowel such as the English indefinite article 'a' is a syllable. It also means that a word with one vowel (and no syllabic consonants) represents a monosyllable, no matter how many consonants it may cluster around itself (for example 'texts' CVCCCC, or street CCCVC are monosyllables). The different onset and coda consonants are affiliated with one syllable in the following way:

[1] Complex margins representation

a. texts b. street

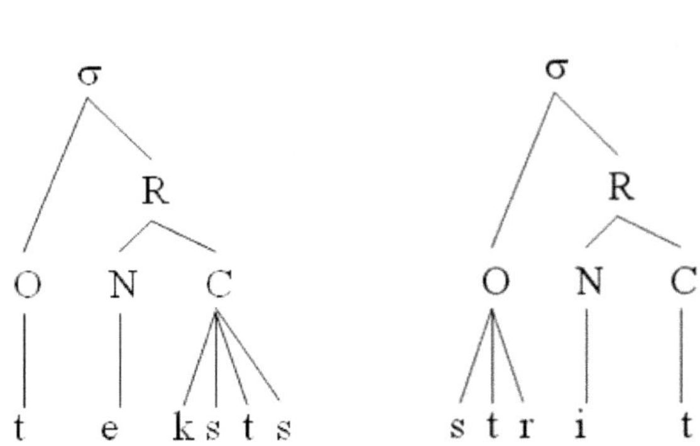

According to Vaux and Wolfe (2009), this view of syllable structure which affiliates all consonants with onset and coda slots arises from the SSP. The principle has been developed as a result of the observation that sonority tends to rise with the onset consonants until it reaches the peak with the nucleic vowel, then it decreases gradually with the coda consonants. Thus, the way consonant clusters are ordered within the syllable is quite important. For instance, as illustrated in Hammond (1999), in the word '*cramp*' [kræmp] the onset sequence [kr] is possible, because it represents an increase in sonority since [r] is more sonorous than [k]. Similarly, [mp] is a permissible coda sequence, as [m] is more sonorous than [p]. A further argument for the SSP is that reversing the order of these segments is only possible if we change the sequence from onset to coda. In other words, [rk] is not a permissible onset but it is a permissible coda (e.g. *lurk*).

Although the effect of SSP is attested cross-linguistically, a number of violations have been observed. Particularly, it has been observed that peripheral segments may violate SSP by exhibiting a higher degree of sonority than the adjacent segments that are closer to the syllable nucleus. This means that a segment may be considered as extrasyllabic if it is subject to extrametricality conditions or also if it violates the SSP. To account for the non-tautosyllabicity of such segments, the notion *appendix* has been introduced.

[2] *A word-final appendix* (Vaux and Wolfe, 2009, 102)

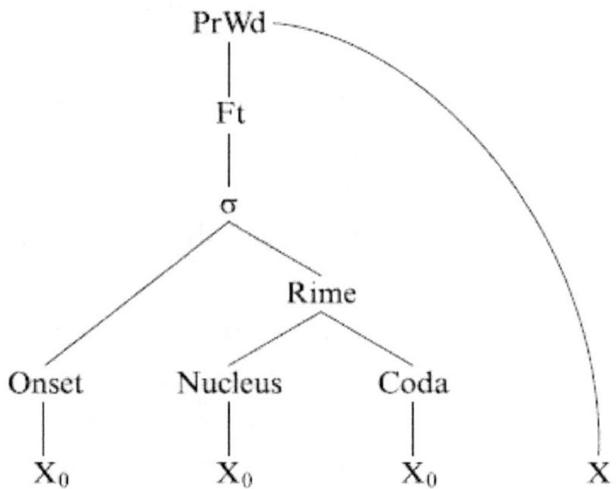

As shown above, considering the final C as an appendix consists in adjoining it to a category that is higher than the syllable in the prosodic hierarchy. This operation spares the analysis the problem of syllable weight, since whether the appendix is moraic or not, its weight does not contribute to the main syllable weight. It also ensures the non-violation of SSP, since the sonority of the appendix is of no concern to the syllable.

One major problem with the appendix theory is that it might allow the adjunction of more than one segment to potentially any node in the prosodic hierarchy. Initially, the main reason for considering a given segment as an appendix is its violation of the order required by the SSP. The very status of an appendix as extrasyllabic frees it from syllabic restrictions such as sonority sequencing and phonotactic constraints. Yet, just as Vaux and Wolfe (2009) argue, with multiple appendix adjunctions, we could potentially expect any sequence of segments to occur in a word. One way to limit this potential is to consider the extrasyllabic segments as independent syllables called "degenerate syllables." They would thus abide by the rules governing the syllable and SSP.

2.1.2 The degenerate syllable

The appendix theory aims to set a segment as non-tautosyllabic. It does so by attaching it to a node higher than the syllable (the foot, the prosodic words, or the prosodic phrase). Another way to account for the final C is to affiliate it with a syllable node that is different from the core syllable node. This is applicable to edgemost consonants in initial or final clusters. An illustration of this approach is given in [3] below, where the universal constraint FT-BIN governs the syllabification process by creating a binary foot that is minimally and maximally bimoraic. [3a] is a representation of what Boudlal (2001) terms a minor syllable. It is a degenerate syllable the consonant of which is licensed by a mora node rather than the syllable node. [3b] and [3c] include representations of the words [bka] (*he cried*) and [kəlb] (*a dog*) from Casablanca Moroccan Arabic (CMA).

[3] Degenerate syllables in CMA (Boudlal 2001, 66)

a. Schema b.bka c. kəlb

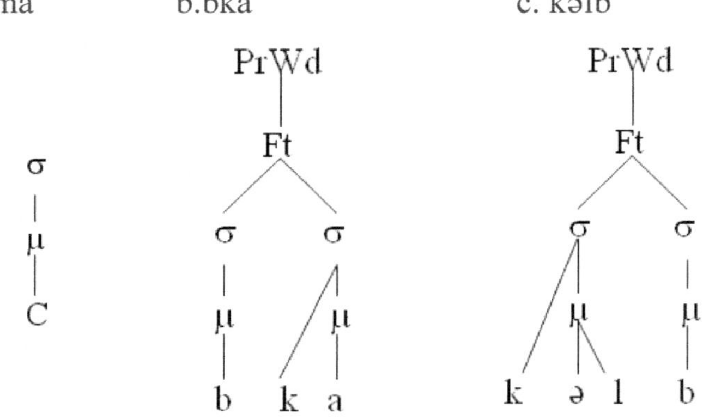

The reason why Boudlal (2001) interprets the degenerate syllable as moraic is the minimal weight requirement; a prosodic word is minimally restricted to two moras. For instance, if in [bka] the first consonant [b] were considered as a member of a complex onset or were considered an appendix, the word's minimal weight would not be met. Another reason for considering [b] as a moraic degenerate syllable is probably historical. The word comes from Standard Arabic [baka], and as argued in Vaux and Wolfe (2009), the historical loss of a vowel is often taken as an excuse for affiliating the remaining consonant with a mora. It is as if the vowel segment were lost, but its mora survives as a floating element.

There are however certain notes that need to be made about Boudlal's (2001) representation of both words in [3], and the analysis with degenerate syllables, in general. First, with regard to the representation of [bka], it is thanks to the first consonant of the cluster that such a moraic analysis is possible. In fact, this does not hold for words such as [ma] (*water*) and [ʒa] (*he came*). It is not possible to consider the initial consonant as a degenerate syllable, because this will form an impermissible onsetless syllable (*[m_{μ}.a_{μ}] and *[$ʒ_{\mu}$.a_{μ}]). Boudlal (2001, 65) does not account for these words and footnotes that they are the only words of such a form. Jouini (2015) showed that regardless of the number of onset consonants, all words rhyming with [ma], [ʒa], [bka], and [kla] could be analyzed without resort to an arbitrary assignment of consonants as moraic degenerate syllables, but rather by recognizing the inherent nature of these words as having underlying long (bimoraic) vowels.

In addition to weight requirements, Boudlal (2001) provides another argument for such a representation of [bka], which is the violation of SSP. The sequence [bk] violates it by virtue of having a first consonant that is more sonorous than the second one. However, this motivation is not attested in the many words in CMA starting in clusters that abide by the SSP, such as [dlu] (*pail*) and [qra] (*he read*).

3 Mora-sharing

By considering the final consonant as an appendix or a degenerate syllable, the aim is to establish the non-tautosyllabicity of the final consonant. This aim, however, misses an important aspect of the TA syllable structure; the final consonant actually contributes to weight. Rjili and Ghazali (2003) used experimental data to show that consonant clusters in Modern Standard Arabic tend to lengthen, and are the equivalent of geminates. That is, equivalencies can be drawn between consonant clusters and geminates. A further equivalent to be added to this group is the final C in CCVC verbs. In other words, [b] in [ktib] has a similar weight to the geminated consonant in [dibb] (*a bear*) and the cluster [bt] in [ktibt] (*I wrote*). Within moraic theory, this observation is treated as follows. First, there is the geminate [bb]. Conventionally, only the first member of the geminate is moraic (i.e. [bb] = 1μ). Since the final [b] in [ktib] is equivalent to [bb], then it is also moraic (i.e. [b] = 1μ). The consonant cluster in CVCC behaves in a similar way in terms of weight; its constituent consonants must share a mora (i.e. [bt] = 1μ). Obviously, when a segment enjoys a separate mora it is *stronger* ([b] and [bb]) while when one mora is shared between two segments, it makes them *weaker*, especially the edgemost one. This explains the prosodic weakness of the final C.

The different attempts at considering the final consonant in a superheavy syllable as extrasyllabic show how vulnerable this final consonant is. Being weak, however, is quite different from being dispensable. This has one explanation: segments do not yield themselves to a binary distinction as to whether they are moraic (necessary) or not (weak, dispensable); they may also be in the intermediate state of sharing a mora. Mora-sharing is obtained by an 'adjunction-to-mora' rule (Broselow, 1992).

[4] *Adjunction to mora in CVVC syllables*

With regard to superheavy CVVC syllables, mora-sharing concerns the final C and the vowel preceding it. Mahfoudhi (2005) incorporates mora-sharing with Piggott's (1999) Remote-Licensing to account for the moraic characterization of Cairene, Mekkan and Tunisian Arabic. He extends mora-sharing to CVCC syllables in TA, only when they occur word-initially or word-internally. Word-finally, he considers final consonants as non-moraic, and treats them as "appendix-like codas that are attached directly to the syllable where they are parsed" (Mahfoudhi, 2005, 37).

[5] Mahfoudhi's (2005) analysis

a. Representation (Mahfoudhi, 2005, 39)

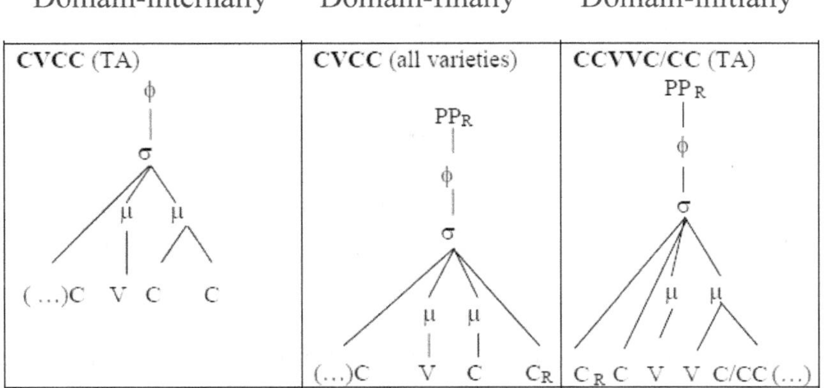

b. Tableau for /ktubtxuuja/ [[ktubt] [.xuu.ja]]PP (*my brother's books*) (Mahfoudhi, 2005, 44)

Candidates	DEP(V)	Noappendix	NosharedMora(CC)
a. [[ktub.t]w **i**[.xuu.ja] w] PP	*!		
b. √ [[ktubt]w[.xuu.ja]w] PP			*
c. [[ktub-t]w[.xuu.ja]w] PP		*!	

While the analysis succeeds in showing that TA is different from other Arabic dialects when it comes to the treatment of CVCC syllables, it does not give much explanation as to how mora-sharing is extended from CVVC syllables to include CVCC. Actually, mora-sharing accounts for CVVC syllables with no apparent restrictions, yet it is not straightforwardly extendable to CVCC syllables. The reasons are diverse. Broselow et al. (1995) and Watson (2007) argue for an asymmetry between the two types of superheavy syllables. They observe that, in many dialects, surface CVCC is more restricted than CVVC, and that most frequently when it occurs word-internally it calls for syllable restructuring through epenthesis (Broselow et al. 1995, 122). [6] illustrates this asymmetry.

[6] Word-internal asymmetry (Broselow, 1995, 123)

	CVVC	CVCC
Cairene	no	no
Makkan	no	no
Sudanese	yes	no
Abu Dhabi	yes	no
Levantine	yes	only in some CC clusters
Other Gulf	yes	only in some CC clusters

It is obvious then that CVCC is more restricted word-internally than CVVC. In dialects where it is allowed in that position (as in Levantine and other Gulf dialects), it is limited to clusters where the first consonant is more sonorous than the second one. Accordingly, Broselow et al. (1995) conclude that CVCC must be trimoraic.

In TA, the asymmetry is not attested. CVCC syllables occur word-internally and word-finally, just like CVVC syllables. Actually, while the dialects that allow word-internal CVCC impose certain sonority constraints on the order of CC sequences, in TA possible combinations exhibit a relatively significant freedom. This leads us to the following conclusion: CVCC syllables in TA are different from their correspondents in other Arabic dialects in that they are less constrained by sonority sequencing. This discards their treatment as trimoraic (cf. Broselow et al. 1995). However, this does not mean that sonority plays no role in TA (as it forces other phonological processes such as metathesis) and the possibility of adjoining the final cluster to one node must not be systematic (cf. Mahfoudhi, 2005). We need an analysis that considers CVCC syllables as bimoraic, yet at the same time, mora-sharing of the final cluster is determined by the relative sonority of the two consonants. Let us first consider the sonority hierarchy, and then TA data including word-internal CVCC will follow.

[7] Decreasing order of sonority

a. Featural

Vowels

Approximants

Nasals

b. Segmental (Selkirk, 1984)

a

e,o,ə

i,u

r (rˁ)

l (lˁ)

m,n

s,sˁ

χ,ɤ,ħ,ʕ,h,ʔ

ð,ðˁ,z,zˁ

f,θ,š

b,d,g

t,tˁ,k,q

The exact placement of certain consonants within the segmental sonority hierarchy is discussed in Angoujard (1990). For the present matter, the hierarchy under [7a] is deemed sufficient. Below are different examples from TA, where the sonority sequence in the CC cluster is highlighted. (In the data below, A=approximant; N=nasal; O=obstruent).

[8] Sonority sequencing and possible CC clusters

a. Falling sonority

AN	ʕilm	*knowledge*
	ħilm	*a dream*
AO	kirʃ	*a belly*
	kalb	*a dog*
NO	bint	*a daughter*
	kanz	*a treasure*
OO	ðˤaʕf	*weakness*

b. Sonority plateau

AA	qawl	*a say*
NN	ʔamn	*security*
	simn	*fatness*
OO	waqt	*time*
	buɤðˤ	*loathing*

c. Sonority reversals

OO	xubz	*bread*
	ʕaks	*opposite*
ON	dihn	*paint*
	fahm	*understanding*
OA	buχl	*laziness*

	sabr	*patience*
NA	ħiml	*burden*
	ʔamr	*matter*

While with CVVC syllables, the final consonant shares a mora with the preceding vowel, with CVCC syllables two representations are possible and, in fact, required. The first is where the final two consonants share a mora, and the second is where the final consonant adjoins to the second mora while the preceding VC sequence shares the head mora. The two possibilities are illustrated underneath [9].

[9] *CVCC mora-sharing representation*

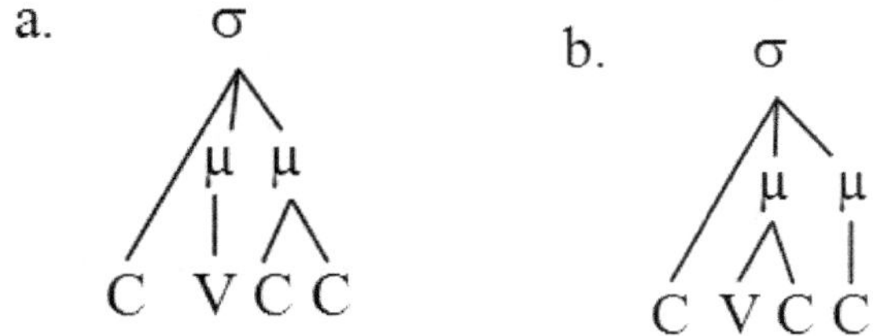

The final C in [9a] shares a mora with the preceding consonant. However, as noted earlier, one of the problems this representation faces is that it imitates mora sharing in CVVC and takes no account of SSP. In CVVC, the sonority of the final C is always lower than the preceding vocalic segment. Thus mora-sharing in final VC never violates SSP. On the contrary, in CVCC structures, the final cluster may exhibit a reversed order where the final C is more sonorous than the one preceding it. In that case, adjoining the two consonants to the same node is not acceptable, given the sonority reversal that they represent. The reason is that mora-sharing among consonants with reversed sonority wrongly predicts that the final C is less sonorous that the one preceding it.

Accordingly, the representation in [9a] is more adequate to structures where the final cluster exhibits a falling sonority or at most a sonority plateau. When the final C is more sonorous (that is, in cases of sonority reversals) it is the representation in [9b] that is adopted, as it clearly separates the two consonants in terms of adjunction, and assigns a separate mora to the more sonorous segment. Therefore, CVCC syllables are to be represented in two different ways, depending on the sonority distance between the constituent consonants of the cluster.

[10] Mora-sharing and sonority distance

a. $CVC_1C_2 \rightarrow C_1 \geq C_2$ (Falling sonority and plateaus) b. $CVC_1C_2 \rightarrow C_1 < C_2$ (sonority reversals)

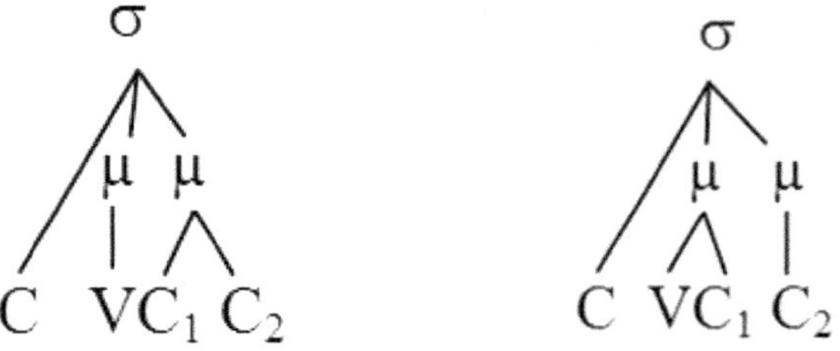

The advantages of the above analysis are many. First, it recognizes CVCC syllables as ordinary heavy (bimoraic) syllables while at the same time allowing tautosyllabicity and discarding notions such as appendice, degenerate syllable and the like. Second, it neutralizes the asymmetry between CVVC and CVCC syllables which is not motivated in TA. Third, it extends mora-sharing to CVCC syllables while taking into consideration SSP which is quite crucial in this respect. In fact, which representation to choose depends on the relative sonority of the final C. In the case of falling sonority and plateaus, the cluster shares a mora ($CV_{\mu}\widehat{CC}_{\mu}$). However, in the case of sonority reversals, the final C enjoys a separate mora and mora-sharing shifts to the head mora ($C\widehat{VC}_{\mu}C_{\mu}$). Finally, the very fact that the final C is affiliated with an independent mora when it is more sonorous is a further evidence for the correlation between moraicity and sonority.

In Optimality Theoretic terms, a set of constraints is needed to account for mora-sharing in CVVC syllables. These constraints are stated below.

[11] *Constraints on final consonants*

$*\sigma_{\mu\mu\mu}$	Syllables are maximally bimoraic (Sherer, 1994).
*APPENDIX (*APP)	Appendix consonants are not allowed (Sherer, 1994).
NOBRANCHINGMORA	(NBM) moras associate to single segments (Broselow et al., 1995).
PARSE-μ	Moras must be parsed into the syllable.
DEPENDENCE-VOWEL	(DEP-V) A vowel in the output has a correspondent in the input form.
SONORITY SEQUENCING PRINCIPLE-SYLLABLE (SSP_{σ})	In a syllable, sonority increases toward the peak and decreases toward the margins (Morelli, 2003, 359; Yu Cho and King, 2003).
SONORITY SEQUENCING PRINCIPLE-MORA (SSP_{μ})	Consonants affiliated with the same mora exhibit a falling sonority.
NO-BRANCHING HEAD MORA (NBHM)	A head mora must not branch (Broselow et al. 1995, 126).
NO-BRANCHING MORA-CC (NBM-CC)	A mora must not be shared between two consonants (dubbed No-CC-Mora in Broselow et al. 1995, 126).

SSP is sometimes called SONSEQ (Bosisio, 2003, 73; Gouskva, 2003, 72). It is violated when sonority increases towards the margin. For the present matter, the violation is caused when the final consonant is more sonorous than the one preceding it. It is considered as a cover constraint for two different sets of constraints: (a) the margin and peak constraints (*Margin*: *M/*a*>> *M/*i*>> ….>> *M/*d* >> *M/*t*; and *Peak*: *P/*t*>> *P/*d* >> … >> *P/*i* >> *P/*a* (Prince and Smolensky, 1993 [2004], 152), and (b) constraints such as *PLATEAU and *REVERSAL

(Morelli, 2003, 360). Crucial enough is the interpretation of SSP as being constructed of two sub-constraints, each governing a type of sonority sequence. SSP_σ controls sonority at the syllabic level while SSP_μ controls sonority at the moraic one. It is the ranking SSP_μ >> SSP_σ that allows consonants exhibiting sonority reversals to be analyzed tautosyllabically.

NBHM is violated when the first (or head) mora in a bimoraic syllable is shared between two segments. The constraint was suggested in Broselow et al. (1995) to ban vowels in CVCC syllables from sharing a mora. In the present analysis, ranking NBHM lower than both SSP constraints results in allowing VC to share a mora. This is deemed a minimal violation in cases where the final C is more sonorous than the one preceding it. NBM-CC is ranked lower than both SSP and NBHM to ensure that the final cluster shares a mora when it does not violate SSP. The constraint hierarchy is presented below. It is the constraint interaction that decides on the optimal candidate at this level.

[12] *The constraint hierarchy governing CVCC*

$*\sigma_{\mu\mu\mu}$>>DEP-V>>PARSE-μ>>*APP>>SSP_μ >> SSP_σ>>NBHM>>NBM-CC>>NBM

The system is illustrated in the tableaux below with the two examples [dars] (*a lesson*) and [sabr] (*patience*). The former word exhibits a falling sonority in the final cluster, as [r] is more sonorous than [s]. The latter shows a sonority reversal since [b] is less sonorous than [r], the final consonant.

[13] Mora-sharing in CVCC

a. *Tableau for* /dars/→ [$da_{\mu}rs_{\mu}$] (*a lesson*) ([rs] = falling sonority)

/dars/	*$\sigma_{\mu\mu\mu}$	DEP-V	PARSE μ	*APP	SSP μ	SSP σ	NBHM	NBM-CC
a. σ μ μ μ d a r s	*!							
b. σ σ μ μ μ d a r i s		*!						
c. ω ϕ σ μ μ μ d a r s			*!					
☞ d. σ μ μ d a r s								*

b. Tableau for /sˤabr/ → [$\text{s}^{\text{ʕ}}\text{ab}_{\mu}\text{r}_{\mu}$] (*Patience*) ([br] = sonority reversal)

/sˤabr/	*σμμμ	DEP-V	PARSE μ	*APP	SSP μ	SSP σ	NBHM	NBM-CC
a. σ μ μ μ sˤ a b r	*!							
b. σ μ μ sˤ a b r				*!				
c. σ μ μ sˤ a b r					*!	*		*
☞ d. σ μ μ sˤ a b r						*	*	

In the first tableau, the final two consonants share a mora. Since SSP is not violated, the minimal violation principle favors violation of NBM-cc over NBHM. Exhaustive segmental parsing yields a bimoraic CVCC where the nucleus is adjoined to the head mora and the coda consonants share the second.

In the second tableau, the coda sequence [br] represents a violation of SSP, as the final [r] is more sonorous than the preceding [b]. As a result, the system opts for branching the head mora. The sequence [ab] in [sˤabr] represents a falling sonority, thus it satisfies SSPμ. The final consonant [r] is adjoined to the second mora, which makes sense given that it ranks high in the sonority hierarchy. The overall structure of the syllable, however, exhibits a sonority reversal, which incurs a violation of SSPσ. This violation is minimal though, as SSPσ is ranked lower than SSP_{μ} in the constraint hierarchy.

3 Conclusion

The aim of this paper is twofold; first, to make the argument that CVCC superheavy syllables in TA should be analyzed as bimoraic syllables just like their CVVC counterparts, and second to stress the necessity of a tautosyllabic analysis that takes into consideration the relative sonority of the rime consonants. These objectives have been met through alternating mora-sharing between the VC and the CC sequences of the CVCC syllable, depending on the type of sonority exhibited by the consonant cluster. Given that sonority is governed by SSP, two sub-types of SSP have been introduced on the basis of the domain of sonority they control; SSPσ controls sonority at the syllabic level while SSP_{μ} requires a falling sonority at the level of the segments affiliated with the same mora. Constraint interaction resolves in the following system: In the case where the cluster represents a sonority fall or a sonority plateau, the two consonants share a mora ($CV_{\mu}\widehat{CC}_{\mu}$) while in the case of a sonority reversal, the final C separately affiliates with the second mora. Thus, the preceding VC sequence shares the head mora ($C\widehat{VC}_{\mu}C_{\mu}$). Last, the analysis presented in this paper neutralizes the asymmetry between superheavy syllables and represents a further argument for the universal markedness of trimoraic syllables.

Works cited

Angoujard, J. P. (1990). *Metrical Structure of Arabic.* Dordrecht: Foris.

Bosisio, N. (2003). Vocoids and their prosodic distribution, with special reference to Italian and Arabic, Durham theses, Durham University. Available at Durham E-Theses Online: http://etheses.dur.ac.uk/4076/

Boudlal, A. (2001). *Constraint Interaction in the Phonology and Morphology of Casablanca Moroccan Arabic.* Doctoral dissertation. Rabat, Morocco: Mohammed V University. Rutgers Optimality Archive – 650.

Broselow, E. (1992). Parametric variation in Arabic dialect phonology. In Ellen Broselow, Mushira Eid & John J. McCarthy (eds.) *Perspectives on Arabic linguistics IV.* Amsterdam & Philadelphia: Benjamins. 7–45.

Broselow, E., M. Huffman, Su-I Chen & Ruohmei Hsieh. (1995). The timing structure of CVVC syllables. In Mushira Eid (ed.) *Perspectives on Arabic linguistics VII.* Amsterdam & Philadelphia: John Benjamins. 119–38

Broselow, E. Chen, S. & Huffman, M. (1997). Syllable weight: convergence of phonology and phonetics. *Phonology 14* (1). 47–82.

Hall, T. (2002). Against extrasyllabic consonants in German and English. *Phonology 19.* 33–75.

Hammond, M. (1999). *The Phonology of English. A Prosodic Optimality-Theoretic Approach.* Oxford: Oxford UP.

Hayes, B. (1989). Compensatory Lengthening in Moraic Phonology. *Linguistic Inquiry 20* (2). 253–306.

Hayes, B. (1991). *Metrical stress theory: principles and case studies.* Samizdat. Los Angeles. Published as Hayes 1995.

Hung, H. (1993). Iambicity, rhythm, and non-parsing. Ms. U of Ottawa. Rutgers Optimality Archive – 9.

Itô, J. and Mester, A. (1992). Weak layering and word binarity. Linguistics Research Center Report 92–09. U of California: Santa Cruz.

Jouini, M. (2014). Constraints on Tunisian Arabic epenthesis. *International Journal of Innovation and Applied Studies 9* (2), 819–28.

Jouini, M. (2015). On the Bimoraicity of Tunisian Arabic Open Monosyllables: A Moraic Optimality-Theoretic Approach. *International Journal of Humanities and Cultural Studies 2*(3), 454–70.

Kiparsky, P. (2003). Syllables and moras in Arabic. In Caroline Féry& Ruben van de Vijver (eds.) *The syllable in Optimality Theory*. Cambridge: Cambridge UP. 147–82.

Mahfoudhi, A. (2005). Moraic Syllable Structure and Edge Effects in Arabic. In M. T. Alhawary and E. Benmamoun, (eds.), *Perspectives on Arabic Linguistics XVII-XVIII* (123–50). Amsterdam: Benjamins.

McCarthy, J. and Prince, A. (1990). Prosodic morphology and templatic morphology. Retrieved 04-11-2007 from http://people.umass.edu/jjmccart template.pdf

Morelli, F. (2003). The Relative Harmony of /s+Stop/ Onsets, Obstruent Clusters and the Sonority Sequencing Principle. In C. Féry & R. van de Vijver (eds.), *The Syllable in Optimality Theory*. Cambridge: Cambridge UP. 356–71.

Piggott, G. (1999). At the Right Edge of Words. *The Linguistic Review 16* (2), 143–85.

Prillop, K. (2013). Feet, syllables, moras and the Estonian quantity system. *Linguistica Uralica* 49, 1–29.

Prince, A. and Smolensky, P. (1993/2004). *Optimality Theory: constraint interaction in generative grammar*. Maiden: Blackwell. (Revision of [1993] technical report, Rutgers University Center for Cognitive Science). Rutgers Optimality Archive – 537.

Rejili, C. and Ghazali, S. (2003). Consonant cluster duration in Standard Arabic. 15th International Congress of Phonetic Sciences, Barcelona.

Selkirk, E. (1981). Epenthesis and Degenerate Syllable in Cairene Arabic. In H. Borer and J. Aoun, (eds.), *Theoretical Issues in the Grammar of the Semitic Languages*. Cambridge, MA: MIT. 111–40.

Selkirk, E. (1984). Phonology and Syntax: The Relation Between Sound and Structure. Cambridge, MA: MIT Press.

Sherer, T. D. (1994). *Prosodic Phonotactics* (doctoral dissertation, U of Massachusetts, Amherst). Rutgers Optimality Archive –57.

Vaux, B. and Wolfe A. (2009). The appendix. In C. Carins and E. Raimy (eds.), *Contemporary Views on Architecture and Representations in Phonological Theory* (101–43). Cambridge, MA: MIT Press.

Watson, J. (2002). *The Phonology and Morphology of Arabic.* Oxford: Oxford UP.

Watson, J. (2007). Syllabification patterns in Arabic dialects: long segments and mora-sharing. *Phonology 24*. 335–56.

Yu Cho, Y. and King, T. H. (2003). Semisyllables and Universal Syllabification. In C. Féry & R. van de Vijver (eds.), *The syllable in Optimality Theory*. Cambridge: Cambridge UP. 183–12.

Speaking Anxiety, Order or Disorder?

Zeineb Ayachi, Institut Supérieur des Sciences Humaines de Jendouba, Tunisia

Abstract

This study, a replication research of Subaşı's (2010) work, is part of a larger study on the exploration of the fear of negative evaluation and self-perception as sources of skill-specific anxiety for a group of ESP Tunisian learners. Contrary to the original study, the fear of negative evaluation whether on its own or while interacting with self-perception was not found to be the source of speaking anxiety. Only self-perception was highlighted as the main anxiety source for this skill. The explanation for such findings emanates from the new Tunisian order yielded by the disorder that took place during the Jasmine Revolution of 2011. In fact, being able to challenge dictatorship was translated in the loss of the feeling of the fear of negative evaluation in expressing oneself. However, the way this group of IT and Multimedia engineering students perceived their performance was detected as the main source of the speaking anxiety. Pedagogical implications on how to deal with such a feeling for an optimum teaching are presented.

Keywords: order; disorder, speaking anxiety, self perception, fear of negative evaluation

Introduction

This work, a replication research of Subaşı's work (2010), is part of a larger study which explores the fear of negative evaluation (FNE) and self-perception as potential sources of speaking anxiety. In the original study of a group of Turkish English major students, both FNE and self-perception were found to be at the origin of speaking anxiety whether in isolation or in interaction with each other. In the present work, only self-perception was revealed to interact with speaking anxiety in a group of IT and Multimedia engineering students. One of the most prominent variables deriving from the setting explained the difference between the two studies.

The study was carried in the 2013/2014 academic year in an IT and Multimedia college in Tunisia. This period may be referred to as the post-revolution era where different perceptions of life, learning, work, relationships, and feelings came into existence. In fact, 2011 was the year when the Tunisian people managed to oust a long-feared dictator. As a result, people now refer to the events, activities or atmosphere as pre-2011, and post-2011. Contrary to the pre-revolution era, where many human rights were violated, the post-revolution era has been characterized by a will to recover the missed rights, including first and foremost the freedom of expression which has become a building stone that allows self-expression in various fields, as well as participation in decision-making (Petersson n.p.).

New concepts emanating from the new spirit of the revolution came to be adopted. In fact, a new disorder trend was established. Many managers who once abused their power were ousted, people from the old regime were persecuted, and authorities were no longer respected. People have become eager to regain their long-abused rights and mainly the freedom of expression. Unions engaged in an endless tug of war with the ministries of the successive governments. Strikes and sit-ins in all sectors shaped the new face of Tunisia. As a result, a new order introduced by the 'No more fear' slogan and established by the revolution disorder stipulated that people should no longer fear anyone or anything.

In line with this new background, the findings of the present study suggest that the anxiety feelings of a group of IT and Multimedia students did not emanate from FNE but from their self-perception as potential speakers of English.

Review of the literature

Good communication in English, as a growing need, has imposed a huge worldwide demand for achieving a good grasp of English among non-native speakers (NNS) (Mahmoodzadeh 466). Developing a good speaking ability has been recognized among NNS as a crucial factor that displays a good command of the language. However, speaking as an oral performance is probably considered the most stressful skill among the four skills from the point of view of both EFL teachers and learners (for example Subaşı, 2010; Yaikhong & Usaha, 2012).

Horwitz et al. indicate that speaking in class is often perceived as "high risk, low gain" (129). This is due to the fact that speaking in class in front of others may be debilitative for EFL learners (Subaşı, 2010; Basic, 2011). This emanates from the fear of making mistakes, losing face as well as the fear of being criticized by the teacher (Young, 1991; Bailey & Nunan, 1996). Therefore, some learners may view learning and speaking a foreign language in the classroom as an eternal problem as a result of the fear of making mistakes (Tang et al., 2013).

Speaking anxiety is not exclusive to foreign language class (McCroskey et al, 1985). It may occur in a person's native language or in a foreign language. Indeed, in a review of the literature, McCroskey et al. report results indicating that Japanese students have high speaking anxiety in both languages (14). Their hypothesis suggested that "if international students are apprehensive about speaking their own language, their fear of communicating in English must be magnified tenfold" (Jung & McCroskey 172). This shows how much apprehension an EFL learner may experience in practicing the target language orally.

FNE as a source of speaking anxiety

Horwitz et al. (1986) define FNE as "apprehension about others' evaluations, avoidance of evaluative situations, and the expectation that others would evaluate oneself negatively" (128). In this sense,

Young (1991) argues that students are "more concerned about how (for example, when, what, where or how often) their mistakes are corrected rather than whether correction should be administered in class" (429).

FNE is similar to test anxiety. However, it has a broader range, because it is not restricted to test-taking situations; it may take place in social situations as well (MacIntyre & Gardner 105). In this context, MacIntyre and Gardner refer to the source of FNE being the close association between one's self concept and one's self expression (105). FNE is observed when foreign language learners experience inability to make the appropriate social impression (Horwitz et al., 128). It is an apprehension towards assessment by others and an attempt to evade evaluative situations.

Subaşı (2010) explored a correlation between FNE and FL anxiety as far as the speaking skill is concerned. She found that FNE was a source of anxiety in Turkish students in the English FL classroom; hence a significant positive correlation between these two variables was displayed ($r=.488$, $p=.000$, $n=55$) (38).

Subaşı's findings also revealed that there was an interaction between students' FNE and their self-perceptions (42). In fact, the students in question felt more anxious in the FL when they realized that their speaking ability was poorer than that of their classmates and native speakers of English.

Self-perception as a source of speaking anxiety

Learners of a foreign language sometimes tend to perceive themselves negatively in the foreign language classroom setting as a result of the inability to speak correctly, and/or understand the target language in its spoken and written forms (Horwitz et al. 128). Likewise, Subaşı (2010) found out that there was a negative correlation between foreign language anxiety and self-perceived ability in the speaking skill (9). Subaşı, (2010) accounted for such findings by the fact that her Turkish EFL learners had low self-esteem, and perceived their communication as less effective than that of their peers or native speakers (45).

The above findings were supported by some researchers and rejected by others. In fact, Gregerson and Horwitz (2002) suggest that sometimes EFL learners set extremely high perfectionist standards which sometimes may not be reached (563). In this case, they are likely to impose very high objectives on themselves which are sometimes difficult to meet. This causes dissatisfaction with one's learning ability and hence induces anxiety. On the other hand, Horváth and Nikolov report that the more learners tend to have perfectionist feelings; the less anxious they are (134).

When observing a negative relationship between anxiety and students' self-rating of their language achievement, MacIntyre et al. (1997) concluded that self-perception not only reveals competence but is likely to evaluate some affective construct (280). Similarly, Cheng's study revealed a negative correlation between foreign language anxiety and self-perception of competence (79). In this regard, self-perception which may involve learners' bias in judging their FL achievement, especially if they believe their level of L2 competence to be very low, is reported as a source for FLA (Horwitz et al., 1986; MacIntyre et al., 1997; Cheng, 2001).

Interaction of variables as a model for the sources of foreign language anxiety

Kitano (2001) is among the researchers who highlighted the interaction of independent variables as a cause of FLA. In a study exploring two potential sources of the anxiety of 212 EFL Japanese students in speaking, namely FNE and self-perceived speaking ability, Kitano found out a positive correlation between FNE and speaking anxiety, and a negative correlation between self-perception of ability and anxiety. However, there was no interaction between FNE and self-perceived ability as a predictor for speaking anxiety.

Subaşı (2010), on the other hand, found different results. In her examination of FNE and self-perception as two potential sources of speaking anxiety, she found out that there was an interaction between FNE and two self-rating scales, namely; Self-rating for the Current Level of Study (SR-CL) and Self-rating Can Do Scale (SR-CDS) which best predicted the speaking anxiety with her 55 Turkish EFL students (46).

In this regard, the present study explored the interaction of such variables with a group of non-English majors. Such an exploration provided a model that predicted the speaking anxiety for this particular group.

Research questions

The present work, by replicating Subaşı's study (2010) on FNE and self-perception as potential sources of speaking anxiety, addressed the interaction of FNE and self-perception in predicting FLA in the speaking skill. In this regard, three research questions replicated from Subaşı's work (2010) were addressed:

1. What is the relationship between the anxiety level of an advanced ESP student and his or her dispositional fear of negative evaluation regarding the speaking skill?
2. What is the relationship between the anxiety level of an advanced ESP student and the self-perception of his or her ability in English regarding the speaking skill?
3. Do fear of negative evaluation and self-perception of ability in English interact to relate to the anxiety level of individual ESP learners in the speaking skill?

Methodology

Participants

The present research was conducted at the Institut Supérieur des Arts Multimédias in Manouba University (ISAMM), Tunisia during the 2013-2014 academic year. 48 subjects (22 males and 26 females) from the third year IT and Multimedia Engineering section, whose age ranged between 23 and 25 participated. Data of two students were discarded because their questionnaires were not duly filled in. The final sample included 46 participants: 26 females and 20 males.

Instruments

Instruments exploring both quantitative and qualitative data were used to evaluate the main sources of the speaking anxiety. The foreign language class anxiety scale (FLCAS) (Horwitz et al., 1986, 129) was used to assess the speaking anxiety level. Two other scales were used to assess the independent variables. One is the FNE, and the other is self-perception which includes three sub-scales; namely Self-Rating Can Do (SR-CD) scale, Self-Rating for the Current Level (SR-CL) scale, and the Self-Rating Expected Perception by the English (SR-EPE) scale. Qualitative data were explored by means of semi-structured interviews and group discussions where results of the research were shared with the participants. Data from the different instruments were triangulated.

Data analysis

Excel spreadsheets together with the Statistical Analysis System (SAS) were used as analytical procedure tools where data were entered in order to investigate the first, second, and third research questions. The different scales were coded and displayed in the form of columns in Excel. Every participant's information respective to every scale was entered in these columns in order to obtain quantitative numerical data. To answer research questions 1 and 2, following Subaşı's data analysis, three methods were used: one is descriptive, the other is correlational, and the third one is interactional. The descriptive method was used in order to identify the participants' level of their fear of negative evaluation, their self-perception evaluation and the level of anxiety they experienced in the speaking skill. This was carried out by computing the mean (M), standard deviation (SD), maximum, minimum, and the frequency distribution of the variables.

The correlational method was used in order to see the possible association between the dependent (FLCA) and the independent variables (FNE and self-perception). In this regard, correlation coefficients were calculated to evaluate the magnitude of the correlation as well as to check whether the direction of the correlation between the independent and dependent variables was positive or negative. A $p < .05$ value was also used in order to examine the statistical significance of the FNE/speaking anxiety and self-perception/speaking anxiety correlation.

The interactional method was carried out to answer the third research question, whereby multiple regression analyses and a two-way ANOVA were used to create a model which identifies which variable among the FNE and the three self-perception ratings predicted English speaking anxiety. Finally, the triangulation of the quantitative data was carried by means of the interview and group discussion analysis.

Results and discussion

Research question 1

What is the relationship between the anxiety level of an advanced ESP student and his or her dispositional fear of negative evaluation?

FNE correlated positively with the anxiety level of the participants in the speaking skill (*r*=.089, p=.555). We should note that the Pearson correlation coefficient is too low to indicate a significant relationship between the two variables. This finding suggests that FNE did not have any effect on the anxiety level pertaining to the speaking skill of the present participants.

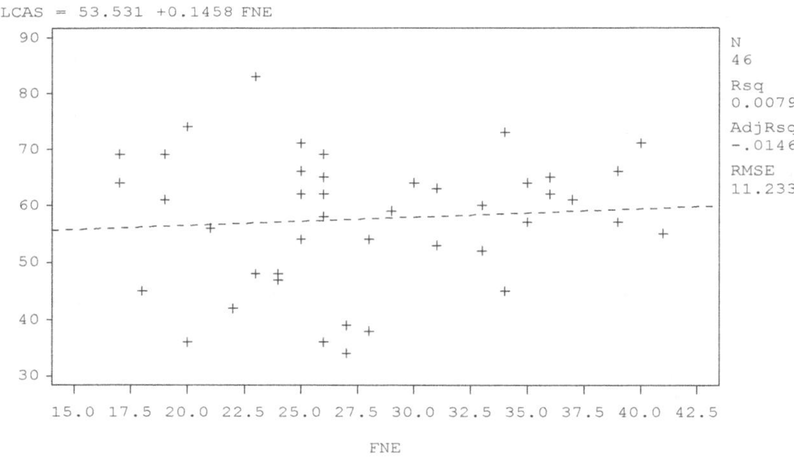

Figure 1. The relationship between FLCAS and FNE

The interview data with the present participants further confirmed this finding. In fact, none of the participants who were interviewed showed a concern about the fear of being negatively evaluated by the teacher, their peers or native speakers.

Such a finding contrasts with that of Subaşı's (2010) who found that FNE was one source of speaking anxiety in the Turkish classroom (44). According to her, the students in question feared the negative evaluation by their peers, and for fear of creating a stupid image of themselves, they preferred to remain silent.

The inconsistency between the results of the present findings and Subaşı's might be attributed to the different participants' majors. In the present study, the engineer students were learning English as a required module while in Subaşı's study, students were learning English as a major subject as they were enrolled in the English Language Teaching (ELT) department of Anadolu University. Therefore, as English was not the current participants' major subject may explain why the latter might have been less subject to FNE as far as the speaking anxiety skill is concerned.

However, although such a hypothesis was supported by some researchers, it was rejected by others. In fact, while Hou (2013), in his study on anxiety of English majors and non-English majors in Taiwan, found out that non-English majors had a higher level of FNE than their English major counterparts. Wei (2013), in his exploration of the sources of anxiety with English and non-English majors in China, found no significant difference in the FNE level between these groups of learners. However, elsewhere, FNE was assumed to be a minor variable affecting the anxiety level of non-English majors.

In fact, researchers like Lee support the idea that non-English majors do not care much about being negatively evaluated regarding their speaking skill (176). Lee found out that FNE was the variable that affected learning anxiety the least especially with Mechanical Engineering students. Lee explained this phenomenon by the fact that these students' major studies were taught in English and that the majority of the textbooks were written in English. They, therefore, focused more on understanding written materials relating to their specialty subjects than on interaction in the English class. Similarly, students in the present survey learned some materials in English in their specialty subjects. An informal discussion with the specialty teachers about their level in English revealed that they had some gaps in English. However, this did not prevent them from teaching some materials related to their specialty in English. The idea of not being proficient in English as far as fluent interaction and pronunciation are concerned while being able to teach some specialty field materials might have influenced these students whose concern was not worrying about what others might think about their abilities, but the main concern was whether they were able to communicate an idea.

Another explanation for the inconsistency of the current findings with those advanced by Subaşı might be due to the different learners' respective ages and university levels. In fact, while the participants' age range in the present research was between 23 and 25, and were in their last year of university study, Subaşı's students' age ranged between 17 and 19, and were in their first year of university study (36). The difference may relate to the maturity level experienced by each type of participants. Being in the last year of university education might reveal more maturity, experience, and self-confidence than being freshmen.

Such findings are partly in line with those advanced by Aydin. In fact, Aydin found out that senior EFL learners were less afraid of making mistakes than their junior counterparts (434). Learners in the present study were senior learners. Their answers in both the quantitative and qualitative instruments revealed a lower degree of fear towards leaving an unfavorable impression, disapproval by others, and making mistakes. However, the fact that senior students are less afraid of making mistakes is not always true. Kitano, for example, in his investigation of the sources of speaking anxiety with a group of English speaking students learning Japanese, found out that FNE affected the level of anxiety with the advanced students more than with the intermediate and elementary students (553).

Research question 2

What is the relationship between the anxiety level of an advanced ESP student and the self-perception of his or her ability in English regarding the speaking skill?

The examination of the scatter plots and Pearson correlations shows that there were significant negative relationships between speaking anxiety and the three self ratings, SR-CD, SR-CL, and SR-EPE displaying a respective statistical significance of $p<.0001$ (see figures 2 to 4 for the scatter plots).

SR-CD and the FLCA

A moderate significant negative correlation is noted between speaking anxiety and the speaking SR-CD Scale (*r*= -.596, p<.0001) (figure 2). Hence, this means that the lower an individual's SR-CD is, the higher their speaking anxiety, a finding in line with Subaşı (2010, 9) and Occhipinti (2009, 80), while contrasting Kitano's (2001, 554) conclusions concerning the lack of significant correlation between SR-CD and speaking anxiety.

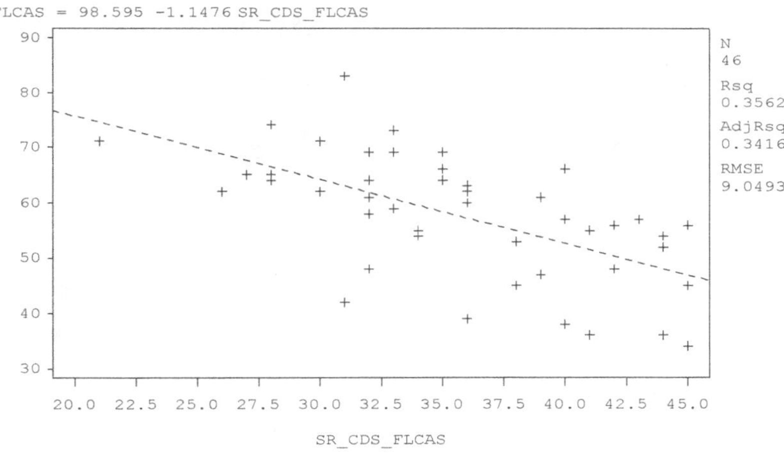

Figure 2. The relationship between speaking anxiety and SR-CD Scale

In the speaking Can Do scale, the present participants deemed that it was a little difficult for them to express themselves on items 13, 14, and 15. This is in line with Takahashi (2010) who stated that these items were difficult even for quite proficient non-native speakers (95). So, it would not be surprising that these items affected the participants' self-perception, and hence their speaking anxiety level as they were non-English majors. On the other hand, in line with Tang et al., findings from the interview data revealed that these students did not perceive themselves to have good pronunciation which increased their speaking anxiety. They judged that their current achievement did not allow them to speak confidently in class.

SR-CL and the FLCA

The Pearson correlation (*r*=-.690, p<.000) which indicated a significant negative moderate relationship between speaking anxiety and SR-CL showed that the lower the SR-CL is, the higher the speaking anxiety. Again similar to Subaşı's findings, the present participants felt anxious in the speaking skill, because they felt that they did not achieve enough proficiency. This means that their current level was below their expectations which made them apprehend engaging in a speaking activity. Such a result supports findings from previous qualitative and quantitative studies, indicating a negative correlation between anxiety and self-perceived competence in a foreign language (Cheng 652; Kitano 555).

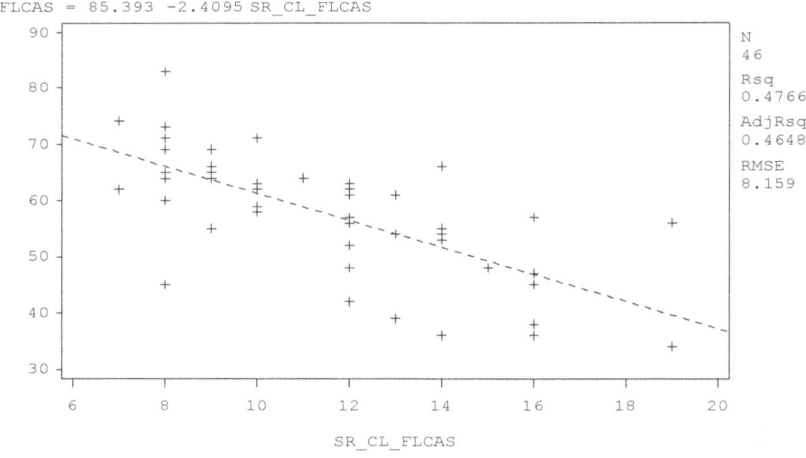

Figure 3. The relationship between speaking anxiety and *SR-CL*

SR-EPE and the FLCA

The negative moderate relationship between speaking anxiety and SR-EPE (*r*= -.559, p<.000) meant that the lower an individual's SR-EPE is, the higher their speaking anxiety, a finding that supports Kitano's (2001) study about learners of Japanese as a foreign language. Qualitative data uncovered some of the sources that were responsible for a low speaking perception when it came to be evaluated by native speakers.

During the interview, a shortage of vocabulary, poor grammar, and bad pronunciation were at the origin of holding a low-perception of one's speaking ability regarding native speakers' expectations, which in turn induced speaking anxiety. Such findings are in line with Young (1991) who suggests that anxiety triggered by the differ-ence between a learner's perceived competence and reality may emanate from the learner's perceived pronunciation compared to that of native speakers. However, the reality is that most "students, unless they are highly motivated, will not sound like a native speaker" (428).

This reverse relationship between speaking ability and one's expected perception by the English may also emanate from the lack of contact with native speakers. Confirming data in the semi-structured interview, participants reported, during the meeting in which results were shared, that they had never had the opportunity to interact with a native speaker face to face. They sometimes interacted with some English-speaking people on some social networks, but this was carried out by chat messages. The present participants really apprehended direct contact with native speakers. This finding is in line with Kitano (2001, 549), Ohata (2005, 6), and Basic (2011, 11) who found out that talking with native speakers was a dreaded activity which may lead learners to wonder whether they were understood by native speakers, and in a worse scenario avoid such an interaction.

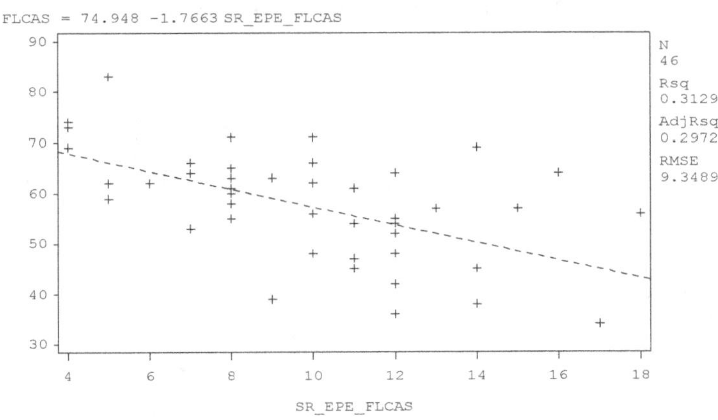

Figure 4. The relationship between speaking anxiety and SR-EPE

Research Question 3

Do the fear of negative evaluation and self-perception of ability in English interact together to relate to the anxiety level of individual ESP learners pertaining to the speaking skill?

The regression analysis together with a two-way ANOVA procedure helped determine which independent variables among the FNE and the three self-perception ratings had the highest impact on the anxiety level of the speaking skill. The impact of the interaction between those independent variables on the FLCA was measured by the squared partial correlation coefficients. Depending on the shared variance, the impact was measured as low (2% to 12.99%), medium (13 to 25.99%) or high (26% and above).

As noted in table 1, the independent variables that displayed the highest impact on the speaking anxiety are as follows by order of importance: SR-CD explaining as much as 39, 5% of the total variance in the participants' FLCA predictors (p=.000). SR-CL, on the other hand, displayed a medium variance of 19% (p=.002). However, SR-EPE accounted only for 2% of the total variance predicting the FLCA anxiety (p=.053). No interaction of variables was noted concerning FLCA. Self-perception, and particularly SR-CD, emerged as the best predictor of speaking anxiety. This leads to the assumption that self-perception as the main source of FLCA both in isolation and in the presence of other variables highlights the importance of the present learners' subjective self-perception as a key factor affecting their speaking anxiety.

Table 1

Model of Predictors of Speaking Anxiety

Source	DF	Mean square	F Value	Pr > F	Squared Partial Corr Type I
FNE_Level	2	117.160	1.79	.1882	.007
SR_CDS_Level	2	623.228	9.53	.000	.363
SR_CL_Level	2	522.809	8.00	.002	.192
SR_EPE_Level	2	217.471	3.33	.053	.016
FNE_Level*SR_CDS_ Level	4	65.563	1.00	.425	.019
FNE_Level*SR_CL_ Level	3	130.139	1.99	.142	.086
FNE_Level*SR_EPE_ Level	1	7.970	.12	.730	.003
SR_CDS_ Level *SR_CL_Level	1	3.215	.05	.826	.046
SR_CDS_ Level *SR_EPE_ Level	2	65.683	1.00	.381	.021
SR_CL_ Level *SR_EPE_ Level	2	135.562	2.07	.147	.064

Such findings contradict Subaşı's English majoring participants' anxiety predictors concerning the speaking skill where she found that FNE and self-perception interacted and impacted FLA, regarding the speaking skill (46). However, the findings of the present investi-gation support Kitano's findings as the latter did not find an interaction between FNE and self-perception regarding the speaking skill (557). Thus, in line with Horváth and Nikolov as well as earlier studies indicating a negative relationship between self-perceived ability and FLA such as those presented by Young (1991), MacIntyre et al. (1997), Kitano (2001), Cheng (2002), and Yang (2012), self-perception was revealed as the best predictor of the speaking anxiety. Therefore, a low perception of proficiency in the speaking skill contributed to a higher anxiety level in that skill.

To sum up this part, findings concerning predictors of the speaking anxiety showed that the two variables FNE and self-perception when combined together using multiple regression analysis could not predict the present participants' speaking anxiety. The absence of FNE and the emergence of self-perception as the main speaking anxiety predictor may be attributed to the latter's awareness of their limitations in English and failure to meet their perfectionist expectations about the target language; a prior feeling to apprehending negative evaluation.

Viewing the context of the study, which took place two years after the revolution in Tunisia, the fact that FNE did not affect the anxiety level of the speaking skill can be due to the changes brought about by the Tunisian revolution, which gave some power to young people. Such empowerment, referred to as community empowerment by Lord and Hutchinson (1993), has valued young people's initiation of the Tunisian revolution. In fact, young people nowadays are praised for not fearing the oppression of the previous regime or any other authority. This context may have provided another explanation for the lack of effect of FNE on the anxiety level of the speaking skill.

Conclusion and pedagogical implications

The main aim of the present study was to replicate Subaşı's (2010) findings concerning FNE and self-perception as potential sources of speaking anxiety. The study revealed different outcomes from those of Subaşı's (2010).

The discrepancy between the findings in the two studies relates to different factors. Some of the inconsistency may be attributed to the different participants' age, majors, as well as to the different social contexts. The absence of FNE as a source of speaking anxiety can be explained by the 'No more fear' slogan directed against all types of authorities in the country since the 2011 revolution. The emergence of self-perception as the main speaking anxiety predictor may be attributed to the participants' failure to meet their perfectionist expectations, a more significant feeling to apprehending negative evaluation.

Anxiety is such a complex phenomenon, and its analysis may be endless as the variables that induce it are multiple, and may change from individual to individual and even within the same individual as they are affected by external factors such as time and space. On the other hand, its measurement, though intended to be as comprehensive as possible, still suffers some limitations. The findings of the present study are not definite, and may not always be consistent with different individuals, and even with the same individuals in different contexts and on different occasions.

Pedagogical implications that emanate from this study suggest that it is necessary to remind language instructors, who view foreign language anxiety as a marginal variable affecting the achievement of their non-English major learners at the level of higher education, that besides the linguistic challenge many of their students face, affective factors can impact their performance. Data from the interview revealed that some participants had some previous unrewarding experiences with their past English teachers. As self-perception was revealed to be the most significant variable affecting the participants' speaking anxiety, several recommendations that pertain to the speaking skill need to be taken into account in order to make these learners and similar ones develop more positive beliefs about themselves and be more confident in their speaking skill.

In a "supportive and friendly environment" (Aida 164; El Khafaifi 217) and "a psychologically secure environment" (Saito & Samimy

247), learners would feel more comfortable in the language class. It is worthwhile to reflect on the type of activities implemented in class as they may be one of the major causes of FLA related to speaking (Young 433). It is also the role of the English teacher to know how to handle the delicate issue of the learners' limitations in the target language as far as pronunciation is concerned. In so doing, teachers can change learners' beliefs about language learning inherent in their perfectionist attitude, which could be one of the factors of their feeling anxious.

Scheduling some interaction with English speaking people in class through networked classrooms would help learners judge their speaking ability more fairly. In fact, in so doing, learners can have more authentic interactions with native speakers. Such natural interactions may serve as a standard against which the learners can evaluate their learning.

Recommendations for future research

This study should be replicated with larger populations including engineer students from different fields, and even engineers in offices from different specialty areas. Another recommendation is to add classroom observation, students' videotaping during the interview, and participants' diaries to the set of the tools used in the present research in order to add more validity to the results.

Works cited

Aida, Yukie. "Examination of Horwitz, Horwitz, and Cope's Construct of Foreign Language Anxiety: The Case of Students of Japanese." The *Modern Language Journal* 78 (1994): 155–68.

Aydin, Selami. An Investigation on the Language Anxiety and Fear of Negative Evaluation Among Turkish EFL Learners." *Asian EFL Journal* 30.1(2008): 421–44. http://w3.balikesir.edu.tr/~saydin/index_dosyalar/testanxiety.pdf. Web. 10 November 2012.

Bailey, Kathleen. M. and Nunan, David. *Voices from the Language Classroom: Qualitative Research in Second Language Education*. Cambridge University Press, 1996. www.booksgoogle.com Web. 8 January 2012.

Basic, Lejla. "Speaking Anxiety. An Obstacle to Second Language Learning?" M.A. thesis. Akademin for Utbildning Och Ekonomi. 2011. http://www.diva-portal.org/smash/get/diva2:453921/FULLTEXT01.pdf. Web. 1 September 2013.

Cheng, Ys. "Factors Associated with Foreign Language Writing Anxiety." *Foreign Language Annals* 3.6 (2002): 647–56.

Cheng, Ys. "Learners' Beliefs and Second Language Anxiety." *Concentric: Studies in English Literature and Linguistics* 27.2 (2001): 75–90.

EL Khafaifi, Hussein. "Listening Comprehension and Anxiety in the Arabic Language Classroom." *The Modern Language Journal* 89, ii (2005): 206–20. http://old.fltrp.com/wyzx/07techer/doc/papers/Listening%20comprehension%20and%20anxiety.pdf. Web. 5 October 2012.

Gregerson, Tammy and Horwitz, Elaine. K. "Language Learning and Perfectionism: Anxious and Non-Anxious Language Learners' Reactions to Their Own Oral Performance." The *Modern Language Journal* 86 (2002): 562–71.

Horváth, József and Marianne, *Nikolov. Eds.* "Predictors of Foreign-Language Anxiety: Examining the Relationship Between Anxiety and Other Individual Learner Variables." *Empirical Studies in English Applied Linguistics* (2007): 123–48.

Horwitz, Elaine K; Horwitz, Michael B. and Cope, Joann. "Foreign Language Classroom Anxiety." *The Modern Language Journal* 70.2 (1986): 125–32.

Hou, Yen-Jou. "Taiwanese College Students' Anxiety About Foreign Language Learning Between English Majors and Non-English Majors." *WHAMpOA – An Interdisciplinary Journal* 65 (2013): 57–80. http://www2.cma.edu.tw/u_edu/journal/65files/%2857-0%29Taiwanese_College_students.pdf. Web. 27 February 2014.

Jung, Hye Yoon and McCroskey, James. C. "Communication Apprehension in A First Language and Self-Perceived Competence as Predictors of Communication Apprehension in A Second Language: A Study of Speakers of English as a Second Language." *Communication Quarterly* 52.2 (2004): 170–81.

Kitano, Kazu. "Anxiety in the College Japanese Language Classroom." *The Modern Language Journal* 85 (2001): 549–66.

Lee, Mei. Ling. "Differences in The Learning Anxieties Affecting College Freshman Students Of EFL, Global Perspectives, Local Initiatives: Reflections and Practices In ELT." Eds. Jaidev, Radhika et al. Centre for English Language Communication National University of Singapore, 2013. 169–82. http://www.nus.edu.sg/celc/research/books/3rdsymposium/169to182-lee.pdf. Web. 22 February 2014.

Lord, John and Hutchinson, Peggy. "The Process of Empowerment: Implications for Theory and Practice." *Canadian Journal of Community Mental Health* 12.1 (1993): 5–22. http://www.johnlord.net/web_documents/process_of_empowerment.pdf. Web 20 April 2014.

MacIntyre, Peter. D. and Gardner, Robert. C. "Methods and Results in The Study of Anxiety and Language Learning: A Review of the Literature." *Language Learning* 41.1 (1991): 85–117.

MacIntyre, Peter. D., Noels, Kimberly A. and Clément, Richard. "Biases in Self-Ratings of Second Language Proficiency: The Role of Language Anxiety." *Language Learning* 47.2 (1997): 265–87.

Mahmoodzadeh, Masoud. "Investigating Foreign Language Speaking Anxiety Within the EFL Learner's Interlanguage System: The Case of Iranian Learners." *Journal of Language Teaching and Research* 3.3 (2012): 466–76.

https://www.ucd.ie/t4cms/Guide70.pdf. Web. 3 April 2012.

McCroskey, James. C., Gudykunst, William. B., and Nishida, Tsukasa. "Communication Apprehension Among Japanese Students in Native and Second Language". *Communication Research Reports*. 2.1 (1985): 11–15. http://www.jamescmccroskey.com/publications/126.pdf. Web. 9 January 2015.

Occhipinti, Alessia. "Foreign Language Anxiety in In-class Speaking Activities – Two Learning Contexts". Thesis. The University of Oslo, 2009. Online https://www.duo.uio.no/bitstream/handle/10852/25584/Daxstamparexoggixultima.pdf?sequence=1. Web. 3 April 2014.

Ohata, Kota. "Potential Sources of Anxiety for Japanese Learners of English: Preliminary Case Interviews with Five Japanese College Students in the U.S." *TESL-EJ* 9. 3 (2005): 1–21. http://www.tesl-ej.org/ej35/a3.pdf. Web. 22 February 2014.

Petersson, Catherine. *Freedom of Expression and The Downfall of a Regime: The Tunisian Revolution and the Transition to Democracy*. Mänskliga rättighetsstudier, 2011. https://lup.lub.lu.se/luur/download?func=downloadFile&recordOId=2371802&fileOId=23718 03. Web. 23 June 2015.

Saito, Yoshiko and Samimy, Keiko. K. "Foreign Language Anxiety and Language Performance: A Study of Learner Anxiety in Beginning, Intermediate, and Advanced-Level College Students of Japanese." *Foreign Language Annals* 29.2 (1996): 239–51.

Subaşı, Gonca. "What are The Main Sources of Turkish EFL Students Anxiety in Oral Practice." *Turkish Online Journal of Qualitative Inquiry* 1.2 (2010): 29–49. http://www.tojqi.net/articles/TOJQI_2_4/TOJQI_2_4_Article_7.pdf. Web. 5 July 2012.

Takahashi, Ayumi. "Foreign Language Writing Apprehension: Its Relationships with Motivation, Self-Perceived Target Language Ability, And Actual Language Ability." *Niigata Studies in Foreign Languages and Cultures* 15 (2010): 89–100. http://dspace.lib.niigata-u.ac.jp:8080/dspace/bitstream/10191/13158/1/15_89-100.pdf. Web. 29 April 2014.

Tang, Xin.; Zhang, Shengqi.; Li, Yucong.; and Zhao, Miqiang. "Study on Correlation of English Pronunciation Self-Concept to English

Learning." *English Language Teaching* 6. 4 (2013): 74–9.

Wei, Jianhua. "The Main Construct of the Chinese Bouyei College Learners' ECA." *Journal of Studies in Social Sciences* 5.2 (2013): 328–351. http://infinitypress.info. Web. 27 February 2014.

Yaikhong, Kriangkrai and Usaha, Siriluck. "A Measure of EFL Public Speaking Class Anxiety: Scale Development and Preliminary Validation and Reliability." *English Language Teaching* 5.12 (2012): 23–35.
http://files.eric.ed.gov/fulltext/EJ1080110.pdf. Web. 28 March 2013.

Yang, Hui Chun. "Language Anxiety, Acculturation, And L2 Self: A Relational Analysis in The Taiwanese Cultural Context." *Electronic Journal of Foreign Language Teaching*. 9 2 (2012): 183–93.
http://e-flt.nus.edu.sg/v9n22012/yang.pdf. Web. 2 May 2014.

Young, Dolly Jesusita. "Creating A Low Anxiety Classroom Environment: What Does Language Anxiety Research Suggest?" *The Modern Language Journal* 75 (1991): 426–39.

La polysémie du verbe porter: de l'ordre vers le désordre et vice versa

Hajer Ochi (Institut Supérieur des Sciences Humaines de Jendouba)
Laboratoire de Recherches Langues, Discours et Cultures

Résumé

La plupart des morphèmes lexicaux et grammaticaux sont polysémiques: ils prennent un sens différent dans certains contextes grammaticaux et/ou énonciation. Victorri et Fuchs (1996) indiquent que plus de 40% de mots dans le dictionnaire *Petit Robert* sont polysémiques. En plus, la polysémie touche essentiellement des mots du vocabulaire de base. Seuls les mots techniques ou savants, et encore pas toujours, sont véritablement monosémiques. La polysémie est donc tout à fait «centrale dans la langue: elle représente la règle plutôt que l'exception» (*ibid.* 13).

La polysémie relève des moyens auxquels la langue a recours pour répondre aux exigences du principe d'économie.

Porter est un des verbes à combinatoire large et qui présente de ce fait un éventail sémantique considérable. Les dictionnaires ne font que répertorier une masse d'effets de sens qu'il est impossible de réduire à l'unité, si l'on part d'un «sens premier» mettant en relation ce verbe, et, par exemple, la notion de poids, ou d'un simple maintien. En outre, quelques acceptions intransitives viennent compliquer le problème, et il est si vrai qu'on ne voit pas bien comment mettre en relation *porter une alliance* et *sa tête a porté contre une pierre*.

Nous essayerons de rendre compte de la complexité du verbe *porter,* en tant que verbe polysémique et distinguer son sens précis qui varie d'un contexte à un autre.

En outre, nous mettrons en relief ses trois statuts à savoir prédicatif, support et en tête d'une structure figée.

Mots-clefs: polysémie, ambiguïté, construction de sens, verbe support, figement.

Le premier à avoir utilisé le mot « polysémie » est Michel Bréal (1897) qui la définit comme un processus dynamique se réalisant dans le temps et engendrant de nouveaux sens: «à mesure qu'une signification nouvelle est donnée au mot, il a l'air de se multiplier et de produire des exemplaires nouveaux, semblables de forme, mais différents de valeur».[1]

1. Les sources de la polysémie:

Des données aussi bien linguistiques qu'extralinguistiques peuvent générer la polysémie. L'un des domaines linguistiques étroitement liés au phénomène de la polysémie est la syntaxe. Dans la pratique courante, il suffit souvent d'énumérer les différents environnements dans lesquels une lexie peut apparaître pour illustrer ses différentes acceptions. La syntaxe considère donc que la polysémie est à étudier en rapport avec les contraintes syntagmatiques liées à l'emploi du mot.

Les tenants de l'école du distributionnalisme sont de fervents défenseurs de ce point de vue. Selon eux, seul l'axe syntagmatique confère un contenu sémantique aux unités linguistiques si bien qu'une unité n'a de sens qu'à l'intérieur d'un environnement syntaxique. Ainsi, déco(n)textualisé, un verbe comme *porter*, par exemple, sera considéré comme dénué de tout sens. Il en ressort que la polysémie d'une lexie comme *porter* n'est définissable qu'à partir d'environnements comme:

(i) *Porter un enfant*
(ii) *Porter aisément, avec difficulté*
(iii) *Porter dans ses bras*
(iv) *Porter le poids d'un péché*
(v) *Porter le destin d'un pays*
(vi) *Porter de la drogue*
(vii) *Porter une arme au poing*

Etc.

En l'absence de l'axe de combinaisons, tous les sens virtuels recensés par l'axe paradigmatique finissent souvent par perdre une

[1] Michel Bréal, (1897), *Essai de sémantique*, chap. XIV, (p. 444).

signification précise.

L'impact de l'emploi d'une unité lexicale dans une structure syntaxique est indéniable, la notion d'*emploi* permet, selon Gaston Gross[2] de rendre compte des contraintes syntagmatiques. «C'est une constatation empirique que tout changement de sens d'un prédicat est corrélé à un changement de schémas d'arguments»,[3] avant d'ajouter que la polysémie d'un *prédicat* est liée à la nature des mots en position d'*arguments*.

Mais le traitement qu'il préconise appelle à tenir compte des contraintes entraînées par l'analyse de certains prédicats. Ces contraintes sont en relation avec la syntaxe particulière des verbes symétriques, la possibilité ou l'impossibilité de pronominaliser le ou les arguments (objets), la résistance de certains schémas syntaxiques au test de la passivation, le degré de figement de quelques combinaisons, etc.

L'inventaire des différentes significations d'un prédicat nécessite que les *classes d'objets* d'un prédicat soient affinées de manière à attribuer à chaque prédicat la catégorie d'arguments qu'il exige:

a) Certains prédicats s'associent à n'importe quel type de substantif. C'est le cas du verbe *intéresser* par exemple:
(*Paul, ce cheval, cette voiture, ce trajet, ce travail*) *m'intéresse*.
C'est également le cas des objets des verbes comme *penser à* ou *parler de*:
Je pense à (Paul, ce cheval, cette voiture, ce travail, cette idée)
Je parle de (Paul, ce cheval, cette voiture, ce travail, cette idée)

b) D'autres prédicats sélectionnent de grandes classes sémantiques (les hyperclasses) qui, selon G.Gross, sont au nombre de six: *humain, animal, végétal, concret, locatif, temporel*.

c) Les autres prédicats, les plus nombreux, nécessitent, pour être décrits, des classes plus fines, appelées *classes* d'objets[4]. Dans notre communication, nous avons choisi le verbe *porter* pour

---

[2] Gaston Gross, *traitement automatique du français*, Paris 13, Laboratoire de linguistique informatique. CNRS, p. 25.
[3] *Ibidem*.
[4] *Aéroplanes*, *constructions*, *arbres* sont des exemples de ces classes.

sa forte polysémie et nous distinguerons trois types d'emploi:

a) En verbe syntaxiquement «libre», ex. *L'élève porte son uniforme.*

b) En verbe support d'une prédication nominale, ex. *qn porte la responsabilité de l'accident = est responsable de.*

c) Elément d'une suite verbale figée, ex. *qn porte ses pas en un lieu.*

2. Porter: verbe prédicatif:

Le prédicat joue le rôle central dans la phrase dans la mesure où c'est lui qui sélectionne les arguments. Si *porter* est un prédicat verbal, c'est qu'il entre dans une séquence libre.

La description syntactico-sémantique tient compte de la délimitation des critères définitoires des différents statuts d'un verbe. En effet, si la suite est libre, l'application des propriétés de recomposition est souvent possible vu que le sens est transparent et compositionnel. En revanche, si la séquence est sémantiquement opaque, son caractère autonome bloque le fonctionnement des modifications.

Examinons ces deux phrases:

(10)-*Michel porte un manteau.*

(11)-*Michel porte bien son âge.*

À partir de ces deux phrases,

-la pronominalisation

-la relativisation

-le clivage: c'est … que

-la passivation.

-le détachement de l'objet.

ne s'appliquent pas de la même façon aux deux cas cités plus haut.

-la pronominalisation:

-*Michel porte un manteau.*

-*Michel le porte.*

-*Michel porte bien son âge.*

-**Michel le porte.*

-La relativation:

-Michel porte un manteau.
-Le manteau que porte Michel est en cuir.

-Michel porte bien son âge
*-*L'âge que porte Michel est bien.*

-Le clivage c'est … que

-Michel porte un manteau.
-C'est le manteau que porte Michel.

-Michel porte bien son âge.
*-*C'est l'âge que porte Michel.*

-La passivation:

-Michel porte un manteau.
-Le manteau est porté par Michel.

-Michel porte bien son âge.
*-*L'âge est porté par Michel.*

-Le détachement de l'objet:

-Michel porte son manteau.
-Le manteau, Michel le porte.

-Michel porte bien son âge.
*-*L'âge, Michel le porte.*

Dans une suite libre, l'application des propriétés de recomposition est largement possible vu que le sens est transparent et compositionnel. En revanche, si la séquence est sémantiquement opaque alors son caractère autonome bloque le fonctionnement des modifications.

3. Porter: verbe support:

Son rôle primordial consiste à porter les marques temporelles et aspectuelles. En d'autres termes, il est un «actualisateur du nom prédicatif»[5]. Il n'ajoute pas de signifié lexical aux noms avec lesquels

[5] Mejri S. (1997), *Le figement lexical*, Thèse d'état, Faculté des Lettres de la

il se combine, mais il sert à les «conjuguer»: à l'instar de tous les prédicats, les substantifs prédicatifs sont «susceptibles d'être inscrits dans le temps, c'est-à-dire actualisés. À la différence des prédicats verbaux, où ces informations sont prises par la conjugaison, les prédicats nominaux ont une double actualisation exprimée d'une part par les déterminants qui les précèdent [...] et d'autre part par des verbes spécifiques que nous appelons *verbes supports*».[6]

Pour caractériser syntaxiquement les verbes supports, Robert Vivès[7] retient les trois propriétés suivantes:

-les contraintes sur les déterminants du nom supporté,
-leur aptitude à former un G.N,
-la double analyse à laquelle ils se prêtent.

À ce niveau de description, J. Giry-Schneider a ajouté deux autres critères qui donnent lieu à la distinction d'une construction à verbe ordinaire de celle d'un verbe support:[8]

-l'interrogation par *que*,
-la possibilité de l'adjonction d'un adverbe.

3.1. Contraintes sur les déterminants du nom prédicatif:
Considérons les deux phrases suivantes:

(1) *–Michel porte son assiette à la cuisine.*
(2) *–Michel porte la responsabilité de l'accident.*

Si dans la première phrase N1: *son assiette* peut supporter différents déterminants:

(1a)-*Michel porte son (une, mon, ton, l'...) assiette à la cuisine.*
Il n'en est pas de même dans le second énoncé; en effet le remplacement du déterminant *la* par l'adjectif possessif *sa*, à titre d'exemple, n'est pas acceptable:
(2a)-*Il porte* (**ma, ta, …*) *responsabilité de l'accident.*

L'impossibilité d'insertion des adjectifs possessifs *ma, ta* ou de

---

Manouba, Université de Tunis, p. 363.
[6] *Ibidem.*
[7] Vivès R. (1983), *Avoir, prendre, perdre: constructions à verbes supports et extensions aspectuelles,* Thèse de 3ème cycle, Université Paris 8, p. 8.
[8] Giry Schneider J. (1987), *Les prédicats nominaux en français, les phrases simples à verbes supports*, Droz, Genève.

l'article indéfini *une* traduit un cas de contrainte syntaxique et de restriction sémantique.

Ceci permet de déduire que le sujet du verbe support *porter* établit un rapport étroit et nécessaire avec le déterminant du nom prédicatif.

3.2. La formation du groupe nominal par la réduction du verbe support:

(3)-Michel porte la responsabilité de l'accident

peut être ramenée par relativation à:

(3a)-La responsabilité de l'accident que porte Michel lui coûtera cher.

ou encore par suppression du verbe support:

(3b)-La responsabilité de l'accident de Michel lui coûtera cher.

La deuxième propriété des verbes supports est leur aptitude à former un groupe nominal.

Ainsi, le verbe support *porter* qui actualise le nom supporté *responsabilité* et l'inscrit dans le temps, disparaît lors de la réduction de la relative.

3.3. Double analyse possible du groupe nominal:

La troisième propriété qui caractérise un verbe support est celle de la possibilité de la double extraction. Le modèle sélectionné: nom prédicatif accompagné d'une préposition et suivi d'un nom, admet normalement la double analyse. Nous essayerons d'appliquer ces transformations aux phrases suivantes et analyser les résultats obtenus.

(4)-*Michel porte la main à son front.*

(5)-*Nathalie porte la responsabilité de l'accident.*

-Premier cas de figure:

(4) *Michel porte la main à son front.*

(4a) *C'est la main à son front que Michel porte.*

(4b)*C'est la main que Michel porte à son front.*

(4c)*C'est à son front que Michel porte la main.*

-Second cas:

(5)-*Nathalie porte la responsabilité de l'accident.*

(5a)-? *C'est la responsabilité de l'accident que Nathalie porte.*
(5b)-? *C'est la responsabilité que Nathalie porte de l'accident.*
(5c)-? *C'est de l'accident que Nathalie porte la responsabilité.*

Nous observons que ce type d'extraction n'est pas toujours acceptable. À l'encontre du premier cas, les propriétés transform-ationnelles font varier un ou plusieurs paramètres dans les phrases qui déterminent le second cas de figure.

3.4. L'interrogation par que:
C'est le paramètre le plus sûr pour l'identification et la détermination d'un verbe support.

À partir de l'énoncé suivant:

(10)- *Michel porte la responsabilité de l'accident.*

On peut obtenir:

(10a)- *Que porte Michel?*
(10b)- **La responsabilité de l'accident.*

Dans cette perspective, J. Giry Schneider résume toute la problématique en un «énoncé question-réponse non acceptable».[9] Le nom prédicatif n'est pas susceptible d'être soumis à la question par *que* car ce même pronom interrogatif a inévitablement comme désignation de «quelque chose».[10] Il est donc quasi-impossible de s'interroger sur l'abstrait en utilisant les moyens de tout ce qui est concret.

3.5. Possibilité de l'adjonction d'un adverbe:
L'adverbe qui se joint à son support verbal, change la signification du prédicat, de diverses manières.

(8)- *Michel porte la responsabilité de l'accident.*
(8c)- *Michel porte (*beaucoup, *peu) la responsabilité de l'accident.*
(8d)- *Michel porte (*bien, * très) la responsabilité de l'accident.*

3.6. La nominalisation d'un verbe support:
Parmi les caractéristiques retenues dans la définition du verbe support, rappelons celle de sa non prédicativité, d'où sa nécessaire combinaison avec un nom qui assumerait la prédication dans la phrase. À cet égard,

---

[9] Giry-Schneider J. (1987), *op. cit.*, p. 29.
[10] *Ibidem.*

il semble clair que ce raisonnement se base concrètement sur le test de la nominalisation.

(9)-*Michel porte la responsabilité de l'accident.*

(9a)-**Le port de Michel de la responsabilité de l'accident.*

Nous avons déduit, grâce aux différentes restructurations, que les critères les plus sûrs, qui nous permettent de définir le verbe support *porter* sont les suivants:

-la propriété de coréférence du sujet.

-la transformation relative.

-la formation du groupe nominal par la réduction du verbe support.

De même, les opérations transformationnelles visent, seulement, à confirmer le statut prédicatif du nom complément.

4-Porter*: en tête d'une suite verbale figée:*

«La première condition nécessaire pour qu'on puisse parler de figement, est que l'on soit en présence d'une séquence de plusieurs mots et que ces mots aient, par ailleurs, une existence autonome».[11] Chaque élément constitutif de l'expression figée peut figurer dans d'autres contextes et former avec son environnement intérieur un concept nouveau et autonome.

Pour notre analyse des séquences verbales figées comportant le verbe *porter*, nous retenons le blocage des propriétés transformationnelles. Les propriétés de recomposition ou de reformulation des constructions libres ne s'appliquent pas de la même façon avec les expressions figées.

Considérons les exemples suivants:

(1)- *Michel a porté ses pas en Amérique.*

(2)- *Pierre a porté les provisions à sa voisine.*

-Pronominalisation:

(1)-*Michel a porté ses pas en Amérique.*

(1a)-**Michel les porte en Amérique.*

(2)-*Pierre a porté les provisions à sa voisine.*

(2a)-*Pierre les a portées à sa voisine.*

---

[11] Gross G. (1996a), *op. cit.*, p. 9.

-Passivation:

(1)-*Michel a porté ses pas en Amérique.*

(1b)-**Les pas sont portés par Michel en Amérique.*

(2)-*Pierre a porté les provisions à sa voisine.*

(2b)- *Les provisions ont été portées à la voisine par Pierre.*

-L'interrogation:

(1)-*Michel a porté ses pas en Amérique.*

(1c)-**Qu'a porté Michel en Amérique*?

(2)-*Pierre a porté les provisions à sa voisine.*

(2c)-*Qu'a porté Pierre à sa voisine*?

-Extraction:

(1)-*Michel a porté ses pas en Amérique.*

(1d)-**Ce sont les pas que Michel a portés en Amérique.*

(2)- *Pierre a porté les provisions à sa voisine.*

(2d)- *Ce sont les provisions que Pierre a portées à sa voisine.*

-Relativation:

(1)-*Michel a porté ses pas en Amérique.*

(1e)**Les pas que porte Michel en Amérique.*

(2)-*Pierre a porté les provisions à sa voisine.*

(2e)-*Les provisions que Pierre a portées à sa voisine.*

À partir de l'examen de cette paire d'exemples, nous pouvons constater que:

-Dans la première phrase: (1)-*Michel a porté ses pas en Amérique* n'admet pas de transformations, toutes les manipulations sont rejetées. Ceci nous permet de dire que les contraintes syntaxiques régissent la structuration interne de la séquence et bloquent toutes les modifications.

Porter ses pas en est une unité polylexicale qui a une existence autonome.

-Pour ce qui est du second emploi, toutes les transformations sont possibles. L'organisation syntactico-sémantique interne de l'expression l'exige. En d'autres termes, les éléments lexicaux constitutifs de l'énoncé en question sont susceptibles de restructurations. L'application de ces tests nous a permis de constater que (2) *Pierre a porté les* provisions *à sa voisine* est loin d'être figée, au contraire, il ne s'agit, en fait que d'une suite libre. Les manipulations syntaxiques prouvent que les structures profondes permettent de discerner une grande différence entre ce qui est polylexical et ce qui ne l'est pas. De ce fait, les critères, que nous venons de mentionner, (passivation, extraction, détachement, etc.) sont susceptibles de distinguer une suite verbale figée d'une autre qui ne l'est pas.

Conclusion:

Nous avons essayé de faire une brève description syntactico-sémantique des trois statuts du verbe polysémique *porter* afin de mettre en lumière ce «mouvement» qu'il effectue en passant d'un statut à un autre et d'un sens à un autre.

Cette analyse syntactico-sémantique nous a permis de nous éloigner des approches traditionnelles.

Ainsi appréhendé, la notion de verbe en linguistique a été remise en question en fonction de telles considérations pour aboutir à une classification en termes de verbe prédicatif, de verbe support et d'une suite verbale figée.

Bibliographie

-Arrivé, M., Gadet, F., Galmiche, M., (1986), *La grammaire d'aujourd'hui*, Flammarion, Paris.

-Beneveniste, E., (1974), *Problèmes de linguistique générale*, vol. I et II, Paris, Gallimard.

-Bréal, (1897), *Essai de sémantique*, Saint-Pierre de Salerne: Gérard Monfort.

-Constentin, C., (2005), «un corpus propice à la problématisation de la polysémie: les Maximes de La Rochefoucauld», in Soutet O. La polysémie, actes de colloque la Sorbonne 17, 18 et 19 novembre 2000, Paris: Presses de l'Université Paris-Sorbonne 415–37.

-Fuchs, C.,

a- (1982), «La paraphrase entre la langue et le discours», in *Langue Française*, n°53, Paris, Larousse, pp.22–33.

b- (1994), *Paraphrase et énonciation*, Ophrys, Paris.

-Giry Schneider J. (1987), *Les prédicats nominaux en français, les phrases simples à verbes supports*, Droz, Genève.

-Gross, G.,

a- (1993), «Trois applications de la notion de verbe support», L'information grammaticale, 59, Paris.

b- (1994), «Classes d'objets et description des verbes», Langue Française, n°115, Paris, Larousse, pp.15–30.

c- (1996), *Les expressions figées en français, noms composés et autres locutions*, Ophrys, Paris.

-Gross, G. & Prandi, M. (2004a), *La finalité, Fondements conceptuels et genèse linguistiques*, De Boeck, Duculot, Bruxelles.

-Gross, G., (2004b), «Pour un Bescherelle des prédicats nominaux», In GROSS Gaston, PONTONX Sophie de, (éd.), «Les verbes supports: nouvel état des lieux » *Linguisticae Investigationes* Fascicule spécial, 27, pp 343–58, John Benjamins CO, Amsterdam. Philadelphia.

-Martin, R., (1992), *Pour une logique du sens*, 2e édition revue et augmentée, Presses Universitaires de France, Paris.

-Mejri, S., (1997), *Le figement lexical*, Publications de la Faculté des Lettres de La Manouba, Tunis.

-Victorri, B., & Fuchs, C., (1996), *Construction dynamique du sens*, Hermès, Paris.

-Vivès, R., (1993), «La prédication nominale et l'analyse par verbes supports», L'information grammaticale, 59, Didier, Paris.

Dialectics of Order and Disorder from World Politics and Media to Philosophy

A New Order of Zionist Lobbying: a Statistical Approach of the Jewish Pressure Groups during Ronald Reagan's Presidency

Mohamed Anouar Barouni, I.S.S.H.J., Tunisia

Abstract

Regular lobbying has characterized the American political life since the American Revolution of 1776. Several ethnic groups were involved in such a process which is described as an orderly and organized branch of pressure upon the American governments. In the first Amendment of the Bill of Rights, lobbying is guaranteed. "Congress shall make no law respecting an establishment of religion, or prohibiting the free exercise thereof; or abridging the freedom of speech, or of the press; or the right of the people peaceably to assemble, and to petition the Government for a redress of grievances" (U.S Bill of Rights, 1791). To point out this phenomenon of lobbying, the Jewish Zionist lobby/ies represent/s the most suitable context through which this ethnic minority in the U.S.A has survived and managed to become at the heart of American political decision-making strategies. As Jewish author and political science professor, Benjamin Ginsberg, pointed out "Since the 1960s, Jews have come to wield considerable influence in American economic, cultural, intellectual and political life. Jews played a central role [...] during the 1980s, and they were among the chief beneficiaries" (Ginsberg, 1993, 1). From 1981 to 1988, which is the period of study in this paper, there has been an unusual and organized system of lobbying traditionally regarded as pro-democrat which turned in favor of Ronald Reagan from the congressional and financial Jewish Zionist lobbies during his presidency. This paper analyzes the shift that Jewish lobbies made from the Democratic Party to the Republican Party, the doubled financial and military support that Israel benefited from in Reagan's presidency and the impact of this shift in balance of power in the Middle East.

Keywords: Order, lobbies, Zionist, Jewish, Congress, Reagan, statistics

Introduction

Theoretically an interest group, pressure group or lobby is a group of people who share the same aim and pursues certain claims towards other groups. In this case, the substantive "interest" assumes a clear connotation just when it is blended with an adjective: "private", "public", "social", "religious", "local" for example. Therefore, it is the adjective who describes the nature and the range of the group (Mattina 2010). For this, Republicans' embracement of Zionist lobbies' aspirations has brought a radical new order in dealing with the American Israeli relations. Lobbies have a direct "influence" on the Form of government, because they play a role in the relationship between the bodies involved in addressing the political system, so in order to understand pressure groups, one needs to look not just at the behavior of the groups but also at the behavior of government. Handling lobby problematic shows the extent of some ethnic minorities' influence over American decision-making. To understand the progressive pressure, throughout American history, that Zionism, as an ideological and political movement, has done in the United States of America, we refer to the arrival of the early Jewish and puritan migrants from Europe to the new world at the beginning of the seventeenth century (Hotten 1874). These communities believed that America could be their "promised land" and since then they have worked in establishing a country that could fulfill this dream despite their small number compared to other waves of immigrants particularly the White Anglo-Saxon Protestants. The Haskala (Jewish Enlightenment) in the eighteenth and nineteenth centuries urged the Jewish communities around Europe and America to assimilate into Western culture. They believed that it was the best way to guarantee the survival of the Jewish heritage (Jewish Virtual Library) and, therefore, they have become a powerful minority. They were aware that the West, particularly the United States and Great Britain, became dominant forces around the world. As a result, the Lobbying in such societies would become a real power not only in these countries but also around the globe. The twentieth century witnessed a rise in these lobbies particularly during World War I and World War II and the aftermath of the creation of Israel (Fleshler 2009). During his 1912 campaign for presidency, Woodrow Wilson remarked that, "the government of the United States is a foster child of the special interests. It is not allowed to have a will of its own" (Wilson 58). The Jewish Zionist pressure groups managed to reach a peak of lobbying during Reagan's presidency starting from 1981.

Lobbying in America

The question of lobbying in the United States goes back to the eve of the Declaration of Independence when royalists and separatists were pushing for their own interests of whether to remain within the empire or to for fight for independence. Since then, lobbying has played a vital role in the American political life. Advocacy groups have appeared to guarantee American and ethnic interests inside and outside of the society. The most prominent ones are the Jewish Zionist groups which are known to be pro-Israel. These groups have intensified their pressure on the American governments and particularly those of the 1940s namely, with Harry Truman as a president who diplomatically recognized the creation of the State of Israel just minutes after Ben Gurion's speech and the proclamation of the state of Israel (Truman Library n.p.). In Spring 1948, Palestine became embroiled in American domestic politics. Jewish votes were important to President Truman in the coming election. Key advisers, especially Clark Clifford, pushed him to stand firmly for UN partition to win those votes (Truman Library n.p.). As May 15th drew closer, a lot of lobbying was made on President Harry Truman. He was advised to recognize the new Jewish state that was certain to be proclaimed when partition occurred.

Secretary of State George C. Marshall's opposition was tremendous as he did not appreciate the idea of recognizing the new state. The Secretary's opposition to recognition of a new Jewish state in Palestine troubled President Harry Truman (Truman Library n.p.) and this led to the strongest trouble between the president and his secretary.

A nation is born

As partition was coming closer, the decision in the United Nations became an approaching fact and reality; President Truman had to decide whether or not to recognize the Jewish state that would be proclaimed on May 15th 1948. On May 12th, he gathered his advisors at the White House. Tempers flared. Clark Clifford made the case for recognition. Secretary of State George Marshall led the opposition, saying he could not vote for President Truman if he pursued recognition (Truman Library n.p.). Truman measured personal, political and strategic concern because he believed that Jewish votes in his country are important and lobbies would always reward his decision (Truman Library n.p.). On May 14th, he decided that America should recognize the new state of Israel. He then acted and recognized the Hebrew state.

In the same day, Prime Minister David Ben-Gurion read the proclamation of the establishment of the Hebrew state. Striking the speaker's table for emphasis, he announced "The name of our state shall be Israel" (Ben Gurion, Speech 1948).

The American statement recognizing the new State of Israel bears President Truman's last-minute handwritten changes. American recognition came shortly after midnight in Palestine, just minutes after the new nation was proclaimed (Truman Library n.p.). President Truman received a letter from Dr. Chaim Weizmann, first president of the new state of Israel, urging him to recognize the state of Israel as a final solution to the question of Palestine (Benson 127). From that date on, lobbying would find its way in the Israel-American relations for the following decades. The 1950s, 60s and 70s were characterized by a Jewish favor of the Democratic Party (Medoff 2002) as this latter would promote the question of ethnicity and fight against discrimination in the American society, an idea that is so much appreciated by the Jews of America and of the world. In response to Harry Truman's decision to recognize the state of Israel, the Zionist lobbies have remained faithful to the Democrats' principles and voted massively in favor of Democrat presidential candidates. But a change would later on happen with Jimmy Carter's second attempt to win the presidency in 1980. Zionist lobbies shifted the balance towards republicanism. That is considered as a new order for the Jewish votes.

The peak of Zionist lobbying in the United States became orderly remarkable with the rise of Republican liberalism among the Jewish community during the end of the 1970s, in particular, at the beginning of the 1980s. President Ronald Reagan would profit from that new order of Jewish economic liberalism and would try to attract Jewish sympathizers in the Congress, especially, by promoting further and stronger relations with the state of Israel. According to The Office of the Historian at U.S Department of State, congressional pressures on that issue were visible with the number of official visits that kept the relations between the American and Israeli diplomats at high levels and of tremendous strategic interest for each other's countries. Other several issues, which include secret affairs and the role of the CIA in promoting a pro-Israeli policy in the Middle East and around the world, were in Reagan's foreign affairs agenda.

The Reagan presidency and the unusual order of lobbying

When Reagan was governor of California he managed to pass a bill in the legislature of that state. This legislative plan allowed several banks and financial institutions to launch investment projects in the State of Israel. From 1973 to 1976 Reagan was an active columnist in The Jewish Press weekly newspaper, readers of which were mainly Orthodox Jew New Yorkers (Jewish Virtual Library n.p.).

Reagan's closest Jewish advisor was Theodore E. Cummings of Los Angeles who served in the Reagan inner circle for several years. During the presidential campaign in 1980, several prominent figures of the American Jewish communities in the States were active in supporting the future president. These Jews included a number of businessmen and intellectuals like Albert Spiegel who headed the Jewish Coalition for Reagan, Max Fisher, a businessman, philanthropist and an advisor of the Republican American presidents since Dwight Eisenhower presidency to Reagan's. Other prominent Jewish figures such as George Klein, Gordon Zacks, and Jacob Stein were close to Reagan. Neo-conservative Jewish intellectuals, such as Eugene V. Rostow, Max Kempelman, Irving Kristol, and Norman Podhoretz were active in the Reagan election campaign and many became influential in the Reagan Administration.

In the 1980 election, 40 percent of the Jews who voted chose Reagan, another 40 percent voted for the incumbent President Jimmy Carter, the lowest percentage for a Democrat in the past 80 years, and 20 percent for John Anderson, indicating that the Democratic Party could no longer take the Jewish vote for granted (Jewish Virtual Library n.p.). An important divide among the Jewish Orthodox voters who chose a Republican candidate over a Democrat was seen for the first time in American electoral history. Congress also had been so much affected by Jewish Zionist lobbies especially after Camp David agreement, the bombing of Osirak nuclear center and the contra affair/Iran gate. Priority was given to the Israeli security in the Middle East as far as the American foreign policy is concerned. In this regard, AIPAC and the American Jewish Congress, the most powerful Jewish lobbies in Congress, manipulated the question of Israeli American relationship. In this context Mark Pelavin, then a legislative assistant with the American Jewish Congress declared "the end of the Cold War, strengthening the U.S.-Israel alliance–he (Reagan) was a pivotal figure and his achievements will be long-lasting" (Jewish Weekly of Northern California n.p.). In 1981, Israel began receiving its full economic aid in grants, and four years later, all its military assistance became grants as well (Harvard Israel Review n.p.). By 1987, the amount of military and economic assistance – $1.8 billion (Harvard Israel Review n.p.) – was at the level at which it would remain for 12 years. The rise in terms of military aids and grants started with Reagan's presidency at $1.2 billion in 1981 and went up to $1.8 billion in 1987 (Harvard Israel Review, n.p.). With additional $ 0.6 billion in 6 years, it meant an approximate amount of $0.1 billion was given each year from 1981 to 1987 (Harvard Israel Review n.p.). It is believed that the Camp David agreement strengthened the American aids to Israel as aids were also given to Egypt (Sharp 2009). This aid was an important matter for American politicians and financial lobbies. There were worries that the share of Israel in the aid might decrease. Therefore, they lobbied in favor of keeping the level of grants to Israel higher than any other neighboring country in the region or even in the whole world. Statistically, the rise was about 50% of aids from 1981 to 1987. (Harvard Israel Review n.p.). This percentage is considered among the highest in the history of foreign aids which were granted by any American government after the Marshall plan in the aftermath of the Second World War.

The strength behind all these aids lies in the priority given by both Congress and Reagan to support the Hebrew state at any cost. Jewish Zionist pressure groups campaigned that a pro-Israel Congress should always remain faithful to supporting Israel through a liberal policy. There should be open hands to the strategic ally in the Middle East. These open hands were not visible during the decades that preceded Reagan's presidency. There were 'restrictions' as far as military aids were concerned. The American governments tried to keep good diplomatic relations with the Arab nations, so the open hand policy was not fully applied. But, after Camp David Agreement, the Jewish American Congressmen and the Christian Zionists were convinced that the old policy of supporting Israel should stop and a new era should start.

The order of lobbying among congressmen/women was at a peak in 1987. They were 37 representatives during Reagan's presidency (Jewish Virtual Library n.p.). Democrat Jewish congress members supported the Republican agenda especially when it came to the question of security of Israel and the liberal economic aids towards it. Conservative Democratic Jewish congressmen devoted so much effort on behalf of the AIPAC and The Conference of Presidents of Major American Jewish Organizations to maintain a stable and considerable influence in that issue. In this very context, the Jewish author and political science professor, Benjamin Ginsberg, pointed out "Since the 1960s, Jews have come to wield considerable influence in American economic, cultural, intellectual and political life. Jews played a central role in American finance during the 1980s, and they were among the chief beneficiaries of that decade's corporate mergers and reorganizations" (Ginsberg 1).

This new order of accelerated support to Israel is considered by several historians, notably Jewish ones, as a turning point in the Jewish lobbying history. The bipartisan lobbying will play an important role in the decades that followed Reagan's two presidential terms by creating a more Zionist-oriented Republican agenda especially with the Bush administrations. This new order is believed to be caused by the appeasement between Egypt and Israel following Camp David Agreement signed by Anwar Sadat, Menahem Begin and Jimmy Carter. This compromise has not satisfied some radical Zionists in the congress and this has shifted Jewish American community towards a Republican candidate in the nineteen eighty presidential election. The question of lobbying and the new order of the pressure groups in the Jewish Zionist American minorities were not exclusively related to this ethnic minority. But, they have rather influenced other Zionist non-Jewish communities, particularly the Evangelicals whose support to Israel in congress; in addition to the foreign policy came for the benefit of the Ronald Reagan's cold war policies as Israel was a Middle Eastern ally to the United States. The president, believed in the conservatism with an Evangelical ideology. The press defended Reagan's policies and there was even a public support since the Jewish Zionist media lobbies presented a very shining image of the president as far as his support to Israel was concerned. It should be noted that a lot of the American mass media were owned by Jewish Americans namely Hollywood during Reagan's presidency. This latter reminded Ronald Reagan of his youth as an actor. The press and the radio were also dominated by Zionist lobbies and in the very context Reagan had an important influence as he was a radio presenter, a columnist and an orator.

Conclusion

The AIPAC lobby over U.S. elections has become a controversy since the creation of this lobby in 1963. It is not something new, it is rather ancient and it has become a ritual and a force embedded in U.S. politics. This lobby has had its share in previous presidential elections in the works of some academics and politicians who dealt with it from different angles. According to some authors and politicians the U.S presidential elections is a democratic process that has no window for any lobbying or corruption. However, other academics have taken the path to reveal hidden forces driving the U.S. elections, mainly, the AIPAC lobby. Some academics took the task of showing the roles of this lobby during several presidential elections including those of

1980. Virginia Tilley, for instance, argued that "AIPAC was exclusively responsible for Bush victory in the 2000 presidential race" (Tilley 124). Paul Fendley argued that The Israeli prime minister has a stronger influence in the American foreign policy in the Middle East than in his own country (92). The presence of AIPAC members and correspondences in the presidency of Reagan made his era a new beginning for Zionist lobbying in the United States of America. Since 1963, the majority of American presidential candidates visited AIPAC during their electoral campaigns. Congress came under heavier and heavier influence of this group as foreign aids are decided and voted by the Senate which was overwhelmingly Republican. Therefore, this institution devoted a lot of efforts in the survival and security of Israel as the nineteen eighties were characterized by a prominent threat to the Hebrew state particularly by the Islamic revolution in Iran and the Lebanese civil war. This strategic value of Israel pushed Reagan's administration to go further in its support for the Hebrew state. This is considered as a new order in the American Israeli relations. Reagan believed that Israel could be a "barrier country" (Rose 82) against any possible Soviet or Iranian expansion in the Persian Gulf and in the entire Middle East. This policy would later open more doors for Israel to position itself in the top priorities of the political and foreign policy agendas of the presidents who came after Reagan whether they are Democrats or Republicans. The shift to bipartisan policies among Jewish-American voters characterized the electoral opinions to guarantee a strong Jewish lobby with any administration.

Works Cited

Ben Gurion, David. *Ben Gurion's Speech 14th May 1948.* Official Gazette: Number 1; Tel Aviv, 5 Iyar 5708, 14.5.1948. Web.

Benson, Michael T. *Harry S. Truman and the Founding of Israel.* Westport: Greenwood Publishing Group, 1997. Print.

Fendley, Paul. *They Dared to Speak Out.* Chicago: Lawrence Hill Books, 1985. Print.

Fleshler, Dan. *Transforming America's Israel Lobby: The Limits of its Power and the Potential for Change.* Washington, D.C: Potomac Books Inc, 2009. Print.

Ginsberg, Benjamin. *The Fatal Embrace: Jews and the State.* Chicago, U of Chicago, 1993. Print.

Harvard Israel Review. Issue 4, Spring 2004. Web.

Hotten, John Camden. *The Original List of Persons of Quality ... who went from Great Britain to the American Plantations.* London: John Camden Hotten, 1874. Print.

Jewish Weekly Friday. *The Role of the American Jewish community in lobbying for Israel during Reagan's political career.* June 11, 2004. Web.

Mattina, Liborio. *I gruppi di interesse.* Bologna: Il Mulino, 2010. Print.

Medoff, Rafael. *Jewish Americans and political participation: a Reference Handbook.* Santa Barbara, ABC-Clio, Inc., 2002. Print.

Rosen, Steven. J. *The Strategic Value of Israel, AIPAC,* Michigan: U of Michigan, 1982. Print.

Sharp. Jeremy. *U.S Foreign Aid to Israel*, Washington, D.C, Congressional Research Service. December 4, 2009. Print.

Tilley, Virginia. *The One-State Solution: A Breakthrough for Peace in the Israeli-Palestinian Deadlock.* Dearborn: U of Michigan Press, 2010. Print.

Weber, Mark. *A Look at the Powerful Jewish Lobby in America*. 2004. Web.

Wilson, Woodrow. *The New Freedom*. New York, Doubleday, 1913. Print.

www.jewishvirtuallibrary.org/jsource/biography/RonaldReagan.html.

www.trumanlibrary.org.

Chevauchement des genres rédactionnels journalistiques

Majdi Chaoiachi, l'Institut supérieur des langues de Tunis

Résumé

Bien que commodes et concevables, les genres n'ont jamais déclaré claires et exactes les frontières qui les séparent. La question du genre n'est pas à négliger, elle participe, selon Bakhtine à l'organisation de la parole «de la même façon que l'organisent les formes grammaticales» (Bakhtine, 1977).

Cette contribution s'inscrit dans le cadre d'une étude analytique sur une coupure de presse tunisienne d'expression française qui couvre le lendemain de la révolution sur le sujet de salafisme. Étant considéré comme une escale d'information, le discours journalistique est un milieu fluctuant et instable dans lequel le chevauchement des genres est une caractéristique omniprésente. En effet, de par sa nature le discours journalistique possède souvent une double facette; d'une part, il est le reflet de la société, une mise en mot des tensions sociales et d'autre part, il est un vecteur social et un moteur d'action sur autrui. Cette complexité s'accentue avec la dichotomie objectivité/subjectivité journalistique amenant ainsi à un empiètement permanent entre les genres d'information et les genres d'opinion. L'étude sera focalisée sur des exemples manifestant l'empiètement entre les articles à caractère informatif et les articles d'opinion. En ce sens, l'embarras que manifeste l'articulation entre l'opinion publique et l'opinion publiée avec la nécessité de l'impartialité journalistique est une explication entre autres de cet empiètement. Toutefois, dans l'un et l'autre sens, l'idée directrice de cette étude est de mettre au clair les stratégies discursives permettant le chevauchement des genres rédactionnels journalistiques. Dans cette perspective, une question principale correspond à notre problématique: Les chevauchements des genres journalistiques, font-ils l'objet d'une nécessité subjective énonciative ou, ils ne sont que la nature inconsciente du langage journalistique.

Mots-clés: discours journalistiques, chevauchement, salafistes, objectivité/subjectivité.

Introduction

La présente contribution pointe un aspect de désordre qui n'est pas exceptionnel, il est plutôt la marche normale des choses. La presse est un milieu fluctuant dans lequel il est difficile de garder des contours et frontières claires entre l'information et l'opinion engendrant ainsi un désordre perpétuel manifesté par un empiètement incessant sur les deux visées journalistiques fondamentales: transmettre une information et donner son opinion.

Ce travail se divise en deux parties: nous présenterons, dans un premier temps, le cadre scientifique dans lequel se situe la question du désordre en l'exposant sous certaines visions théoriques en la matière. Dans une deuxième étape, nous allons prendre pour analyse des coupures de presse tirées du journal *La presse* dans lesquelles transparait clairement l'empiètement énonciatif entre les genres d'opinion et les genres d'information.

1. Le chevauchement des genres: perspective théorique

La question du genre rédactionnel dans la presse écrite développe deux points essentiels. D'abord, un problème de choix entre les différentes méthodes de l'analyse du discours dans la mesure où, on peut se demander s'agit-il d'une analyse purement linguistique; énonciation, pragmatique, rhétorique, etc.? Ou, faut-il prendre en compte les données extralinguistiques, unités rédactionnelles de la presse écrite à l'instar de brevet, éditorial, interview, reportage … etc.?

La diversité de genres rédactionnels et ses origines historiques dépassent une simple classification linguistique pour des échelles extralinguistiques. Lits et Dubied (1999), auteurs d'un «*Que sais-je*?» sur le fait divers,[1] rappellent que le concept des genres n'est pas séparable de ses racines historiques. Pour Grosse et Seibold (1996),[2] il ne s'agit pas seulement d'un fait historique et linguistique, la diversité du genre s'explique par la diversité des lecteurs, dont les quotidiens se distinguent par les genres qu'ils favorisent. Jufer et

---

[1] Annik Dubied, Marc Lits, 1999, *Le fait divers*, P.U.F., coll. «*Que sais-je?*».

[2] Grosse Ernst Ulrich, Seibold Ernst, 1996, *Panorama de la presse parisienne*, Berlin: Peter Lang.

Herman (1999),[3] en se focalisant sur le genre noble de la presse écrite, essayent de montrer son importance à travers une analyse énonciative centrée sur le rapport éditeur/lecteur. Selon leur étude, les journaux se distinguent par leurs positions éditoriales.

Maurice Mouillaud et Jean François Têtu (1989)[4] préconisent l'idée que l'événement est une catégorie référentielle par excellence pour étudier un journal:

> La maquette et le péritexte de chaque journal répartissent sémantiquement les articles en rubrique, elles-mêmes inséparables d'une grande classification en grandes familles événementielles: nouvelles politiques, catastrophes (naturelles /écologiques), accidents d'avion, voyages/ visites (présidentielles, ministérielles.[5]

Un autre problème côtoie régulièrement les genres journalistiques, celui de la difficulté de classification. Ce flou de classification est parfois incompréhensible dans la mesure où ces genres ont des limites et des différences très claires ainsi qu'un nom et un titre spécifique (*éditorial, dépêche, reportage, commentaire, analyse, courrier des lecteurs, revue de presse, etc*). Toutefois, nous avons souvent des ressemblances de forme et de contenu qui ne font qu'aggraver cette incertitude.

Généralement, on distingue deux genres du discours journalistique majeurs selon la division classique du texte de presse; l'opinion et l'information. Sous cet angle, De Brouker (1995)[6] distingue deux grands genres rédactionnels: les genres de l'information tels que *dépêche, brève, compte rendu, reportage, interview, portrait, enquête,* etc. et les genres de commentaire tels que, *commentaire explicatif, commentaire interprétatif, éditorial, le billet, la caricature, la chronique, etc.* Selon Adam, la distinction de De Brouker repose sur trois critères essentiels: d'abord, un critère purement sémantique qui se base sur le sujet, ensuite un autre critère argumentatif et pragmatique et finalement un critère énonciatif.

---

[3] Thierry Herman, Gilles Lugrin, 1999, *Formes et fonctions des rubriques dans les quotidiens romands - Approches théorique et quantitative,* Fribourg (Suisse): Institut de journalisme et des communications sociales.

[4] Maurice Mouillaud Jean François Tétu, 1989, *Le journal quotidien*, Paris, Puf.

[5] *Ibidem.*

[6] José De Brouker, 1995, *Pratiques de l'information et écritures journalistiques*, Paris, CFPJ.

Selon Moirand (1999), la question du genre relève de la classification binaire des dires de presse entre l'écriture d'information et l'écriture d'opinion. Elle la reformule[7] en "énonciation objectivisée" et "énonciation subjectivisée".

Maryse Souchard[8] va dans le même sens en distinguant les formes neutralisantes ayant un rôle informatif sans l'intention du journaliste de la forme subjective où le discours est assumé par le journal:

> Il donnera, dans l'article d'information, le texte comme le discours de l'Autre et interviendra le moins possible dans le déroulement discursif. Par contre, dans l'éditorial, dans l'article d'opinion, le discours s'affirmera comme médiatique, au sens où il cessera de rapporter le discours de l'Autre pour inscrire des positions, des analyses, des réflexions.[9]

Martin-Lagardette (1994)[10] qui partage le même point de vue de De Brouker, ajoute deux autres catégories rédactionnelles: la fantaisie (*écho, billet*), et le genre noble (*enquête, reportage, interview*).

Dumont, Grevisse, Marion et Ringlet[11] proposent une division tripartite des différentes unités rédactionnelles. Nous y trouvons d'abord les catégories où le journaliste remet en forme l'information (*Le communiqué, la dépêche d'agence et la conférence de presse)*. Ensuite, les dix grands genres (*enquête, interview, écho, billet d'humeur, éditorial, critique, chronique judiciaire*), et enfin, les formes narratives (*fait divers, papier d'ambiance, reportage*).

Toutes ces études visant la classification des différentes unités rédactionnelles se mettent d'accord sur le flou qui entoure ces unités dont les limites se chevauchent:

> Dans cette perspective, telle catégorie présentera des frontières plus ou moins floues avec telle autre (la tribune et la chronique, l'article de commentaire et l'éditorial, l'écho et le billet d'humeur par exemple), des

---

[7] Sophie Moirand, 1999, *Variations discursives dans deux situations contrastées de la presse ordinaire, les Carnets du Cediscor* 6.

[8] Maryse Souchard, 1989, *Le discours de la presse. L'image des syndicats au Québec (1982, 1983),* Montréal, Le préambule (L'Univers du discours).

[9] *Ibidem.*

[10] Jean-Luc Martin-Lagardette, 1994, *Guide de l'écriture journalistique, écrire, informer convaincre*, Paris, Syros.

[11] Frédéric Antoine, Jean-Franois Dumont, Benoît Grevisse, Philippe Marion et Gabriel Ringlet, 1995, *Ecrire au quotidien, Pratiques du journalisme*, Louvain-la-Neuve Evo-Communication.

> voisinages de forme (le portrait et la caricature); des analogies avec d'autres catégories qui la rendent inclassable; un fait divers peut être donné sous forme de brève, monté en filet, se développer en reportage et même interview et commentaire avant d'être repris et basculer dans la chronique judiciaire.[12]

Après avoir réuni toutes ces classifications, et face à cette complexité, Adam (2001) explique le problème des genres par les pratiques langagières textuelles et contextuelles capables de créer une multiplicité rédactionnelle qui commande la typologie des catégories journalistiques, « *Pour l'analyse du discours que nous préconisons, la notion centrale de genre est indissociablement linguistique et historico-culturelle*[13] ». D'après Adam, les genres sont des configurations prises sur deux principes contradictoires: Le principe de clôture (passé, répétition, convention, reproduction), et le principe d'ouverture (futur, variation, innovation). Il rejoint ainsi l'idée de Maingueneau (1984) qui explique la diversité des genres par des conditions socioculturelles qui sous-tendent le déroulement discursif des textes de presse.

> Rien d'étonnant si les typologies, dès qu'on les scrute d'un peu près et qu'on veut les appliquer, volent en éclats laissant apparaître un immense entrelacs de texte dans lesquelles seules les grilles idéologiques d'une époque, d'un lieu donné, ou les hypothèses qui fondent une recherche peuvent introduire un ordre.[14]

2. Approche analytique

(1) Mosquée d'El Fath à Tunis — Traque policière
Abou Iyadh court toujours...

> Hier après-midi, à la mosquée d'El Fath, à l'avenue de la Liberté à Tunis, le dirigeant salafiste djihadiste, Abou Iyadh, de son vrai nom Seif Allah Ben Hassine, a fait un prêche, après la prière d'El Dhohr, Sur l'esplanade de la mosquée, plusieurs dizaines de manifestants salafistes menaçants scandaient des slogans louant l'Islam. Petit à petit, la foule se disperse, non sans se poser des questions: déjà qu'avant-hier, la police n'a pas arrêté Abou Iyadh qui aurait assisté aux funérailles d'un des salafistes tués durant

---

[12] Jean-Michel Adam, 1997, *Op.cit.*

[13] Jean-Michel Adam, 2001, *Genres de la presse écrite et analyse de discours", Semen* 13, mis en ligne le 30 avril 2007, URL: http://semen.revues.org

[14] Dominique Maingueneau, 1984, *Genèses du discours,* Liège, Mardaga, 16.

> la journée du vendredi, voilà qu'aujourd'hui le scénario se répète. Abou Iyadh court toujours. Jusqu'à quand le gouvernement va-t-il jouer au chat et à la souris avec les salafistes? Les citoyens s'impatientent. (La Presse: 18-09-2012)

Cet article, tiré du journal *La Presse*, a un caractère informatif qui relate la traque policière d'Abou Iyadh, chef du mouvement salafiste. L'énonciation est fondée sur une valeur descriptive consistant à cadrer l'atmosphère spatiotemporelle *«hier après-midi, à la mosquée d'El Fath....* Nous y trouvons également une mise au point sur le personnage principal de l'énonciation autour duquel tourne l'évènement. La description informative de l'événement se termine à la ligne 5 avec la mention implicite que le recherché n'est pas interpelé par les forces de l'ordre (*Petit à petit, la foule se disperse, non sans se poser des questions*). A la ligne 7, le journaliste rappelle un autre événement celui de la présence du recherché aux obsèques d'un autre salafiste. Cet article à caractère informatif semble apporter une information, porte aux niveaux, implicite et explicite, l'opinion du journaliste. Au niveau explicite, nous avons une seule qualification négative *«menaçants»* qui peut être considérée comme un adjectif axiologique selon la terminologie avancée par Orecchioni.[15] Dans le reste de l'article, l'énonciation se fonde sur un reproche envers les forces de l'ordre du seul fait qu'ils soient responsables de la fuite d'Abou Iyadh. Le reproche commence par une forme ironique «*le gouvernement va-t-il jouer au chat et à la souris avec les salafistes?*». L'ironie met en symétrie le début et la fin de l'évènement qui commence par un aspect brutal, *«plusieurs dizaines de manifestants salafistes menaçants»* et finit par *«la foule se disperse, sans se poser une question»*. La forme négative «*la police n'a pas arrêté Abou Iyadh*» peut être considérée comme un acte de langage indirect selon la terminologie de Searle, qui peut être traduit implicitement par «la police devrait, doit, aurait dû arrêter Abou Iyadh». Avec l'expression *«voilà qu'aujourd'hui le scénario se répète»* le reproche prend une forme plus franche. Cette expression fait entendre un caractère itératif et cela à travers la combinaison entre l'adverbe du temps «*aujourd'hui*» et le verbe «*répéter*». L'idée de réitération sera

[15] Catherine Kerbrat-Orecchioni, 1977, *La connotation,* Presse universitaire de Lyon.

renforcée davantage par un regard vers le futur à travers l'expression *«court toujours»* qui donne à l'événement une envergure temporelle non bornée sur l'axe temporel. Le reproche prend ensuite une forme interrogative *«jusqu'à quand?»* avec une forme ironique *«le chat et la souris»*. A la fin de l'article, l'expression *«les citoyens s'impatientent»* met l'accent sur la nécessité de capturer Abou Iyadh, une affaire qui est devenue la préoccupation de toute la communauté langagière à qui s'adresse l'article. Il s'agit ici d'une forme de légitimation énonciative par laquelle le journaliste s'efface afin d'élargir la problématisation vers tous les citoyens dont il se présente comme le porte-parole et ce qui est déjà l'une des caractéristiques fondamentales du discours journalistique[16]. Cet article est un exemple parmi d'autres dans lequel nous pouvons voir clairement le chevauchement des genres d'opinion et d'information.

(2) Champ civique - Salafistes dans la cité
A la conquête de l'espace public

> 500 mosquées sous contrôle, des écoles sous influence, des associations généreuses et un marché florissant ...
>
> Aujourd'hui, le nombre des salafistes est impossible à cerner. Il se multiplie et se laisse dépasser par la diversité de leurs profils et l'étendue inestimable de leurs conquêtes. En haut de l'échelle, le ministère des Affaires religieuses recense 500 mosquées sous contrôle salafiste, quelques jours seulement après en avoir compté 400. Elles constituent désormais des lieux de prière, d'endoctrinement, de planification et de retranchement en cas de poursuite policière. (La Presse 02-03-2012)

Un deuxième exemple nous montre comment la production journalistique fonctionne avec un désordre perpétuel. Cet article censé être un compte rendu basé sur une enquête quantitative du nombre des mosquées qui sont sous le contrôle des groupes salafistes. Les seules informations résultantes de cette enquête sont *«500 mosquées après 400* […] *il y a quelques jours»* ainsi que la multiplication sans un nombre exact du nombre des salafistes qui va de pair avec la prolifération des écoles et des associations inhérentes au mouvement salafiste. Le reste de l'article met l'accent sur le danger que présente

---

[16] Patrick Charaudeau, 1997, *Le discours d'information médiatique. La construction du miroir social*. Paris, Nathan.

cette évolution incessante. Dès le titre, l'expression *«des associations généreuses»* porte une critique intense envers les sources de financement occultes qui supportent le mouvement salafiste. Le danger salafiste est présenté à travers les expressions *«le nombre des salafistes est impossible à cerner, Il se multiplie et se laisse dépasser par la diversité de leurs profils et l'étendue inestimable»*. Le danger transparait également à travers un vocabulaire belliqueux *«conquête de l'espace public, leurs conquêtes, plani-fication et de retranchement en cas de poursuite policière»*. En creusant plus profondément, le journaliste relie la source de l'information au ministre des Affaires religieuses *«le ministère des Affaires religieuses recense»*. Toutefois, l'expression «*En haut de l'échelle*» dénote explicitement la fonction administrative occupée par le ministre, et renvoie implicitement, au mouvement salafiste, voulant dire ainsi; «*en haut de l'échelle du mouvement salafiste*».

Conclusion

Le chevauchement des genres n'est pas l'apanage des articles politiques, il s'agit d'une caractéristique omniprésente dans toutes les formes de la production journalistique. Nous pouvons naturellement déceler le positionnement énonciatif du journaliste dans tous les genres rédactionnels. Notre ambition n'est pas d'apporter une réponse à la question de chevauchement des genres dans le discours journalistique, nous avons limité le travail à une description d'un désordre qui ne pourrait être que la marche normale des choses vu le carrefour énonciatif dans lequel se situe le discours journalistique, entre le politique, le social et le religieux ainsi qu'entre l'information et le lectorat. La plasticité conceptuelle que présentent les dires de presse laisse entendre que les limites entre l'information et l'opinion se veulent impossibles dans un fluctuant pareil au discours journalistique. Ce chevauchement entre les différents genres journalistiques. Notre but était de montrer comment les angles théoriques auxquelles nous avons recours n'arrivent pas à établir une classification nette et claire, à vrai dire, un ordre bien clair et une répartition nette de l'aire scripturale.

Bibliographie

Adam Jean Michel, 2001, *Genres de la presse écrite et analyse de discours*, Semen 13, mis en ligne le 30 avril 2007, URL: http://semen.revues.org

Adam Jean-Michel, 1997, *Unités rédactionnelles et genres discursifs: cadre général pour une approche de la presse écrite,* in Pratiques n° 94, Metz.

Antoine Frédéric, Jean-François Dumont, Benoît Grevisse, Philippe Marion et Gabriel Ringlet, 1995, *écrire au quotidien, Pratiques du journalisme,* Louvain-la-Neuve Evo-Communication.

Charaudeau Patrick, 1997, *Le discours d'information médiatique*. La construction du miroir social. Paris, Nathan.

De Brouker José, 1995, *Pratique de l'information et écriture journalistique*, Paris, CFPJ.

Dubied Annik, Marc Lits, 1999, *Le fait divers,* P.U.F., coll. «Que sais-je?».

Eliseo Veron, 1988*, Presse écrite et théorie des discours sociaux production, réception, régulation"*, in La presse, produit, production, réception, Patrick. Charaudeau éd., Hatier.

Herman Thierry, Gilles Lugrin, 1999, *Formes et fonctions des rubriques dans les quotidiens romands - Approches théorique et quantitative, Fribourg (Suisse):* Institut de journalisme et des communications sociales.

Kerbrat-Orecchioni Catherine, 1977, *La connotation,* Presse universitaire de Lyon.

Maingueneau Dominique, 1984, *Genèses du discours*, Liège, Mardaga.

Martin-Lagardette Jean-Luc, 1994, *Guide de l'écriture journalistique,* écrire, informer convaincre, Paris, Syros.

Moirand Sophie, 1999, *Variations discursives dans deux situations contrastées de la presse ordinaire,* les Carnets du Cediscor 6.

Montant Henri, 1994, *Commentaires et humeurs*, Paris, CFPJ.

Mouillaud Maurice Jean François Tétu, 1989, *Le journal quotidien*, Paris, Puf.

Souchard Maryse, 1989, *Le discours de la presse. L'image des syndicats au Québec (1982, 1983),* Montréal, Le préambule (L'Univers du discours).

Ulrich Grosse Ernst, Seibold Ernst, 1996, *Panorama de la presse parisienne*, Berlin: Peter Lang.

Why are Order and Chaos Part of Man's Inescapable Doom?

Aya Somrani, Northern Borders University, KSA

Abstract

The New World Order, and Hegel`s Management Theory are two crucial concepts within the issue of order and chaos. First of all, the New World Order is a political agenda created by a group of people holding key positions in the world, like owners of oil companies or weapon makers, to make more profit from worldwide economic changes. As for Hegel`s theory, it is a political ideology utilized by nations to resolve political or economic problems. If order is immune to time flux, it will not be disturbed by disorder. However, Man cannot help but accept chaos as paradigm of the universal phantasmagoria: our world is constructed of illusionary images, which interfere in our interpretation of existence. Some eyes naturally turn to order as the best option for perfect life; while others consider pandemonium, or chaos, as a threat to communities' profiles, for turmoil is, generally, considered as negative for social stability.

In fact, the concepts of order and disorder oscillate between fact and fancy. Several races sought for order in different ways, since the dawn of existence; from Plato's Atlantis, and Thomas Moore's Utopia, (which are examples of perfect kingdoms) to the Elizabethan Great Chain of Being, and Freemasony New World Order of today.

The American author Thomas L. Friedman wrote in his article "Order vs. Disorder", Sunday Review: "If it feels as though the world of disorder is expanding against the world of order, [...] there's an unfortunate logic to it {disorder}". This idea has been supported by Hegel's theory, which considers the claim that, Order stems from the sense of responsibility and need for security. For this reason, Man sets constitutional nations so that communities avoid ontological jeopardy.

Some technocrats admit that social dyslexia is shrewdly exploited to impose desired harmony. Therefore, world magnates try to spread diseases and terrorism, in order to reduce communities' number and select the best subjects, for the purpose to serve their agenda which is an agenda demanding only the intellectual elite, or a group of influential people.

Keywords: Freemasons, history, communities, order, chaos, New World Order, Hegel.

Introduction

What if order and disorder were responsible for our existence? Technically, we are not at the level to challenge millennia of clockwise evolution on earth. Generally speaking, ceaseless eon flux wields a sovereign power on our being (existence) and becoming (future) status. The outcome of Man's journey, in understanding the universe, is a supreme awareness that life depends on a range of ethics and codes in order to survive. It has been confirmed historically, in hundreds of occasions, that the presence of order is essential as part of self-preservation against external chaotic forces. Waged wars, as well as worldwide racial discords, may stand as best examples of order's necessity, as the last sanctuary, and the ultimate decision to reject the perils of disorder.

Nonetheless, disorder is sometimes resorted to as a cure to solve social crisis. Hegel's crisis management theory serves as a good example in this case. Such theory is based on solving social crisis, through the analysis of the influence of social calamities on Man's awareness (Cohen and Arato 469).[1] This article will discuss the conditions and methods requiring the coexistence of order and chaos. The main theme will be about the goals and objectives of order as well as disorder, and the reason for Man's need to both concepts for the continuity of species' history. Likewise, the following sections will depict the necessity of disorder within social organization, and the way chaos cures humans' institutions protecting them from extinction. Therefore, the idea of order and chaos will be debated along the historical timeline, illustrating Man's efforts to build a good present and a better future.

I. The Impact of Order on the Profile of Communities

It is globally considered that order is vital for communities' security. Order can be responsible for safety, social welfare, as well as future development. Man's history displays a panorama of humans' firm endeavors to maintain order in all its manifestations, be it through fiction or. Namely, orderliness is axiomatically treated as one of civilized measures to rank communities and civilizations. Typically, any nation that is affected by disorder is seen as a barbarian one, and

---

[1] Jean Cohen and Andrew Arato, *Civil Society and Political Theory* (Massachusetts: MIT Press, 1994).

it is automatically segregated from the elite of refined cultures. For this reason, the notion of order has always dominated the version of communities, which are alleged to be developed.

I.1. Portrayal of Order within Fictional Societies

An infinite number of order-bound texts emerge under the utopian genre. In this manner, utopias are based on verisimilitude. Every utopia builds on the previous one. For instance, as Moore's *Utopia* builds on Plato's *Atlantis*, Jonathan Swift's *Gulliver's Travels* also follows some aspects of Moore's *opus*. Literary works can be classified into, amongst others, secular, feminist or religious utopias; such as Homer's Amazons or *Islandia* by Austin Tappan Wright, St. Augustine's *City of God*, and *Crystal Age* by W.H. Hudson, along with hundreds of other worthwhile works.

Philosophically, Plato's meticulous Republic, produced around 380 B.C., is one of the eminent paragons of order. Literally, the Republic outlines tips explaining the method to establish a perfectly ordered government, as portrayed by the Greek philosopher Socrates. In this *opus,* Socrates considers order as one of the basic pillars of a just state or what he calls the *Kallipolis.* According to him, order defines justice and justice defines a happy life. Correspondingly, an ordered, ethical city is happier than a chaotic, unjust one. Equally, he maintains that a stable balanced soul is healthier than a disordered one. In this way, wisdom is order. So, the platonic Republic's basic foundation is orderliness.[2]

Nevertheless, there is no flawless nation and no ideal soul in the world. Plato's Republic subverts what is accredited to social turmoil, like poetry, and transcends organized political regulations. Yet, we have almost never witnessed the flaws of poets as a source of instability. Consequently, the philosopher's views are more subjective than objective, for they fit his point of view not people`s opinion (Haslanger 2).

---

[2] For a critical discussion, see Sally Haslanger, "Plato on Happiness: The *Republic*'s answer to Thrasymachus" *Ancient Philosophy* at https://ocw.mit.edu/courses/linguistics-and-philosophy/24-200-ancient-philosophy-fall-2004/lecture-notes/repsum.pdf.

Furthermore, Plato's adapted model, Atlantis, the majestic most-organized community in the ancient world, is still a paradigm for many countries to follow, and a mystery to be unveiled by archeologists, who strive to discover Atlantean organizational standards. Plato's *Timaeus* describes Atlantis as a real empire situated in the Atlantic Ocean near Pillars of Hercules. In fact, Plato claims that he has heard Atlantis story reported by Critias, one of his father's friends. The Atlantean state is shown as a perfectly structured realm, inhabited by an intelligent and skillful breed, rendering the kingdom as a leader in its time. Here, the depiction of the golden age of Atlantis does not seem realistic, but mere oral stories transmitted by ancestors.[3] Despite Plato's exact description of the empire, its ideal regulations and features remain far-fetched, because no kingdom can be immune from chaos forever.

Similarly, Thomas Moore's *Utopia*, referring to an incomparably flawless kingdom ruled by king Utopus, prevails as another instance of order. The portrait of Utopia displays well-arranged community, populated by obediently peaceful and cultivated subjects, who cherish the laws of the monarchist system of their territory. However, such seamlessly designed establishment is not as ordered as Thomas Moore tries to convey. It seemingly undermines women's locus as an essential component of collective life. In addition, it admits slavery. So, it is not an outstandingly unmatched social organism, as Moore attempts to demonstrate. Utopia is just a reaction against Moore's reality that embodies a corrupted community, for the writer is unhappy with the ill-being and imperfection of his time. Moore's artifact excludes the historical evolution, for it kills the sense of social improvement.

As a genre, utopia means the desire to create a better world. The question asked here is to what extent is utopist order beneficial for Man's institutions? Order accentuates the concept of harmony in society. It seeks egalitarianism. Yet, it is employed in fiction as a reaction against greed, lack of love, and lack of wisdom. Therefore, order is utilized, in literary texts, as an ironical device to criticize

---

[3] See, for example, Lewis Spence, *The History of Atlantis* (London: Rider and Co., 1929).

social flaws. Within this framework, the concept of order is not accentuated as a positive ideal, but as a negative attack against public wickedness.

Despite these values of utopian order, it is apparently understandable that faultless human establishments treat people like animals. Such regimes impose certain rules on its subjects which direct their lives, depriving them of their self-independence. Perfect-ion overstresses egalitarianism disregarding individuals' variety for the sake of uniformity. It is almost impossible, not only to create an Eden on Earth, but also to achieve total control over the public.

I.2. Order Applied to Civic Life

The ideology born of order stretches to Man's everyday life to maintain control over the masses. The Aristotelian notion of the Great Chain of Being (*La Scala Naturea*) was particularly developed during the Middle Ages and the Tudor Period and had a colossal effect on the European people. It is a systematic taxonomy, with a theological dimension, which classifies creatures and people's ranks up to their alleged importance, and spiritual nature, starting with God and then progressing to angels, demons, and several earthly beings, with stones at the nethermost of the order. E.M.W. Tillyard explains the theory's dominion over the social life of sixteenth century English people in his book *The Elizabethan World Picture*. He admits:

> If the Elizabethans believed in an ideal order animating earthly order, they were terrified lest it should be upset, and appalled by the visible tokens of disorder that suggests its upsetting. They were obsessed by the fear of chaos and the fact of mutability; and the obsession was powerful in proportion as their faith in the cosmic order was strong. […] To an Elizabethan it [chaos] meant the cosmic anarchy before creation. (24)

The chain's organism is, conceivably, worshipped by English subjects. For this reason, it is legally banned for any citizen to breach the chain's regulations. In short, every person must remain in his birth status, of poverty or wealth, without the ability to evolve, or havoc will tear down all the population. That is why the Elizabethan public, as argued by Tillyard, undoubtedly expects divine penalty in case the Chain's order is infringed, which evidently means a devastating apocalypse for them. As noted, this communal organizational structure impels social immobility. For example, the individual who is born a pauper should, purportedly, remain poor till the end of his or her actual life cycle. As a result, the individual's aptitude, skills, as well as free will, are eradicated. Besides, the subject's fate is also determined, in advance, by society.

Consequently, the Great Chain of Being is an order-device exploited by magnates, as a suitable way for them to uphold supremacy. Hence, civic order is not only employed for the service of security, but also to wield power, for it is suitable to the aristocratic class not to be disturbed by commoners' mobility which may be threatening to their interests and status.

Almost the same scheme is incarnated in the New World Order or *Novus Ordo Seclorum* as stated in the Masonic manifesto. Around the seventeenth century, the flow of Freemasonic philosophy out of lodges' veiled secrecy, to the light of public consciousness, marks a significant shift in worldwide communal conditions. In fact, the New World Order is an ideology whose target is to create a united global government, free from international boundaries. It aims at a radical transformation in all humans' institutions, which is referred to by some opponents (like American critics Michael Barkun and Chip Berlet), as conspiracy theory.

The new planned regulations aim at substituting the universally-known religions, with the worship of reason instead of Divinity. According to Freemasonry, religions limit humans' brains in dogmatic beliefs. Religions make individuals intellectually restricted. So, they will no longer be promoted regarding the hasty technical progress. At this stage, the elite maintains that reason no longer needs theology. Freemasonry stands against monotheistic religions. Thus, the so-called conspirators intend to make these religions outlawed within the New World Order so that reason will be worshipped. Epperson argues that "the basic tenets of Christianity, which were the base for the Old World Order, will have to be eliminated" (19).

Some commentators suppose that the world is prone to a global plot by Freemasons under the about the illuminati agenda, to build a unique new world under the rule of the elite. In particular, Epperson posits that "history has been a series of planned events led by a conspiracy based upon a worship of Lucifer" (58–9), the devil, as the New World is established. He continues that there will be changes in society, which will "efface all law, and end by dissolving all society" (114). In other words, it is claimed that the state will raise children instead of their parents. Women will have total freedom, and divorce will be easier than before. Those who are in favor of the New Order will be powerful, and those who are against it will be enslaved; "in the end they [the people] will lay their freedom at our [the controllers] feet and say to us 'make us your slaves, but feed us [...] the people of the world will give up their freedom to the 'controllers" (qtd. in Epperson 16–19).

Many texts refer to mind control as a tool to steer citizens' will, by dint of the All-Seeing Eye emblem. In his work *Brave New World*, Aldus Huxley states, "controllers use brainwashing to control the minds and behavior of entire populations" (303). It is thought that the new order would relieve humans from torturing feelings throughout mind wash. Due to this mechanism, individuals will not feel hatred, fear, sadness, or even love. They will operate just like robots. According to Freemasonry, such procedure is a good way to make people socially beneficial and reduce war rates on Earth. However, writers like H.G. Wells defend the New World Order system. In his book *New World Order*, he claims:

> Most of our systems of belief rest upon rotten foundations, and generally these foundations are made sacred to preserve them from attack. They become dogmas in a sort of holy of holies. [...] The defenders of all the dogmatic religions fly into rage and indignation when one touches on the absurdity of their foundations. (28)

The solution is, according to Wells, to adjust people's way of thought by dint of new collaborative establishments:

> The reorganization of the world has at first to be mainly the work of a "movement" or a Party or a religion or cult, whatever we choose to call it. We may call it New Liberalism or the New Radicalism or what not. It will not be a close-knit organization, toeing the Party line and so forth. It may be a very loose-knit and many faceted, but if a sufficient number of minds throughout the world, irrespective of race, origin or economic and social habituations, can be brought to the free and candid recognition of the essentials of the human problem, then their effective collaboration in a conscious, explicit and open effort to reconstruct human society will ensue. (73)

As far as the public network is concerned, Wells maintains the following credence:

> At times the Have-nots have been so uneducated, so helplessly distributed among their more successful fellows that they have been incapable of social disturbance, but whenever such developments as plantation of factory labour, the accumulation of men in seaport towns, the disbanding of armies, famine and so forth, brought together masses of men at the same disadvantage, their individual resentments flowed together and became a common resentment. The miseries underlying human society were revealed. The Haves found themselves assailed by resentful, vindictive revolt. (23)

The key is the creation of a collectivist society, and a worldwide shared consciousness. The production of a collective world; however, as Wells points out: "But many of us are coming to realize that all existing governments have to go into the melting pot" (63). Thence, the new world's rules rely on verisimilitude that destroys peoples' diversity, producing clones of the same model. Likewise, slavery approximately has the same locus in Masonic convictions. Wells notes:

> We human and beings are facing gigantic forces that will either destroy our species altogether or lift it to an altogether unprecedented level of power and well-being. These forces have to be controlled or we shall be annihilated. But completely controlled they can abolish slavery - by the one sure means of making these things unnecessary. (31)

This kind of order is spreading its ideals as well as its main symbols, namely the eye and the pyramid, around the world through many chains of interaction. In fact, the eye means knowledge; it is the icon of Antichrist, who is believed to be the future ruler. Likewise, the pyramid represents the steps achieved by Freemasons to the top where the eye is installed, indicating the final stage of founding the New World on the remnants of the Old world.[4] Some critics, like the political thinker Michael Barkun, declare it to be a conspiracy supporting despotism against human races, while others think that this order enlightens people's souls and protects species on Earth. In both cases, the New World Order is altering bureaucratic political thought,

---

[4] See, for example, Robert Howells, *The Illuminati: The Counter Culture Revolution-From Secret Societies to Wilkileaks and Anonymous* (London: Watkins Publishing, 2016).

along with intercontinental power balance.

II. Chaotic Effect on Humans' conditions

As a sociological notion, chaos has multiple aspects. It may be positive or negative, since its context varies according to its managers' objectives. It can be exploited for the benefit of humanity or against it. Turmoil also swings between what is physical and what is metaphysical. It is not only connected to the examination of the nature of creatures and elements, but also related to theoretical scrutiny.

II.1. Chaos in fiction

In fiction, chaos is attributed to magic as demonstrated in Phil Hine's book *Condensed Chaos: An Introduction to Chaos Magic*, concerning Western occultism. In this volume, Hines defines chaotic magic as sinister repetitions boosting one's hubris and ego strength. He claims that chaos has rites functioning via the circle of chaos used by Freemasons. To start the rites, a person must draw a circle with blood, or sand, reciting spells all along the process. Next, one stands inside of that circle, exposing oneself to odd forces. Once the rites are finished, the magician will have demons who will accompany him for the rest of his life, offering him service whenever needed.

In mythology, chaos is linked to cosmic creation as seen in Hesiod's *Theogony,* painting chaos as a shapeless entity, giving birth to life and mythological gods. Hesiod admits that anarchy is the source from which the universe is born. The poet's insertion that sublime gods are the children of chaos, accentuates holiness of anarchy in mythological tradition. Here, chaos is linked to a heavenly sense of sublime divinity (34–46).

In several cases, turmoil is associated with dystopia, chiefly signifying the opposite side of utopian order. It includes Orwell's *1984* and *Animal Farm*, Huxley's *Brave New World*, Suzanne Collins *Hunger Games,* and *Time Machine* by H.G. Wells. These literary works, along with many others, present different worlds wherein each one excels in its chaotic features, teaching us a lesson of communities' ruin by dint of chaos.

II.2. Civil Disorder

Civil disarray, generally, refers to unrest and strife; a sign of disapproval of socio-political matters, or can be an attempt to achieve freedom from the prevailing system. In his article "Order Vs. Disorder", Thomas L. Friedman notes: "If it feels as though the world of disorder is expanding against the world of order, [...] there's an unfortunate logic to it" (Friedman, online).

Friedman's observation reflects that disorder takes a new significance nowadays. Communal havoc – from riots, wars, diseases, pollution, revolutions and so forth – is manipulated in such a way as to steer social order in a particular direction. Specifically, some critics and technocrats assume that chaos is a diplomatic tool devoted to applying a political unsafe agenda on the world's inhabitants, embodied in the New World Order. Yet, Freemasons believe that the derivation of order from disorder, named '*ordo ub chao'*, is the brotherhood's highest motto. In the Freemasonic conception, chaos is "a Masonic symbol of the ignorance and intellectual darkness from which man is rescued by the light and truth of Masonry," according to Albert Mackey's *Encyclopedia of Freemasonry*, wherein he adds that, "order out of chaos, is a motto of the Thirty-third Degree" (1348).

In fact, the 'Thirty-third Degree' in the Masonic fraternity, is an honorary rank conferred to a member for an exceptional service to Freemasonry, and who has already received the Red Hat under the title of Knight Commander. This degree is granted by the Scottish Rite, which is a body of brotherhood, classified after the York Rite. Opinions concerning the New World Order differ between Masons and anti-masons. For anti-masons, such order is a conspiracy, against humanity, meaning the emergence of a totalitarian international government to rule Earth. For this reason, John Coleman explains in *Conspirators' Hierarchy* that "Free Masons' agenda for World Order depends on a small and loyal population" (128).

Coleman's view indicates that Masons aim to eliminate unworthy (weak) people through the creation of poverty, diseases, or terrorism, and overwhelm them with a world of daydreams, by dint of media drugs. The goal is to select the gifted and smartest people, while most of the rest will be terminated, or will disappear during their challdnge against the imposed system of life, for they will realize their inability to reach the required order of existence. Hence, they will acknowledge their unworthiness to endure life on the planet. At this level, every clan on Earth invents its own ideals of order and disorder, to save itself counter to time changes, and power imbalance (international wars for colonization) that warns against humans` extinction.

III. Hegel's Crisis Management Theory

It is ostensibly controversial to think of anarchy as a social healing phenomenon. Yet, a philosophical trend has invented a hypothesis expressing mayhem as a communal therapy. Within this framework, George Hegel's ideology has the function of steering mankind's mental power to its best uses. In fact, Hegel's notion focuses on social systems to cure social problems. Social systems enclose communities, society, and subjects.

According to Vladimir Tomas Mika, and Milos Ondrusek:

> The crisis management theory (i.e. Hegel`s Theory) is trying to find generalized principles and rules valid in variableness of managing of those systems which are threatened or impacted by the crisis situations. This theory explores and studies the processes of the organization management in the crisis situation, which have a general validity. It is trying to find the system of rules and principles which would be independent on the individual willing and thanks to which it would be possible to set up the system of principles, methods, and order of instructions for efficiency crisis management. (433)

The solution to solve matters in crisis theory resides in the study of the social background and the external forces that destroy the system's functions. In other words, Hegel's notion is based on the population's feelings to resolve social disasters. For instance, if the government needed to prohibit gun use, it should not announce it explicitly, since the idea will face public resentment. Instead, Hegel's theory suggests that the problem must be solved with disorder. As such, the state must display the perilous results of gun use to steer the masses` opinion without resort to violence. So, rulers should employ media and special groups of people to display the sense of crimes, as well as oppression with guns, as playing the major role in arising the crisis. In this way, the public will accept the government's proposition willingly and stop using guns. The key to handle communities' matters is by directing the majority's antagonism and disorder, for the national good. Therefore, the social system is cured by dint of chaos instead of order.

Hegel's theory of crisis management exploits subjective feelings before it looks for the influential factors hindering the system's organization. Likewise, to eliminate negative impacts of social dilemmas or economic disasters, and restore the collective organism, crisis management must be applied in a chain formula. The healing process is cyclical. The chart should start from the communal functions' analysis, then situate the tasks to deal with. Later, comes the phase of prevention and people's preparation. At this stage, public feelings are tested. Next, the level of relief that depends on individuals' reaction to instructions, resulting in the needed response that is the government's goal, leading to reparation of social network, and restoration of functions. But, Hegel's philosophy can be held back by radical opponents, who lack experience and skills as crisis managers. In this way, managers' competence, mental evolution, and historical knowledge must be considered within the study of the social disaster.

Conclusion

Order and turmoil are both responsible for Man's doom, because they determine one's existential value. Hence, survival equally depends on both sides to reach aimed ontological safety. Yet, these concepts must be employed in the right way, to promote our future. Otherwise, the result is an annihilating apocalypse feeding on hatred and bloodshed. Anarchy and order are two cardinal halves of the same body, functioning alternatively to keep the continuity of Man's collective core. Whether subjective or objective, views connected to order and disorder are endlessly various, but flow in the same trajectory when Man's survival is put into question. At the end, anarchy's significance stands as a proof of the assets laying in what we may collectively deem as negative or harmful.

Works cited

Barkun, Michael. *A Culture of Conspiracy*, California: University of California, 2003. Print.

Cohen, Jean, and Arato, Andrew. *Civil Society and Political Theory*, Massachusetts, 1994. Print.

Coleman, John. *Conspirators' Hierarchy: The Committee of 300*. New York, Library of Congress, 1997-2006. Print.

Friedman, L. Thomas. "Order vs. Disorder." *Sunday Review*. August, 23rd, 2014.

http://WWW.nytimes.com/2014/08/24/opinion/sunday/thomas-l-friedman-order-vs-disorder-part-3.html?_r=0. Web. 10 October 2015.

Epperson, A. Ralph. *The New World Order*. New York, Publius Press, 1990. Print.

Howells, Robert. *The Illuminati: The Counter Culture Revolution-From Secret Societies to Wilkileaks and Anonymous*. London: Watkins Publishing, 2016. Print.

Huxley, Aldus. *Brave New World*, Harper Perennial. Arizona, 2002. Print.

Mackey, Albert. *Encyclopedia of Freemasonry and its kindred Sciences*. Ohio, Masonic

Company, 1912. Print.

Spence, Lewis. *The History of Atlantis* London: Rider and Co., 1929.

Tillyard, E.M.W. *The Elizabethan World Picture*. London, Penguin, 1943. Print.

Vladimir, Tomas Mika and Milos, Ondrusek. "Actual Problems of Crisis Management theory." *Internationa Scientific Conference 2010*.

www.meste.org/konf/archiva/Man2010/pdf/…/MikaOndrusek.pdf Web. 12 October 2015.

Wells, H.G. *The New World Order*. New York, Wells, 1940. Print.

List of Contributors

Ons Abdi, *professeur agrégée*, has been teaching in the English department of the Faculty of Letters, Kairouan, Tunisia, since 2009. She is a PhD candidate and her research interests include SLA, EFL writing and contrastive rhetoric.
Contact: ons.abdi@gmail.com

Bachar Aloui is an Assistant Professor at the University of Jendouba, Tunisia. He holds an M.A. in linguistics from the University of Ottawa, and a Ph.D. in literature from the University of Montreal, Canada. He is currently interested in literature under the sign of trauma and, particularly, the relationship between the psychoanalytic economy of linguistic encryption and tropological/historiographical effusions of traumatic memory.
Contact: b.aloui@umontreal.ca

Sihem Arfaoui, Ph. D., is an assistant professor at the High Institute of Human Sciences of Jendouba, on a contract with NBU, K.S.A., a position she has held since 2015. In addition to being a department head since 2011, she teaches a variety of literary subjects ranging from modern literature to the rise of the novel and Victorian literature and a research seminar for English students about to graduate. Her research interests include ethnic writings and comparative studies. Her recent publications have appeared in Sami Ludwig, ed., *American Multiculturalism in Context: Views from at Home and Abroad* (2017) and Sylvie Camet, ed, *Decentrement et Travail de la Culture* (2016).
Contact: aa_sassou@yahoo.com

Zeineb Ayachi is a lecturer of English and linguistics at the Institut Supérieur des Sciences Humaines de Jendouba, Tunisia. She holds a PhD in Applied Linguistics and has a 22-year teaching experience. Zeineb's main areas of research include Psycholinguistics, ESP, curriculum development, implementation and evaluation, and communication through networked classrooms.
Contact: zeineb.ayachi@yahoo.fr

Mohamed Anouar Barouni graduated from the Faculty of Letters and Arts of Manouba in 2003. In 2004, he was recruited by the Ministry of Higher Education as he excelled in the C.A.P.E.S national exam. He has been teaching British and American cultures and translation since 2004 at the Higher Institute of Human Sciences of Jendouba. He works as freelance translator and a translator to the court of Jendouba. He wrote a dissertation

entitled "Tony Blair's Promises and Records from 1997 to 2002". He translated a book (Khatimu El- Eddyen by Dr Jaabiri, 2015) into English. The English version of the book is "The Last Religion".
Contact: dbarouni@yahoo.fr

Farhat Ben Amor is a professor assistant of English Literature at the Faculty of Arts and Humanities of Kairouan. He got his PhD award from the Faculty of Letters, Arts and Humanities of Manouba, in January 2015, on John Keats's poetry. Humanism, at large, constitutes his basic field of interest.
Contact: Farhatbenamorfarhat@gmail.com

Majdi Chaouachi Actuellement enseignant de la langue française à l'ISSH de Jendouba, il a poursuivi ses études universitaires à l'Institut supérieur des sciences humaines de Tunis afin d'obtenir en 2006 une maitrise en langues et civilisations anciennes puis un mastère en 2009 en langue et civilisation et littérature française à la Faculté des sciences humaines et sociales de Tunis. En 2012, il a été inscrit en thèse en linguistique générale à l'Institut supérieur des langues de Tunis avec un travail intitulé «Désignations et représentations des extrémistes salafistes dans la presse écrite tunisienne d'expression française».
Contact: ndoutreligne98@yahoo.fr

Asma Dhouioui, Ph. D, is an assistant professor of English and American Literature in the English Department of The Higher Institute of Languages of Tunis (I.S.L.T.), University of Carthage, and a member of the research unit: Language and Cultural Forms. Her doctoral dissertation is entitled: "Blood, Milk and Bones & Alternative sociability in Toni Morrison". Miss Dhouioui's research and teaching concerns vary from African-American literature, postcolonial literature, to Romantic poetry, Modern/ Postmodern poetry, in addition to Arabic Literature, and Comparative Literature.
Contact: asmadhouioui@yahoo.com

Noureddine Fekir teaches at the Institut Superieur des Langues de Tunis, Tunisia. His main interests include contemporary theory, stylistics, and world poetry. His doctoral dissertation (2000) is entitled: E. E. Cummings's Anti-Poetic Uni/Verse: A Cultural Study of the Mind and the Wor(l)d. He has published a number of articles on postcolonial poetry and a book entitled: *The Miracles of the Sound in the Qur'an: A Stylistic Study.*
Contact: fekir64@gmail.com
Farah Stiti Haddad, professeur agrégée en langue et littérature modernes

depuis juin 2011 et doctorante (cotutelle de thèse entre la faculté des sciences Humaines et Sociales de Tunis et la Sorbonne -Paris IV-), exerce depuis Septembre 2011 au sein de l'Institut Supérieur des Sciences Humaines et Sociales de Jendouba.
Adresse e-mail: Farah Stiti farah.stiti@hotmail.com

Welid Hmeissia, Welid Hmeissia, English language teacher at the I.S.E.A.H.Z, University of Tunis; holder of a B.A. from the Ecole Normale Supérieure of Tunis in 2012 and an M.A. from the Faculty of Letters, Arts and Humanities of Mannouba in 2014; and currently conducting research on John Millington Synge's plays and prose.
Contact: welid.hmeissia@gmail.com

Mounir Jouini has a Ph. D in Linguistics from the University of Carthage and is currently teaching linguistics courses at the Higher Institute of Languages, Nabeul. He has participated in a number of conferences in Tunsia and abroad and has publications in phonology.
Contact: mounirjwini@yahoo.com

J.S. Mackley is Senior Lecturer in English and Creative Writing and Programme Leader for English at The University of Northampton in the United Kingdom, as well as Assistant Adjunct Professor at Richmond University, The American International University in London. He received an MA in Late Medieval Studies and a Ph. D in Literature, both from the University of York, and is a Fellow of the Higher Education Academy. His academic publications include *The Legend of Brendan: A Comparative Structuralist Study of the Latin and Anglo-Norman versions*, a chapter in the *Routledge Companion to Literature and Food*, and a critical edition of *Who's the Murderer?* or, *The Mystery of the Forest*, a gothic novel by Eleanor Sleath. His research and publications focus on folklore, Medieval, Gothic and contemporary fantasy literature. His novels include *The* Gawain *Legacy.*
Contact: jon.mackley@northampton.ac.uk

Hajer Ochi assistante à l'Institut Supérieur des Sciences Humaines de Jendouba. Laboratoire de Recherche *Langues*, *Discours* et *Cultures* (Université de Jendouba). Doctorante en Linguistique Générale, inscrite à l'Institut Supérieur des Langues de Tunis.
Adresse e-mail: hajer.ochi@yahoo.fr

Narjess Saidi d'Outreligne, maître assistante en littérature française et comparée à l'Institut Supérieur des Sciences Humaines de Jendouba,

Tunisie. Elle a publié de nombreux articles et deux critiques littéraires aux éditions de l'Harmattan, *De l'Orient des Mille et Une Nuits à la magie surréaliste*, et *Les techniques d'expression dans Zayni Barakat de Ghitany*. Elle est chef de projet auprès du Ministère de l'Enseignement Supérieur pour la qualité dans l'enseignement, elle est aussi responsable du premier Centre de Langues et de Certifications en Tunisie, elle est chef de projet de MOOC qui est à sa deuxième session.
Adresse e-mail: ndoutreligne98@yahoo.fr

Aya Somrani is an English teacher specializing in British and American Literature. She taught at the Faculty of Legal Sciences, Economics, and Management in Jendouba, in 2015, and a former teacher in the High Institute of Arts and Humanities, in 2010. She achieved her Master's Degree in 2015, from the Faculty of Arts and Humanities, Manouba. She is currently teaching English literature in Northern Borders University in Saudi Arabia.
Contact: somrani_aya@yahoo.fr

www.ingramcontent.com/pod-product-compliance
Lightning Source LLC
Chambersburg PA
CBHW060750210726
48292CB00014B/2297

* 9 7 8 1 9 1 7 1 3 0 1 1 0 *